# THE STRUCTURE OF THE KEYNESIAN REVOLUTION

## GHANSHYAM MEHTA

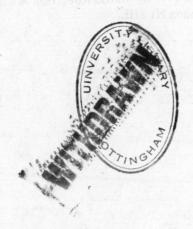

## MARTIN ROBERTSON

First published in 1977 by Allied Publishers Private Ltd., India.

Published in the U.K. 1977 by Martin Robertson & Co. Ltd., 17 Quick Street London N1 8HL.

ISBN 0 85520 219 X

*To*
*Maithili*

# Contents

# Contents

# Preface

This preface is dedicated to Berkeley, to its salubrious intellectual climate which fosters a love for learning and in which students and professors unite in the unending quest for more knowledge. Those who have lived and studied at Berkeley will always remember it as the mecca of intellectual activity. I am grateful for having had the opportunity to study there.

This study was submitted as a Ph.D. dissertation to the University of California, Berkeley. It was accepted in the Fall of 1971. Later, changes were made to deal with the recent developments in the literature and to assess their implications for the methods and conclusions of the book.

I am very grateful to Professor Benjamin Ward. Without his inspiration, guidance, and friendship this study would not have been undertaken. Any good that may be found in this work is due to him. I need hardly add that I alone am responsible for any errors or shortcomings.

GHANSHYAM MEHTA

*Chapter I*

# Kuhn's Historiographical Framework

When Keynes published his *Treatise on Money* and the *General Theory of Employment, Interest and Money* the world was in the midst of a severe depression. The events of those bleak years produced an intellectual crisis in economic science. There was a widespread feeling that the established theoretical picture of the economic world had become effete. It was felt that there was an imperious need to construct a new system of generalizations that could adequately explain the strange and puzzling phenomena of unemployment and trade depression that few could understand.

Initially the Keynesian theory met with stiff resistance from some members of the economics profession. Within a short time, however, it attained to that dominant and hegemonical position that the classical theory had occupied since the times of Smith and Ricardo. Its success was phenomenal.[1]

The object of his thesis is to use the new theory of Thomas Kuhn as a tool to study the structure of the Keynesian Revolution.[2] Kuhn has developed a new theory of the development of scientific knowledge and has applied it in the natural sciences. He has shown that this theory casts considerable light on the structure of revolutions in the natural sciences.

A study of the Keynesian Revolution from the Kuhnian point of view is useful in two respects. On the one hand, it permits the application of Kuhn's theory to the social sciences, a task which Kuhn himself has not carried out. The growth of knowledge in the social sciences may display special characteristics and may necessitate revisions or amplifications of Kuhn's ideas. Consequently, a work like this should be interesting to epistemologists and historians of science concerned with the extent to which the growth of knowledge in the social sciences can be assimilated to the growth of knowledge in the natural sciences.

[1]For an interesting account of how the economics profession received the Keynesian theory, see J. Galbraith (23).
[2]T. Kuhn (52).

On the other, the upheaval associated with the theories of Keynes will always be fascinating to historians of economic thought. They should welcome any new approach that illumines the nature of the development of the theory of income and output.

This study of the Keynesian Revolution differs from other studies in that it is explicitly based on an historiographical framework. The historical material pertaining to the growth of a science cannot be studied with a Lockean *tabula rasa*. All the facts seem equally relevant to the enquirer who approaches empirical material without a "theory". As theories have to be used to apprehend material from the empirical world the historian has to take care to properly articulate and explicitly formulate the theory which he employs.

Most of the economic literature pertaining to the Keynesian Revolution is deficient in this respect. Economists have evinced great interest and have exercised considerable ingenuity in studying the Keynesian Revolution. But most economists have not operated with a systematically formulated theory of the growth of knowledge. The result is seen in the kinds of question that they think it is worthwhile to find the answers to.

First, both the supporters and critics of the Keynesian theory have been keen on pointing out that there were many anticipators and adumbrators of the Keynesian theory. The object is to prove that Keynes's ideas were not "completely original".

Second, there is a tendency to think that it is important to find out when and by whom a certain discovery was made. The emphasis is on finding out the "first" person who made the discovery.[3] There is no recognition of the fact that "knowledge" is a social phenomenon analysable only by sociological categories.

---

[3]No attempt shall be made here at an exhaustive proof of this assertion. Anyone with even a perfunctory knowledge of the Keynesian literature will recognize how prevalent and widespread this tendency is. Only one example will be given here. Viner states explicitly that he will confine himself only to the out-of-the-way anticipators of the Keynesian ideas. Viner has disinterred many early and obscure adumbrators of the Keynesian ideas. But as Viner has not based his research on a fully articulated theory of the growth of knowledge it is not clear what relevance these "facts" have for the meaning of the Keynesian Revolution. See R. Lekachman (55).

The classical economists did not think that their theories were eternal and immutable truths. Although they knew that their theories were substantially correct, they were aware that in many areas the predictions from the theory could not be made to match exactly with observational results. There is a tendency in the literature to attach excessive importance to the amorphous doubts expressed by many "classical" economists about the validity of their theories. The object is to show that many of these "classical" economists had theories that were not very different from the Keynesian theories. There is no recognition of the fact that scientific development may not be *unidirectional* and that successive generations of scientists frequently operate in *different* and *incommensurable* environments. Historians fail to realize that the classical economists may have been living in a different and incommensurable world and that, consequently, it is a mistake to view the achievements of an older science from the vantage point of the theory that is currently believed in. Within the cognitive field of every theory there are dissonant elements. Not operating on a fully justified theory of the growth of knowledge historians of economic thought have frequently misinterpreted the existence of these dissonant elements.[4]

In effect, economists have been using a crude "development-by-accretion" model of the growth of science. According to this view science grows by a process of accretion or accumulation. It is averred that each successive generation of scientists moves closer and closer by an accretive process towards the "true" view of reality. Unfortunately, the growth of knowledge is impeded by errors, prejudices, and obscurantist notions. The "erroneous" doctrines are those that are incompatible with the ones we hold today. The historian, consequently, has to trace modern theories to their origin and to describe the way in which the progress to the "true" view of reality has been halted by the erroneous doctrines of older scientists.

Kuhn challenges this view of the growth of science. Kuhn argues that further historical research makes it harder, not easier, to determine the scientist who "first" made a certain discovery. The reason for this, Kuhn affirms, is that knowledge grows by a *social process*. According to Kuhn, historical research also

---

[4]Many examples of this shall be given in the succeeding chapters.

shows that the assumption of the unidirectional nature of science is unfounded.

> If these out-of-date beliefs are to be called myths, then myths can be produced by the same sorts of methods and held for the same sorts of reasons that now lead to scientific knowledge. If, on the other hand, they are to be called science, then science has included bodies of belief quite incompatible with the ones we hold today. Given these alternatives, the historian must choose the latter. Out-of-date theories are not in principle unscientific because they have been discarded. That choice, however, makes it difficult to see scientific development as a process of accretion.[5]

The concept of a "paradigm" plays a fundamental role in Kuhn's theory. These paradigms are significant scientific achievements that are sufficiently open-ended to inaugurate coherent research traditions. "Normal science" is the paradigm-based research of scientists.[6]

Normal scientists (i.e. those whose research is based on paradigm) do not aim at fundamental novelty of either a theoretical or factual nature. Instead they attempt to force nature into the conceptual boxes supplied by the paradigm.

> The success of a paradigm . . . is at the start largely a promise of success . . . Normal science consists in the actualization of that promise, an actualization achieved by extending the knowledge of those facts that the paradigm displays as particularly revealing, by increasing the extent of the match between those facts and the paradigm's predictions, and by further articulation of the paradigm itself.[7]

The activity of normal scientists can be compared to puzzle-solving. In solving a puzzle the puzzle-solver knows that a

[5]Kuhn (52, pp. 2–3).
[6]It is a great mistake to identify Kuhn's paradigm with a "theory" as that term is used in current philosophy of science. For an instructive discussion of paradigms the reader is referred to Margaret Masterman's article "The Nature of a Paradigm" in A. Musgrave and I. Lakatos (53).
[7]Kuhn (52, p. 24).

solution exists. He knows what to expect. His ingenuity consists in actually finding the solution according to the "rules of the game".

Scientists working on the basis of a paradigm have implicit confidence in its validity. Normal scientific activity takes place only when the relevant members of the science or one of its sub-specialties have agreed on the fundamentals of the subject. Once agreement on the fundamentals of the subject has been obtained, scientists can devote themselves to esoteric research. This is why normal science is so efficient. It restricts the imagination and permits detailed and recondite research on some portion of experience.

Normal science exists because paradigms are open-ended. They leave all sorts of puzzles for the normal scientists to solve.

This means that a paradigm can never explain all the phenomena that come within its range. Ordinarily when certain facts are discovered that do not accord with paradigm-based expectations, scientists do not abandon their paradigms. The failure of a certain puzzle to come out right is at first only seen as a reflection on the scientist who has failed not the paradigm itself. It is believed by the members of the profession that by exercising sufficient ingenuity the puzzle can be solved.

But there are some puzzles that are recalcitrant to normal articulating activity. Such intractable puzzles occasion a *crisis* in the science. In the initial stages those who are wedded to the old paradigm believe that suitable extensions and modifications of the paradigm will be sufficient to solve the puzzle. When success is not achieved, scientists change their perception of the problem. What was formerly only a puzzle now becomes an anomaly. At this stage there arises what Kuhn calls "a proliferation of articulations". Increased attention is devoted to the problem-area and there is a tendency to go off into "speculative" directions in an attempt to deal with the anomalous situation.

It is only when a new paradigm is put forward that the anomaly is seen as a counter-instance that "falsifies" the old paradigm. If the new paradigm has been successful in dealing with the anomaly it will command the allegiance of many of the new members of the profession or its sub-discipline that has been affected by the crisis. Many scientists who have worked with the old paradigm for a long time will be unable to make the

Gestalt switch that is necessary in order to be persuaded or converted to the new paradigm. But if a sufficiently large majority of the profession declares its allegiance to the new paradigm, a new era of normal science will be initiated. A crisis in Kuhn's theory must be seen, therefore, as a *social* response to an anomalous and ambiguous situation.

Kuhn defines a revolution as the replacement of one paradigm by another. It is an essential part of Kuhn's thesis that scientific knowledge grows by a revolutionary process in which paradigms are thrown over. It is for this reason that Kuhn says that scientists frequently operate in different and incommensurable environments. The incommensurability is due to the fact that the new paradigm cannot be simply grafted on to the existing stockpile of scientific knowledge. To use Butterfield's felicitous phrase, the new paradigm requires that a new "thinking cap" be donned by the scientists. Changing the "gestalt" in which scientists view the world is not an easy process. It is for this reason that new paradigms meet with stiff resistance from adherents of the old paradigms.

Kuhn regards science as an ineluctable social process. The individualistic historian does not take sufficient cognizance of the fact that scientists operate in a definite social milieu. Kuhn, on the other hand, regards scientists from the modern Parsonian point of view.[8] He treats scientists as mutually interacting actors with shared value-orientations. The social system of science shares many characteristics with the other social systems of society.[9] The continuity and stability of the value-system of society is maintained through the socialization process. The social system of science has to perform a similar function. It is for this reason that Kuhn lays so much stress on text-books. Text-books are a part of the reward-system of science. They are instrumental in bringing about the continuity and stability of "paradigm-orientations". By studying text-books the student or prospective scientist learns the rules of the game and internalizes other paradigm-orientations. As the recruitment

[8]In the postscript to his book Kuhn says (p. 176) that if his book were being re-written he would start by discussing the community structure of science.

[9]For a highly stimulating discussion of the social system of science from the Parsonian point of view, the reader is referred to N. Storer (91).

of scientists involves a socialization process, the subsequent practice of normal scientists seldom evokes disagreement on fundamentals. According to Kuhn, the majority of scientists are "well-adjusted?", that is to say, they appropriately internalize paradigm-orientations. As the norm-orientations have been internalized, scientists are motivated to play the "game" of science in a way that is both personally gratifying and so necessary for the growth of normal science. The successful and normatively proper solution of puzzles is rewarded; whereas deviant behaviour is punished.[10] From a sociological point of view this is why normal science is so efficient.

> Whatever scientific progress may be, we must account for it by examining the nature of the scientific group, discovering what it values, what it tolerates, and what it disdains. That position is intrinsically sociological.[11]

It is this sociological approach of Kuhn that we intend to use in this study. One aim of this study is to make a contribution to the "Keynes *versus* Classics" debate by demonstrating that the Keynesian Revolution was a revolution in the sense of Kuhn.[12] Its main novelty consists in its delineation of the structure of the paradigm-shift that revolutionized macro-economic theory.

The description of the paradigm-shift to be presented in this study is based on a new interpretation of Keynes' *Treatise on Money*. On the basis of this new interpretation I shall argue that the decisive break with the classical tradition occurred in 1930 when the *Treatise* was published.

If this new interpretation is correct, economists' view about the nature of the development of economic theory during the early thirties will have to be changed. Ordinarily when one talks about the Keynesian Revolution, one has the *General Theory* in mind. The *Treatise* is regarded merely as one book

---

[10]Of course, reward does not mean pecuniary reward but the reward of professional recognition. Economists like Joan Robinson and Galbraith have complained that they do not get any professional recognition for their deviant economic views.

[11]Lakatos and Musgrave (53, p. 238).

[12]There has been some discussion of the application of Kuhn's ideas to economics by Gordon (25) and Coats (6).

that Keynes wrote before he had sloughed off the integument of classicism. An important aim of this study is to oppugn this view about the development of economic theory. Unlike other works on the Keynesian theory, the focus of this investigation will be on "*Treatise versus* the Classics". Proceeding on the *a priori* conviction that the *Treatise* was Wicksellian, and that it did not even contain a theory of effective demand historians have misrepresented the nature of the response to that book. If the interpretation of the *Treatise* presented in this study is correct the post-*Treatise* debates among economists like Joan Robinson, Hayek, Keynes, and Robertson must be seen as inter-systemic or inter-paradigm debates. The post-*Treatise* debates exemplify Kuhn's assertion about the incommensurability of paradigms. According to Kuhn, adherents of different paradigms have a tendency to "talk thru each other". In our chapter on the post-*Treatise* developments in monetary theory it is this aspect of Kuhn's theory (i.e. the tendency of scientists during a crisis to "talk thru each other") that we shall try to bring out.

The *Treatise* was written when economic theory was in a state of crisis, in the sense of Kuhn. Protracted unemployment in Britain during the twenties had attenuated the faith of economists in the fecundity of the classical paradigm. It is interesting to note that those who first experienced the anomaly were not normal scientists. The initial attacks on the classical paradigm were made by men many of whom were outside the economics profession.

At this time many normal economists did not think that the "puzzle" of unemployment and trade depression was in anyway inconsistent with paradigm-based expectations. They felt that the anomaly could be dealt with by suitable extensions of the paradigm. As we shall see, in their attempts at paradigm-articulation these normal economists reached results that were similar to the results of those "speculative" men who felt that commercial phenomena had falsified the classical paradigm.

It is this *social response* to an anomalous situation that will receive much attention in the sequel. Keynes' *Treatise* must be seen as part of this social response. Within such a sociological framework the question of the anticipators and adumbrators of the Keynesian ideas is not really important.

SUMMARY OF SUCCEEDING CHAPTERS

In applying the theory of Kuhn to the Keynesian Revolution three problem-areas must be discriminated: classical normal science, the crisis of classical normal science, and Keynesian normal science. The focus of the following investigation will be on the second problem-area and very little will be said about Keynesian normal science.

The second chapter will describe the basic structure of classical normal science. An attempt will be made to state the central paradigm of the classical economists. Some of the puzzles that arose in the articulation of the paradigm will also be considered. The second chapter has two parts. In the first part the "aggregate output paradigm" of the classical economists will be presented. In the second the "money paradigm" will be described. Needless to say, it is not our objective to deal in an exhaustive fashion with classical normal science for that would entail a study longer than the one to be undertaken.

Chapters 3 and 4 are concerned with important aspects of the crisis in economic theory in the twenties. In chapter 3 the "speculative" solutions of economists and others to the crisis problem will be delineated. The influence of these "speculative" solutions on the formation of new perceptual styles will be emphasized. Chapter 4 will also study the solutions of economists to the crisis problem. The interesting thing about these solutions is that they are more accurately regarded as articulations of the old paradigm than subversive of it, as in the case of solutions studied in chapter 3.

Chapter 5 constitutes the heart of this dissertation. It explores further the crisis situation. It offers a new interpretation of Keynes' *Treatise on Money*. If this novel interpretation is correct, economists' views about the nature of the paradigm-shift in the thirties will have to be changed.

In chapter 6 the implications of this new interpretation are worked out. If Keynes' *Treatise* was indeed a paradigm, the post-*Treatise* debates can be regarded as inter-paradigm debates. Chapter 6 will attempt to bring out Kuhn's argument that adherents of different paradigm frequently talk "thru each other".

# Chapter II

## PART I

# Classical Normal Science

## INTRODUCTION

The object of this chapter is to lay the groundwork for succeeding chapters by describing the salient ideas of classical normal science. There is a problem in identifying the relevant paradigm because of the ambiguity in the concept of paradigm.[1] On the one hand, there is the sociological paradigm which stands for the entire constellation of beliefs, values, techniques, and so on shared by the members of a scientific community. On the other hand, the term "paradigm" may refer to some element within that constellation. In this sense, the term "paradigm" refers to the exemplary past achievements of scientists, the concrete puzzle-solutions that guide the subsequent development of normal science.

For our purposes, it will be sufficient to use the term "classical paradigm" in this second more restricted sense. We shall be concerned only with those aspects of the classical system that are relevant in understanding the structure of the Keynesian Revolution. Much of the classical system deals with the problems of distribution and growth and is only indirectly related to the work of Keynes. Our interest will be centred on the aggregative output and money paradigm of the classical economists. It is true, of course, that in order to properly study the classical system, one would have to study the system in its entirety. But this ambitious task is beyond the scope of this book.[2]

The appellation "classical normal science" should not be misconstrued. In the first place, it does not preclude the existence of points of view not fully consonant with the paradigm; nor

---

[1]See the discussion in Kuhn (52, pp. 174–210).
[2]For modern accounts of the classical system, see some of the works cited in the postscript.

does the applicability of the designation require the absence
of anticipators and adumbrators of the Keynesian ideas. From
Kuhn's point of view, the real desideratum for a normal research
tradition is the existence of coherence.

## SMITH'S THEORY

The chapter on mercantilism in Book 4 of the *Wealth of Nations*
constituted the paradigmatic statement of classical monetary
theory. In that chapter Adam Smith reviewed and criticized
the mercantilist theory of money. In its simplest form this
theory states that $M = W$, i.e. money is wealth. The wealth of
nations, consequently, depends upon the amount of money that
they possess. Other commodities are less durable than money
which consisted at that time primarily of precious metals. As
other commodities are perishable and liable to waste away,
they are imperfect forms of wealth. Unless a country had gold
and silver mines and could produce these metals internally, the
only way available to them to increase the wealth of their nation
was to have a favourable balance of trade with other countries.

It is this theory of money and wealth that Adam Smith
attacked in his famous chapter on mercantilism. Smith said
that the wealth of nations depends upon the amusements, con-
veniences and luxuries that the land, labour, and capital resources are capable of producing, and that this process is facilitated
by the division of labour. Smith advanced a *nominalist* theory
of money.

> That wealth consists in money, or in gold and silver, is a popu-
> lar notion which naturally arises from the double function of
> money as the instrument of commerce, and as the measure of
> value. . . . It would be too ridiculous to go about seriously
> to prove, that wealth does not consist in money, or in gold
> and silver; but in what money purchases, and is valuable only
> for purchasing. . . . It is not for its own sake that men desire
> money, but for the sake of what they can purchase with it.[3]

It took economists another hundred and fifty years or so to

[3]A. Smith (83, pp. 139–155).

develop a rigorous nominalist theory of money. But the germ of the nominalist theory is to be found in the work of Smith: money is the measure of value and the instrument of commerce and money is useful not for its own sake but for the sake of the commodities it enables us to buy. Smith's theory of money implies the antimercantilist proposition that the quantity of money does not significantly affect the wealth of nations. As money is the instrument of commerce, the amount of money required depends upon the value of the trade that is to be transacted. If the actual amount of money exceeds the amount required, money will be transported from where it is cheap to where it is dear. Transportation is particularly easy in the case of precious metals like gold which contain a value that is large relatively to their bulk. On the other hand, if money is scarce, barter transactions will replace transactions in money. Furthermore, paper substitutes for money can be easily introduced.

Smith does not seem to have been aware of the proportionality proposition of the quantity theory: average prices are always proportional to the quantity of money. He did not use this proposition to show that the work done by money is independent of the quantity. This articulation of the classical theory of money was undertaken by John Stuart Mill. Mill asserted categorically that there is nothing so intrinsically insignificant in the economy of society than money except in the character of a contrivance for doing more commodiously what would be done less commodiously without it. Adam Smith was more interested in the policy conclusions to which his analysis led than the analysis itself. He was primarily interested in showing that the government should not concern itself with the quantity of money and should allow it to be determined by the play of market forces. Smith argued that the market will distribute the precious metals according to the effectual demands for those metals in different countries.

Classical monetary theory must be understood as a reaction against the mercantilist theory of money. Up to the time of Marshall, monetary theorists felt that they had to show how their theory was different from the older theory, why it was superior to it, and then to re-interpret the facts in terms of the new theory. Classical economists have been accused of misrepresenting the true nature of mercantilist theory. Keynes,[4] for example, charged them with the failure to see that their concern with the quantity of money was merely a result of their concern over the level of interest rates. According to Keynes the mercantilists had an inchoate liquidity preference theory and were concerned about the effect on investment of a high level of interest. On the other hand this is what Schumpeter said:[5]

First, though pieces of genuine analytic work can be found occasionally and attempts at analysis more frequently, the bulk of the literature is still essentially pre-analytic; and not only that, it is crude.

The question about the "true" nature and significance of mercantilist theories cannot be settled here. Schumpeter's characterization of their literature as "pre-analytic" and even "crude" makes it difficult to speak about a mercantilist paradigm. Much of the mercantilist literature emanated from unprofessional and uneducated minds at a time when economics had not obtained its identity as a profession. Nevertheless the main orientation of mercantilist literature was economic, and a widespread social consensus was achieved on the main tenets of mercantilist doctrine.

Whatever the true nature of mercantilist theory may be, it is clear that Keynesian theory is ontologically closer to mercantilist doctrine than the classical theory of money is to the mercantilist theory. No one has denied the patent fact that the classical theory is superior to mercantilist theory in its fecundity for producing puzzles. In this respect the classical theory is superior. Nevertheless the Keynesian theory of money forces us to admit that the mercantilists in their intuitive and "pre-analytic" way had a "truer" conception of the "real" nature of economic processes than their analytically superior successors. This circumstance illustrates Kuhn's argument that functional progression in science is frequently accompanied by ontological regression[6].

[4]J. M. Keynes (47, chapter 23).
[5]J. A. Schumpeter (80, p. 348).
[6]T. Kuhn (52, pp. 205–206).

## THE CLASSICAL THEORY OF OUTPUT AND SAY'S LAW

The first point to note, as Ludwig Mises[7] has indicated, is that the law of markets was formulated by Say as a reaction against certain garbled doctrines that were held by businessmen and laymen during the mercantilist era. These crude doctrines attributed bad trade to a shortage of money and to general overproduction in accordance with mercantilist principles. Adam Smith said that "no complaint, however, is more common than that of a scarcity of money".[8] Adam Smith initiated the attack on these theories by arguing that money is only an instrument of commerce and that it is not synonymous with wealth. Money cannot be scarce for long as the deficiency can be made up, more easily than in the case of other commodities, by the introduction of barter transactions and paper substitutes.

Say's Law was originally intended to refute the addled view that sellers cannot find markets for their products because money is scarce. It expressed in a more precise and rigorous form the ideas that Smith had in mind. Consider the following passage:[9]

> The commodity, which recurs so repeatedly in use, appears to vulgar apprehensions the most important of all commodities, and the end and object of all transactions, whereas it is only the medium. Sales cannot be said to be dull because money is scarce, but because other products are so . . . . Should the increase of traffic require more money to facilitate it, the want is easily supplied . . . money itself soon pours in, for this reason, that all produce naturally gravitates to that place where it is most in demand.

Say articulated Smith's antimercantilist theory of money and wealth. Smith had asserted that produce naturally flows to the place where it is most in demand. Say's articulation of Smith's theory is based on the important macro-economic insight that different industries are interrelated and that they furnish markets for each other's products. Say formulated the important pro-

[7] H. Hazlitt (38).
[8] Smith (83, p. 151).
[9] J. B. Say (77, p. 134).

position that production is the source of demand. This is true even for a money economy because although it is the case that in order to purchase one must have money, one cannot procure the money without producing something.

Having advanced the important proposition that production is the source of demand Say proceeds to develop the consequences of this view. "As no one can purchase the produce of another except with his own produce, as the amount for which we can buy is equal to that which we can produce, the more we can produce the more we can purchase."[10] In other words, the proposition that production, and not money, is the source of demand implies the proposition that production is identical with demand. This conclusion is based on the assumption of insatiability of wants. Say is aware of this and has the following to say:[11]

> Experience as well as reason shows that a production, *a thing necessary or agreeable* to man, is only despised when one has not the means of buying it . . . . Not to want a useful thing is not to have wherewith to pay for it.

Hence the conclusion follows that "a product is no sooner created, than it, *from that instant*, affords a market for other products to the full extent of its own value."[12] The reasoning by which Say reached this famous conclusion seems to be the following. Smith had already demonstrated that money is not wealth but only the instrument of commerce. As money is only the means by which created values are exchanged, there can be no validity in the specious arguments of those who ascribe bad trade to a scarcity of money. Production is the source of demand, and as the only reason that people do not demand other goods is that they do not have the wherewithal to purchase them, increased production, necessarily and immediately gives rise to an equivalent demand. This is the original meaning of the famous law that supply creates its own demand.

Greater understanding of Say's theory will be obtained if we consider some of the puzzles that arose in the articulation of that

---

[10]J. B. Say (78, p. 3).
[11]J. B. Say (78, p. 28).
[12]J. B. Say (77, p. 134).

theory. The first question that arose was whether the theory was consistent with the factual evidence. Sismondi had objected to Say's theory on factual grounds. "Upon that principle", Sismondi declared, "it becomes absolutely impossible to comprehend or explain the best demonstrated fact in all the history of commerce, viz. the choaking up the markets."[13] Say turned the tables against Sismondi by declaring that the factual evidence is indeed conclusive but that the conclusion is against the proponents of the view that general overproduction can occur. Sismondi had adverted to the fact that English goods were flooding foreign markets where it was difficult to sell them. The low prices consequent upon the "oversupply" had occasioned great suffering in some industries. Using his theory that productions buy productions Say replied these commercial phenomena do not prove that general overproduction has occurred. The very fact that English goods are overproduced implies that foreign goods are underproduced. The sluggish demand for English goods is only the result of insufficient production abroad because demand can only originate from production.

Similarly, in the case of domestic production Say did not deny that there may be relative overproduction. Shoes, for example, may be overproduced. This means that the producers of shoes are experiencing difficulties in finding buyers. But this is the same thing as an underproduction of other goods because production is identical with demand.

It is interesting to consider further the way in which Say removed the cognitive dissonance (whether real or apparent) between his theory and the facts from the commercial world which were alleged to be inconsistent with his theory. Say's position was not that the "puzzle" of general overproduction can be ignored because the phenomenon which answers to that description occurs so infrequently that it is not of sufficient theoretical importance. Say held the stronger view that "general overproduction" is an impossibility. As we shall see presently, Mill resolved the dissonance in a more sophisticated manner.

It is appropriate at this stage to consider the distinction between "Say's Identity" and "Say's Equality" introduced by Becker and Baumol.[14] Becker and Baumol contend that the

---

[13]J. B. Say (78, p. 7).
[14]Becker and Baumol (4, pp. 355–375).

term "Say's Law" has been used in a variety of senses. They are interested in formulating a proposition which can be used to characterize the views of the classical economists on the subject of aggregate output. Say's identity states that the aggregate demand for all commodities (excluding money) is always equal to the aggregate supply, *regardless* of the level of prices and interest rates. Say's identity in this sense states the same thing as Say's Law in the sense of Lange.[15] Say's Equality states that the aggregate demand for commodities equals the aggregate supply not despite of, but because of, price and interest variations. Thus, while Say's Identity states that the demand for money balances is always equal to the supply at all price levels, Say's Equality states that with each level of the stock of money balances is associated a unique price level at which the demand for money is equal to the supply. At any other price level a Patinkinian real-balance effect will be brought into operation which will drive the price-level back to its equilibrium level.

According to the interpretation presented in this paper Say's views cannot be interpreted in terms of "Say's Equality".[16, 17] Say did not show any awareness of an equilibrating mechanism that operates through the effect of changing price-levels on the real value of money balances. On the contrary, he states explicitly that no sooner is a product created than it, from that very instant, provides a vent for other products.

Another interpretation of Say's theory has been given by Schumpeter.[18] Schumpeter's position is that Say was thinking

[15]Lange, McIntyre and Yntema (95).

[16]While not disagreeing with the interpretation presented in this paper, Becker and Baumol feel that even Say had a dim awareness of Say's Equality and that he stated it in a "peculiar" and indirect way. Their assertion is based on the following statement made by Say (*Treatise*, p. 134) "Should the increase of traffic require more money to facilitate it, the want is easily supplied . . . all produce naturally gravitates to that place where it is most in demand." That all produce naturally gravitates to the place where it is most in demand is a view which even Smith had stated, as we have seen. But neither Smith nor Say showed any awareness of the significance of price-level variations in this connection. The assertion by Becker and Baumol is a good example of how facts are distorted to fit *a priori* convictions.

[17]Patinkin (66, p. 650) does not think that the concept "Say's Equality" has any value whatsoever. He asserts that no evidence can be adduced to show that any classical writer thought in terms of the "equality".

[18]J. A. Schumpeter (80, pp. 615–625).

primarily of the "long run" in formulating the law. In stating that Produce opens a vent for produce, Say was not thinking in terms of an identity but in terms of an equilibrium condition to be satisfied in the long run. The evidence given above which is based on direct quotations from Say's works surely contradicts Schumpeter's interpretation. But Schumpeter is not disconcerted by the textual evidence.

> The first point to be made is that, though Say's Law is not an identity his blundering exposition has led a long series of writers to believe that it is one . . . . Once more, however, Say him- self is to blame for this interpretation. In this excessive zeal for establishing the practical importance of his theorem, he expresses himself in several places as if indeed the monetary value of all commodities and services supplied (exclusive of money) would have to equal the monetary value of all commo- dities demanded, not only in equilibrium but 'always and neces- sarily' . . . . He was an addict to the Ricardian Vice.[19]

This *device* of disregarding textual evidence by invoking supra-textual considerations is used by Schumpeter at other places in his *History*.[20] Schumpeter employs this device whenever he finds that an economist says something that "he should not have said". Schumpeter thinks that Say's "blunder- ing exposition" and "reckless statements" misled other writers into thinking that he believed in Say's identity. It is interesting to observe that Say himself would not have agreed with Schum- peter.[21]

> What is it that distinguishes us from the Economists of the school of Quesnay ? It is the pains we take to observe the connexion of the facts which regard wealth, the rigorous exac- titude we impose upon ourselves in the description of them.

From an historiographical point of view Schumpter's "device" is of questionable validity and of dubious value. The episte- mological assumption that underlies it is that of the unidirectional

---

[19] J. A. Schumpeter (80, pp. 618–619).
[20] See his discussion of Fisher.
[21] Say *op. cit.*

nature of scientific development. The implicit assumption is that scientists at all times attempt to understand the nature of the "same underlying reality". The object of science, according to this view, is to come closer and closer to a "true" apprehension of this "reality". This epistemological assumption lends plausibility to the Schumpeterian "device". Once the assumption of the unidirectional nature of science is dropped, and scientists are seen as puzzle-solvers that frequently operate in *different environments*, the anomalous and enigmatic facts become the natural and expected facts. Operating on this new theory historians will not search assiduously to find a sentence (or sentences) that shows that their favourite scientists had an awareness, however dim and inchoate it may be, of some of the issues that we regard as important today. In this way historians may be able to obtain a better understanding of the true nature of classical economic theory than if they persist in trying to relate the work of classical economists to modern economics by either showering exuberant epithets on the so-called anticipators and adumbrators because they devoted, let us say, one or two sentences to the problem, or by making use of the "device" when they do not find such sentences.

Our conclusion is, therefore, that Schumpeter's argument must be rejected as it is based on an epistemological assumption that is unacceptable. A sentence or two may be written in a "careless" manner. But to say that one's basic theory or approach has been written in a "careless" manner, and that one's meaning is frequently different from what is expressed makes much less sense. After all the historian does not have a special access to the "minds" of scientists. He has to rely on public expressions made by the scientists.

Patinkin[22] also inclines to the view that Say's Law must be interpreted as an equilibrium condition and not as an identity. Patinkin, however, does not use the methodologically reprehensible "device" to prove his case. His argument is that, in support of his thesis, Say adverted to the fact that production in France in about 1800 was five or six times as high as in the miserable reign of Charles VI. In this very limited sense it is indeed true that Say had a "long-run" theory in mind.

[22]Patinkin (66, p. 649).

Even after Say's brilliant enunciation and defence of his theory, universal consensus could not be obtained with respect to its main tenets. Eminent economists, who had contributed much to the progress of economic science by their original and brilliant speculations, continued to dissent from it. The alleged occurrence of "general gluts" prevented acceptance of a doctrine so palpably true but apparently in irreconcilable conflict with the factual evidence. It is at this juncture of affairs that John Stuart Mill entered the debate.[23] Mill perceived the necessity of probing into the fundamentals of the subject if there was to be any hope of securing accord. Mill pointed out that there are several senses in which it may be said that commodities have been overproduced. First, commodities may be said to be overproduced relative to the *power* of purchase. Second, commodities may be said to be overproduced relative to the *desire* to purchase. Furthermore, desire may be thought of in a particular sense and a general sense. Mill admitted that there may be overproduction relative to particular desires. For example, it is perfectly conceivable that too many cars are produced. Mill also admits that it is conceivable, though highly unlikely, that this may be the case with all commodities. "The error", Mill affirmed, "is in not perceiving that though all who have an equivalent to give *might* be fully provided with every consumable article which they desire, the fact that they go on adding to the production proves that this is not *actually* the case."[24] By this argument Mill proved that there cannot be overproduction of all commodities relative to the desire to purchase. Recall that Say had argued that the reason people "despise" goods is that they do not have the wherewithal to purchase them. If there is the power to purchase goods there will also be the desire to purchase goods. Mill's argument is much more subtle. He was probably driven to it on account of Malthus' insistence on the torpidity of human wants.

His proof that there cannot be general overproduction of commodities relative to the power of purchase is substantially the same as Say's. "What constitutes the demand for commodities

---

[23]Both Ricardo and James Mill took over Say's theory without substantial modifications. For a particularly forceful exposition of Say's theory, see "Commerce Defended" in D. Winch (93).

[24]J. S. Mill (60, p. 559).

is simply commodities . . . . All sellers are inevitably and *ex vi termini* buyers."[25]

Even after proving, on unimpeachable theoretical grounds, that the doctrine of general overproduction is absurd, Mill felt that a further *empirical articulation* of Say's theory is necessary. By "empirical articulation" we do not mean "verification" in the traditional positivist sense (either "verification" in the sense of Ayer and Neurath or "falsification" in the sense of Popper). Empirical articulation means using the theory to organize and classify empirical experience, and to create a "theory-fact world" which has certain distinctive properties. The empirical articulation of Say's theory Mill carries out by undertaking a theoretical articulation of Smith's monetary theory. Mill saw that the essence of money is that it breaks up into two transactions what, under a barter system, would be effected in one transaction. Furthermore, Mill perceived that this peculiarity of money has implications for the "puzzle" of "general gluts" that Say had overlooked.

What they called a general superabundance was not a superabundance of commodities relatively to commodities, but a superabundance of all commodities relatively to money. What it amounted to was that persons in general, at that particular time, from a general expectation of being called upon to meet sudden demands, liked better to possess money than any other commodity.[26]

Using this insight Mill proceeds to interpret the facts in terms of Say's theory.[27]

At such times there is really an excess of all commodities above the money demand: in other words, there is an under-supply of money. From the sudden annihilation of a great mass of credit, everyone dislikes to part with ready money . . . there may really be, though only while the crisis lasts, an extreme depression of general prices, from what may indiscriminately be called a glut of commodities or a dearth of money. But

[25]J. S. Mill (60, pp. 557–558).
[26]J. S. Mill (61, pp. 71–72).
[27]J. S. Mill (60, p. 561).

it is a great error to suppose, with Sismondi, that a commercial crisis is the effect of a general excess of production. It
is simply the consequence of an excess of speculative purchases
. . . and the remedy is not a diminution of supply but a
restoration of confidence.

Mill's position is that there may be an "undersupply" of money
without there being a "dearth" of money, and that there may be
an "excess" of commodities without there being "overproduction". It is probable that in making these distinctions Mill intended to state that "undersupply" and "excess of commodities"
are short-run phenomena, and that "dearth" and "abundance"
are long-run phenomena. Elsewhere Mill stated that "the
essentials of the doctrine are preserved when it is allowed that
there cannot be a permanent excess of production".[28]

The distinction between the long run and the short run is a
perplexing one. When Becker and Baumol, Schumpeter,
Viner and others argue that the classics "really" meant Say's
Law to be true only in the "long run", they are saying that the
classical theory is complementary with that of Keynes, and thus
indirectly depreciating Keynes' work. This attitude is based
on the implicit epistemological assumption that science is unidirectional. On this assumption it is plausible to say that some
scientists work on one portion of "reality" and that later scientists work on some other portion of reality. Science results
when all these contributions are juxtaposed.

Our interpretation is derived from cognitive dissonance theory.[29] Scientists seek to achieve cognitive consonance within their
cognitive field. For various reasons dissonant cognitive elements
are invariably present within the scientist's cognitive field. As
Kuhn has said there are always some phenomena which a theory
cannot explain. When a scientist perceives dissonance, he has

---

[28]J. S. Mill (61, p. 74).

[29]Festinger's (16) theory that cognitive dissonance is uncomfortable and
creates pressures towards its elimination can easily be dovetailed with Kuhn's
theory. In fact, Festinger's theory provides the rationale for Kuhn's theory.
In contrast, Popper's theory of falsification is inconsistent with Festinger's
theory. The argument that scientists seek to subject their theories to more
and more stringent tests implies that scientists always move towards cognitive
dissonance.

to deal with it. One way to mitigate dissonance is to change one's cognition of the new dissonant element in such a way that it becomes more consonant with one's belief system. Mill's empirical articulation of Say's theory exemplifies this method of alleviating dissonance. The argument that Say's theory holds only in the "long run" is a dissonance-allaying device[30] and was used by Mill for that purpose. This is not an aspersive characterization of Mill's writings. Every scientific theory has to deal with dissonant elements. No description of the work of scientists is complete if attention is not paid to the devices used by scientists to reduce dissonance.

It is this grave lacuna in the economic literature that the present analysis is intended to fill. Many economists operate on the basis of a crude positivist theory of knowledge. They would reject the idea that scientists have to use dissonance-reducing devices. They would assert that scientists should accept theories only after carefully considering all the facts at their disposal and so forth.

Mill himself was aware that any difference of opinion on the doctrine of general overproduction involves "radically different conceptions of political economy". For, if the doctrine is incorrect, economists would have to develop a theory of demand in addition to the theory of production. Mill did not think that such a new theory of demand was needed, whether in the "short run" or in the "long run". This is the essential point. Mill did not think that *a new theory* was needed to explain the "short run" phenomena. This clinches our argument that the use of the term "long run" was merely a dissonance-assuaging device.

## ARTICULATION OF THE CLASSICAL PARADIGM
## THE NEO-CLASSICAL THEORY OF EMPLOYMENT

As we have seen, the main pillar of the Smith-Say-Mill paradigm was the proposition that supply creates its own demand. A

[30]In his book T. Hutchison (46) describes many other devices used by economists to prevent their theories from being falsified. According to Hutchison to state that a theory is true only in the "long run" would be to state a "meaningless" proposition because such a proposition can never be directly compared with experience.

corollary of this view is the denial of the existence of equilibrium income.  In the Keynesian system, there is a unique equilibrium level of income determined by the intersection of the aggregate demand and supply schedules.  The concept of equilibrium income, and the idea of the relationship between saving and investment on which it is based cannot be meaningfully formulated within the domain of Sayian economics.

Sismondi, Malthus and the other dissenters from the classical paradigm referred to commercial crises as providing evidence for their contention that overproduction in the aggregate is possible. From their point of view these were exceptions to some of the implications derived from Sayian economics.  But, from the point of view of classical normal science, they were puzzles to be solved by sufficient ingenuity on the part of scientists.  To the normal scientists, commercial crises were not subversive of paradigm-based expectations.  They were not regarded as counter-instances.  On the contrary, the proponents of Say's Law argued that commercial crises provided incontrovertible evidence in favour of their paradigm, provided that these commercial phenomena were interpreted in terms of conceptual categories supplied by the paradigm.

The main concern of the neo-classical economists was with questions of value, distribution, and the efficient allocation of resources.  For this purpose they usually took it for granted that normally and in the absence of exceptional circumstances, there would be adequate demand to employ all the resources.  For, clearly, the question of the efficient allocation of resources is usefully discussed only when it is assumed that the resources are fully employed. Under circumstances of less than full employment of the resources, the marginalist and maximization principles which are at the heart of neo-classical economics are much less analytically useful.

Much of neo-classical economics is based on the *assumption* of full-employment. But the development of the marginal utility theory of value and the marginal productivity theory of distribution provided further evidence in favour of Sayian doctrines. Neo-classical economics explained the rationale of Say's Law by analysing the operation of markets under the assumptions of wage and price flexibility.  Price flexibility included interest rate flexibility. Interest rate flexibility would ensure that saving would be equal to investment. Even Adam Smith was aware that when there is saving the total consumption is not reduced, only its distribution changes. What the savers have released from consumption will now be consumed by the labourers employed in the production of new capital goods. The neo-classical economists put this doctrine on a more rigorous basis by showing that when there is an increase in the voluntary saving of the people there will be a fall in the rate of interest. This fall will make it more profitable to increase the amount of capital, and this, as Bohm-Bawerk showed, will elongate the structure of production. Hence, investment will increase. Interest rate flexibility would thus ensure the equality of saving and investment.

If prices and wages are perfectly flexible, the labour market will be in equilibrium at the point where the demand and supply schedules intersect. This intersection point will determine both the equilibrium (full-employment) level of employment and the equilibrium real wage which will precisely be equal to the marginal disutility of labour at that volume of employment. We then obtain the equilibrium level of output from the production function.

Crucial to the analysis was the marginal productivity theory of distribution, one of the great achievements of the neo-classical school. Using this theory, it could be shown that the labour market will determine the full-employment level of income and interest rate flexibility would ensure that the amount of saving and investment would always be equal at this level of income. Hence, we can conclude that although the neo-classical economists did not overtly discuss Say's Law, their analysis of markets operating under conditions of price flexibility only strengthened the conclusions derived from Say's Law. From Kuhn's point of view, the neo-classical theory of employment must be regarded as a theoretical articulation of the Smith-Say-Mill paradigm.

The major economists after Mill accepted Say's Law. According to Fisher, for example, a change in the quantity of money "normally" and in the "long run" produces a proportional effect on the level of prices. Consider the following statement by Fisher.[31]

[31]Fisher (17, p. 155).

We now proceed to show that (except during transition periods) the volume of trade, like the velocity of circulation of money, is independent of the quantity of money. An inflation of the currency cannot increase the product of farms and factories, nor the speed of freight trains or ships. The stream of business depends upon natural resources and technical conditions.

"Normally" the quantity of money has a proportional effect on prices because the level of output is already assumed to be at the level of full-employment. Hence, the validity of Fisher's quantity theory depends on the assumption of Say's Law. In the "abnormal" periods when the level of output is subject to variation the above relationship will not be true, as Fisher himself pointed out. His theory of the "transitional" period is intended to take care of the exceptional cases.

Marshall's views on the subject of aggregate demand are similar to those of Mill. Consider the following passage from his *Pure Theory of Foreign Trade and Domestic Values*.[32]

The whole of a man's income is expended in the purchase of services and of commodities. It is indeed commonly said that a man spends some portion of his income and saves another. But it is a familiar axiom of economics that a man purchases labour and commodities with that portion of his income which he saves just as much as he does with that which he is said to spend.

Marshall supported Mill's proposition that commodities constitute means of payment for other commodities. Production is the source of demand. Consequently, there is always enough purchasing power to clear the markets. Like Mill, Marshall conceded that in times of commercial disorganization, when confidence is shaken, "though men have the power to purchase they may not choose to use it."[33]

We conclude that Marshall's recognition of the possibility of a lack of effective demand was restricted to exceptional conditions. Consequently, for Marshall, "normally" and in the "long run", Say's Law is valid.

Pigou, one of Marshall's disciples, articulated Say's theory by proving that only frictional unemployment can exist in a world

[32]Quoted in Eshag (14, p. 85).
[33]Eshag (14, p. 86).

of perfectly plastic wage rates. Following Mill and Marshall, Pigou developed his theory in his two books *Industrial Fluctuations* and *Theory of Unemployment*. According to Pigou, the business cycle is only a temporary disturbance in a system which normally automatically tends to full-employment. During these disturbances the demand function for labour shifts and leads to disequilibrium in the labour market at the original wage rate. If the shift is downward, for example, more labour will be supplied than demanded at the given real wage rate. If only money wages would fall, argues Pigou, real wages will also fall. The fall in real wages increases the amount demanded of labour and restores equilibrium. Consequently, "with perfectly free competition . . . there will always be at work a strong tendency for wage-rates to be so related to demand that everybody is employed".[34]

Pigou, like Say, Recardo, and Mill before him, does not deny the existence of unemployment. According to Pigou, the unemployment that exists is only frictional, in the sense that continual changes in demand conditions cannot be matched by appropriate changes in wage rates because of frictional resistance to these changes. The *level* of demand is irrelevant to employment. This was an important elaboration of the proposition that supply creates its own demand. Ricardo explained unemployment by the maladaptation of production to consumption or an "internal disproportionality" within output. Pigou explains unemployment by *changes* in the level (and direction) of demand. Consequently, "normally" and in the "long run" the economy will operate at the level of full-employment.

Of all the neo-classical writers (with the exception of Hobson) Wicksell seemed to have the greatest doubts about the validity of Say's Law in the "short run". In his *Lectures on Political Economy*, Wicksell asserted that any theory of money worthy of the name must be able to show why the supply of goods is not equal to the demand for goods as a whole. This clearly shows that Wicksell was thinking in terms of Say's Equality (in the sense of Becker and Baumol). As we have seen, even Mill was aware of Say's Equality of the fact that the demand for goods as a whole may not be equal to supply. But, for Mill, this was

[34]Pigou (67, p. 252).

a rare phenomenon occurring only in exceptional circumstances and, therefore, not requiring serious modifications in Say's theory.

Wicksell, however, felt that an extension or articulation of Say's theory was required to explain the phenomenon. His theory of the real balance effect and the cumulative process was designed to provide this explanation. According to this theory, the demand for goods as a whole is equal to the supply *because of* (not regardless of) variations in prices and interest rates.

## CONCLUSIONS

It is clear from the preceding discussion that classical and neo-classical economists were aware of exceptions to Say's theory. This is true not only with respect to the dissenters from the classical orthodoxy such as Malthus and Sismondi. Even the supporters of Say's Law were aware of exceptions. This fact seems to support the "development-by-accretion" model of the growth of science, and the continuity and gradualness of the transition from Sayian economics to non-Sayian Keynesian economics.

But this is only because of the assumption made that science as a whole produces progressively more "truthful" statements about economic reality. Once this assumption is abandoned, it becomes easier to see that science may contain incompatible bodies of belief. The view that supply creates its own demand formed the basis of an elaborate theoretical structure to which many classical and neo-classical economists contributed. Some of the important elements of this structure, such as, interdependence of industries in the macrosystem, the dependence of demand upon production, the marginal productivity theory of distribution and the saving–investment theory of interest have been considered in the preceding pages. A great majority of the most eminent economists of this period supported most (if not all) of the conceptual ingredients involved in Say's Law. In addition to the theoretical elaboration, the empirical articulation of Say's theory was also successfully carried out by these economists.

This basic core of the classical and neo-classical system was quite different from the Keynesian system. Yet these out-of-date classical beliefs were produced for the same sorts of reasons and held for the same sorts of reasons as the Keynesian ones today. The opponents of Say's Law pointed out many problems with Say's theory, and these objections provided some of the puzzles which the normal scientists had to solve. Consequently, from the point of view of Kuhn's theory the existence of alternative points of view, supported by minority groups within the scientific community, is the source of puzzles for the large majority of normal scientists. We conclude, therefore, that the existence of non-Sayian ideas in the underworld of classical economics does not prove the continuity of the transition from Sayian to non-Sayian economics. If the transition was gradual and continuous, as is sometimes supposed, why was there such an extraordinary resistance to Keynesian ideas on the part of some economists? Why did the nature of economic research and economic teaching via text-book change so radically? Questions like these can be multiplied and they can be most embarrassing to the incrementalists. But once the Kuhnian point of view is accepted, the nature of the Keynesian Revolution can be much better understood.

# PART II

# The Nature of Money

## Section I

### KNAPP'S THEORY OF MONEY[35]

In criticizing the mercantilist theory of money Smith had stated that "money is merely the instrument of commerce and the measure of value". The theory of the absolute value of money was replaced by a theory that money only has relative value. Smith adopted a nominalist position. But he was certainly not aware of the implications of such a position. For about a hundred years after Smith advanced his theory, economists did not probe into the fundamentals of the subject. They were content with listing some of the functions of money and saying that "money is what money does".

It was not until the beginning of this century that an effort was made by economists to understand the real nature of money. The most exhaustive, systematic, and authoritative work in this area was done by Knapp who advanced the state theory of money. The work of Knapp has been ignored by economists interested in the Keynesian Revolution. From their point of view Knapp's work is interesting because he did not "anticipate" any of the Keynesian ideas.

[35]The definition of some technical terms in given below:

| | | |
|---|---|---|
| Authylic | = | Validity depends upon weight. |
| Proclamatory | = | Validity depends upon proclamation. |
| Morphic | = | In the form of discs or pieces. |
| Giral | = | "Credit" or bank means of payment. |
| Pensatory | = | Payment is made by weighing a commodity. |
| Hylogenic | = | Metal can be converted into money at a certain rate. |
| Specie Money | = | (1) Unlimited coining of the metal. |
| | | (2) Coined pieces have a minimal metallic content. |
| | | Thus specie money is always metalloplatic and hylogenic. |
| Autogenic | = | Money is not converted from a metal. |
| Platic | = | Nature of the money pieces. |
| | | A nickel is metalloplatic. |
| | | A dollar bill is papyroplatic. |
| | | An example of paratypic money is hylogenic papyroplatic money. |

Knapp is not concerned with the problem of the price-level or the purchasing power of money. Nor is he interested in developing a theory of the way in which money influences and is influenced by the economic system. He states explicitly that the state theory of money must not be confused with the economic theory of money.

His avowed purpose is to develop a theory of the essential nature of money. The method appropriate to such an enquiry is the axiomatic method. Knapp uses a method that may be called Aristotelian. By this we mean that his method has the following three attributes. First, he uses Aristotle's logic of classes. The terms "money", "socially recognized exchange commodity", and "means of payment" are names of certain classes of objects. The class of means of payment is not a subclass of the class of all socially recognized exchanged commodities because there are means of payment which are not "commodities" though they may be socially recognized. Money, however, is a subclass of the class of all means of payment.

Second, he uses Aristotle's method of definition *genus et differentiam*. This means that in order to "define" the essence of some class of objects one must describe the genus that contains that class and the differentiating characteristic that distinguishes this species from other species belonging to the same genus. For example, orthotypic money belongs to the genus of morphic proclamatory means of payment. Its differentiating characteristic from other species of the same genus, such as autogenic papyroplatic means of payment is that orthotypic money is hylogenic.

Finally, he subscribes to Aristotle's view that in order to understand something it is necessary to distinguish between its essential and accidental characteristics and those attributes (Aristotle's proprium) that may always accompany a thing but which may not form part of the essence of the thing. For example, morphic means of payment are usually proclamatory, not pensatory. The property of being proclamatory is a proprium. But it does not belong to the essence of morphic means of payment.[36]

Most monetary theorists in the nineteenth century were

---

[36]An example of a morphic pensatory means of payment is given by Knapp (51, pp. 28–29).

"theoretical metallists".[37] This means that they would have subscribed to Roscher's view that the false definitions of money
consist of those that consider it to be something more, and those
that consider it to be something less than the most salable commodity. But the term "metallists" is ambiguous and is unsuited
for the kind of rigorous analysis that Knapp was undertaking.
He used the term "authylism" to denote all those payment
systems in which some "material, measured in some physical
manner is used as a recognized exchange-commodity".[38] In
authylic payment systems the means of payment is an exchange-
commodity. This implies that authylic payments are pensatory
payments, i.e. payment is made by weighing a certain commodity.
Autometallism is the most important form of authylism. But
Knapp insists on the fact that authylic means of payment, and
the autometallistic in particular, are only an instance of means
of payment in general. It is Knapp's basic contention that nothing
whatsoever can be inferred about the essential nature of money
from the authylic payment systems.

In order to prove this proposition Knapp first demonstrates
that lytric debts are nominal. Lytric debts are "debts which
are expressed in units of value and are discharged with a means
of payment (lytron)".[39] As lytric debts are expressed in units of
value the question arises whether the units of value is defined
"really" or nominally. As an authylic system is pensatory
the unit of value in authylism is defined "really", i.e. the
unit of value is defined in terms of the material composing
it. For example, if silver is used as an authylic means of payment
the value of a debt will be measured in "ounces of silver".
Autometallists argue on the basis of such authylic systems that
the unit of value can always be defined really. This Knapp
denies. Suppose that a lytric debt is incurred at a certain
point of time when silver is being used as an authylic means of
payment. The autometallist asserts that the debt can only be
discharged by the transference of a certain quantum of silver of
stipulated fineness and weight. As long as a silver standard
is operative it is indeed true that the debtor can only extinguish
his debt in this manner. But silver *need not be* a means of pay-

[37]Schumpeter (80, p. 699).
[38]Knapp (51, p. 7).
[39]Knapp (51, p. 11).

ment at the time when the debt has to be discharged. The state may decree that the silver standard is to be changed to a gold standard. In this case the debtor does not have to pay in silver. He will pay in gold.

> Lytric debts under autometallism are therefore "real" debts as long as the material for a payment remains the same. As, however, the introduction of another means of payment is from the State's point of view always possible, they are in that case "nominal" debts.[40]

This is Knapp's famous concept of historic linking or historic back-reference. Three steps are involved in such a back-reference. First, the state must name and describe the new means of payment. For example, if the state wishes to change to a gold standard it will name and describe the gold as being a certain kind of metal and so forth. Second, the state must name the new unit of value. It may decree, for example, that such and such a weight of gold is to be the unit of value. It then expresses the means of payment as multiples or fractions of this new unit of value. In this case the name of the new unit of value and the actual means of payment will be the same, namely "an ounce of gold". Finally, the state lays down a price for the old unit of value in terms of the new. For example, it may ordain that gold will exchange for silver in terms of the new ratio laid down in the new lytric constitution.

If the conversion rate declared by the state is different from the ruling market price at which the two commodities are exchanged, some private parties will be hurt by this change in the lytric machinery.

> Now when the State alters the means of payment, though at first still within the limits of authylism (that is, by the introduction of a new material in place of the old) does anyone lose? Of course; and why not, if the State has paramount reasons for its actions.[41]

When one authylic means of payment is replaced by another

---

[40]Knapp (51, p. 15).
[41]Knapp (51, pp. 17–18).

what the creditor receives in terms of the new means of payment depends upon the conversion ratio laid down by the state. But the fact remains that the creditor still gets paid in something which has "intrinsic value". But the concept of historic back-reference also applies to cases in which an authylic payment system is replaced by a chartal payment system. Now chartal payment systems are morphic and proclamatory. The validity of the pieces depends on proclamation not on their content or weight. An example is papyroplatic autogenic money (like the familiar one-dollar bill). When an authylic payment system is replaced by a chartal payment system, the creditor does not get paid in something which has intrinsic value. So at least the metallist would say.

In order to deal with this problem satisfactorily Knapp developed his theory of real and circulatory satisfactions. First, we have to assume that the concepts of "exchange" and "commodity" are primitive concepts. They cannot be defined within the system of lytrology (just as the sign for negation cannot be defined within the propositional calculus). Second, it is necessary to grasp the distinction between an "exchange commodity", "a socially recognized exchange commodity", and a "means of payment". The authylic assertion that a means of payment belongs to the class of exchange commodities is false because there are means of payment (papyroplatic autogenic means of payment, for instance) that are not exchange-*commodities*. Again the assertion that an exchange-commodity belongs to the class of means of payment is false because it may not be socially recognized.

A "socially" recognized exchange-commodity is, of course, always a means of payment, and therefore included in the concept "means of payment". On the other hand, it is untrue that every means of payment is a socially recognized exchange-commodity. It is indeed always socially recognized and also is always used for exchange: but it is questionable whether it is always a *commodity*. In order to be a commodity it must, in addition to its use in the manner provided by law, also be capable of a use in the world or art and industry, and this is not the case with all means of payment (emphasis added).[42]

[42]Knapp (51, p. 4).

Notice how carefully Knapp has laid the foundations of the lytric framework. His ultimate task is to apprehend the "soul" of money and in order to do this he has to define the concept of a means of payment by carefully distinguishing it from other related concepts.

The possibility of "real" satisfaction is undoubtedly a necessary condition for any commodity becoming a socially recognized exchange-commodity. If metals had not been indispensable in handicrafts, autometallism would never have arisen. But there is "real" satisfaction in every commodity which is taken in exchange. A man, who barters a sheep for wooden dishes, takes the dishes only because they give real satisfaction, i.e. he can use them. But the dishes do not thereby become socially recognized exchange-commodities. The possibilities of real use is therefore essential if a commodity (e.g. a metal) is to be chosen as a socially recognized exchange-commodity; but this property is *insufficient* to make it a means of payment (emphasis added).[43]

Notice that Knapp says that "there is real satisfaction in every *commodity* which is taken in exchange" and not that "there is real satisfaction in every *object* or *good* taken in exchange". His entire theory of the *validity* of money is based on this idea. Furthermore the idea that for a commodity to become a socially recognized exchange-commodity, it is necessary that it should be able to give real satisfaction, and that this property is not sufficient to make it a means of payment enables him to identify the source of the *validity* of means of payment.

The nature of circulatory satisfaction should now be clear.

With the satisfaction derived from exchange (circulatory satisfaction) the position is quite different. It is a *necessary* and *sufficient* condition of every means of payment, and of the autometallistic in particular (emphasis added).[44]

Money is defined by Knapp as a morphic proclamatory means

[43]Knapp (51, pp. 5–6).
[44]Knapp (51, p. 6).

of payment. It is "morphic" because it is in the form of pieces or discs, and its validity is not established pensatorially but by proclamation. If the preceding argument is applied to money it is seen that the lytric properties of money enable it to yield circulatory satisfaction when it is used in exchange. The preceding argument proves that the platic properties (i.e. its nature as a piece or disc) of money cannot determine the lytric properties.

Knapp[45] defines "lytric value" as "the value that results from a comparison with the universally recognized means of exchange", and then goes on to say that "from, this again, it follows that we cannot in this sense speak of the value of the means of exchange itself". Only those commodities have lytric value which are not themselves means of exchange. Commodities possess lytric value not because they possess lytric properties, but precisely because they do not. Money is able to invest commodities with lytric value because of its lytric powers or "faculties". But because it possesses these lytric faculties or powers of enduing the world of commodities with lytric value, it must itself be outside this world of "value". Money *platically* considered may have lytric value. But as the lytric properties of money cannot be deduced from the platic properties, money *qua* money does not have lytric value.

But if the lytric properties of money cannot be deduced from the platic, how does money come to possess these properties? In other words, what is the source of the validity of money? Knapp's answer is that "money is the creature of law" and that the state secures the validity of money. By the "validity" of money Knapp did not mean the purchasing power of money. As should be clear from the preceding discussion the "validity of money refers to the lytric powers possessed by the means of payment which enable it to yield circulatory satisfaction.[46] As Ellis puts it, one must distinguish between the "value it has" and "its having value". Validity refers to the second property of "having value". The expression "the value it has" refers to the purchasing power of money. Unless the means of payment is endowed with the property of "having value" it can-

[45]Knapp (51, p. 9).

[46]Knapp's argument has been frequently misunderstood. For a discussion of these misinterpretations the reader is referred to H. Ellis (13, pp. 13–21).

not have the further property "the value it has". Knapp's thesis was that although money has no lytric value, it has the property of "having value" and that the state endues it, so to speak, with this property.

According to the interpretation presented here Knapp's essential contribution was the development of a nominalist theory of money. His insistence that the state is the only creator of the validity of money is a secondary matter. Many other writers, however, have criticized this part of his theory. Schumpeter, for example, ridicules Knapp's theory by saying that it is as valid as the assertion that the institution of marriage is a creature of law[47]. This is what Ellis says in answer to the question whether Knapp's theory is valid or not.[48]

> Generally speaking, I think the answer is certainly yes, under modern conditions. It is government action which maintains the valuableness of our money and secures its par circulation. (His great mistake is in refusing to recognize that the state does not *always* create money.)

The objection that in certain primitive societies (without any government) money exists can be refuted by the argument that a society of men without a government or state is an impossibility as some political theorists have maintained. Ellis' other objections have more force. In the hyperinflation in Germany "cigarette money" supplanted the state-sanctioned money. There are certain conditions under bimetallism when the overvalued money will drive out the undervalued money in accordance with Gresham's law. In this sense it is true that money may have its origin in custom or trade practice.

## Section II

The chartal theory of money advanced by Knapp has the following characteristics. It is a nominalist theory of money. It regards money as the bearer of the unit of account. Chartal theory

---

[47]Schumpeter (80, p. 1090).
[48]Ellis (13, pp. 21–23).

attributes the existence of money to the proclamation by the state of a unit of account and the designation by the state of a bearer of the unit of account. Second, the chartalist maintains that all economic transactions involving money are to be regarded as debt contracts. The state enforces these debt contracts by securing the validity of money, i.e. its acceptability at par with the unit of account. Third, the chartalist maintains that the ability to give circulatory satisfaction is a necessary and sufficient condition of a means of payment, including authylic means of payment. This implies that the lytric properties of money cannot be deduced from the platic. The chartalist believes that the autometallists err in their attempt to differentiate between "real money" possessing intrinsic value and spurious "paper money" which does not have intrinsic value. Finally, the chartalist holds that money has no lytric value because money *qua* money does not give real satisfaction.

It is the object of this section to study the ways in which Knapp's nominalist theory of money was extended and refined by monetary theorists, especially by German monetary theorists.

The first group of theories to be considered is that of the idealistic nominalists. The idealistic nominalists agreed with Knapp on the nominality of money. They objected to the chartalist facet of Knapp's theory. They inveighed against Knapp's view that the state in "big-brother" fashion oversees each and every economic transaction. It will be recalled that Knapp regarded all money transactions as debt contracts that are enforced by the state. The idealistic nominalists upbraided Knapp for this apotheosis of the state. The idealistic viewpoint is ably set forth by Professor Liefmann. (13, p. 42)

Money in the narrower and more rare sense is the real representative means of payment, the money-signs. Money in the broader sense indispensable to the explanation of economic processes is the ... abstract unit of computation. ... The concept of money in the "real" sense is of lesser importance.

Professor Liefmann says that "money is an idea, an abstract entity". As it is in the mind the state has no power over money. The idealistic nominalist does not deny that the state has power over money in the sense that it can create more money. What he is saying is that what the state creates is not "really money", only inferior money, or perhaps the mere physical appearance of "money". The idealistic nominalist treats the value of money in a similar fashion. Lanzburg, for example, believes that although money has "value" it has no "concrete value". It is indubitable that the term "value" is being used in a sense that is different from the ones we have encountered so far, though what it precisely connotes is not clear. Perhaps all the idealistic nominalist means is that because people think about money in calculating economic value, money "really" is "in the mind".

The materialistic nominalists agree in the main with the chartalists and the idealistic nominalists. But they avoid the exaggerations of both. Amon, Wagemann and Nussbaum were the ablest exponents of this variety of nominalism. According to this theory there are two defining properties of money. There must be the abstract unit of account and the physical money-pieces which are expressed as multiples or fractions of that unit of account. Money, therefore, is a medium of exchange and a standard of value. According to Wagemann "money is the bearer of value units with general and unqualified paying power". Wagemann also refers to money as the "epitome or condensation of value experiences".

It would be an error to believe that the problem has been solved merely by asserting that money is a medium of exchange and a standard of value. The question arises as to what the true nature of "price" is. Are the money prices of commodities quantities of *money pieces* or sums of *money units?* The essence of the monetary theory of Amon is that these concepts are analyitcally different. Amon contends that "abstract" prices and "concrete" prices are not the same just as the abstract mark is fundamentally different from its reification or physicalization in the form of the marks that Germans actually handle. The money-pieces, the physical money-things must not be identified with the abstract elements of the *Wahrung* (i.e. the abstract unit of account and its multiples or fractions). Thus to say that the price of a bottle of Rhine wine is four marks is ambiguous and liable to lead to confusion. Strictly speaking, the price of wine is to be expressed as a multiple of the value unit. It may happen, and does often happen, that the abstract elements of the *Wahrung* are reified in the form of "mark appearances". But this one—one correspondence may not hold. For example, in the eighteenth century in England one pound sterling consisted of twenty shillings. But there was no piece or disk corresponding to the abstract element of the *Wahrung*. This is why the materialistic nominalists insist that money is the *physical* bearer of value-units.

While Knapp and other chartalists hold that money is a creature of law, the materialistic nominalists believe that the origin of money is frequently to be found in custom or trade practice.

Knapp's views on the value of money may be stated in the following way. Money does not have value, but has utility because of its validity. While Knapp denies that money has "value", Wagemann feels that it must have "value". His argument is that if money does not have value, as Knapp maintains, how can he explain its influence on the world of goods? How else can it be connected with that world except through its "value"? The puzzle can be resolved, Wagemann affirms, if one perceives that money has "value" in a different sense from that in which commodities have "value". Money is a phenomenon of mass psychology. Money is social, not political. Money has "value" for one individual for the reason that it has "value" for another individual. To put it paradoxically, money has value precisely because one can get rid of it. This is how Ellis sums up Wagemann's theory.[49]

> But desire for money in one individual is unique in that it is finally explained solely by a like desire in other individuals. Here is a case of true mutual interdependence of real circularity in causation, and we are involved in no vicious circle of logic.

The difference between the theories of Knapp and Wagemann must not be exaggerated. Although Knapp said that money does not have value and Wagemann said that money must have value, they were both fundamentally saying the same thing. They were referring to the peculiarity of money which enables it to yield "circulatory" satisfaction. Now the concept of circulatory

[49]Ellis (13, p. 49).

satisfaction is not as simple as it seems to be. As shall be seen presently it created many problems when theorists considered the applicability of the Marshallian supply-and-demand apparatus to money. The difference between the views of Knapp and Wagemann lies in the fact that the former regarded money as a creature of law and the latter considered it to be a social entity.

## PUZZLES IN THE ARTICULATION OF
## THE NOMINALIST THEORY OF MONEY

It must be remembered that after the Jevonian Revolution economists had generally agreed that the value of commodities is determined by demand and supply. Microeconomic theory after Jevons was formulated in terms of subjective value principles. After the nominalists had developed a sound theory of the nature of money the question naturally arose whether the new supply and demand analysis could be applied to money. Of course, even writers before Jevons had said that the value of money depends upon demand and supply. Mill, for example, said that the value of money depends on demand and supply. But in saying this Mill meant merely that the value of money is explained by the quantity theory of money, the left side of the quantity equation standing for supply and the right for demand. But as Mill believed in the cost of production theory of value he argued that demand and supply are only the *proximate* determinants of the value of money. The ultimate regulator, as in the case of commodities in general, is the cost of production of the monetary metal. But Mill and the majority of monetary theorists in the nineteenth century were metallists. They regarded money as being on a par with other commodities and subject to the same laws of value-determination. Having very vague and fuzzy ideas about the essential nature of money they said that the quantity theory of money is an "objective" supply and demand theory of the value of money. But the terms "supply", "demand", and "money" were not subjected to rigorous analysis.

It is only when the nominalists attempted to apply the Marshallian supply and demand apparatus to money that difficult problems arose. The heart of the problem was to explain the peculiar property of money which enables it to yield circulatory satisfaction. Money does not have the power to satisfy wants but has the power to purchase things that do have that power. But then in what sense can it be said that someone "demands" money? It makes sense to talk about the "demand" for cars because cars have utility or value and the demand is based on the properties that cars have of yielding real satisfaction. But Knapp had shown that the lytric properties of the object that is regarded as money cannot be deduced from the platic. Suppose, for example, that we have an argyroplatic autogenic means of payment. In this case it makes sense to speak about the "demand" for silver as long as one is only thinking of the platic use of silver in the arts and industry. But the "moneyness" or lytricity of silver is independent of its platic properties. Consequently the monetary demand for silver is not a derived demand. But in that case does it make sense to speak about the monetary demand for silver? As real satisfaction can only be derived from the platic use of silver in the arts and industry, and if such a platic use of silver precludes its lytric use for the purpose of obtaining circulatory satisfaction, does it not follow that the very applicability of the concept of demand becomes doubtful when the object is desired only so far as its lytric use is concerned?

Virtually all the major monetary theorists felt that there was another even more devastating objection to the concept of the demand for money. The concept of the demand for money is useful because in conjunction with the concept of the supply of money it can be used to derive the value of money. But the problem is that the demand itself depends upon that value. Hence, argued these theorists, it cannot be used to explain that value.

> Obviously no one can tell what utility he derives from a dollar in his reserves . . . until he knows what the dollar will buy: and this is just what we are trying to explain.[50]

These theorists have been severely criticized by Patinkin[51] and others for their alleged failure to distinguish between "individual experiments" and "market experiments". Patinkin

[50]Ellis (13, p. 67).
[51]Patinkin (66, pp. 11–12).

is more interested in showing how "false" their views were than in understanding why these theorists felt as they did and what sort of arguments they used to support their contentions. Kuhn says that the new historiographers "rather than seeking the permanent contributions of an older science to our present vantage, they attempt to display the historical integrity of that science in its own time".[52] It is in this light that we must study their theories.

Consider the case of Ellis who strongly espoused the view that the "demand for money is a non-entity"[53] and that the marginal utility explanation is circular. It is not at all clear that Ellis confused "individual experiments" with "market experiments". Consider the following passage:[54]

> The *process* by which equilibrium (is arrived at is that) at a given level of prices, anyone who possesses more dollars than he desires to hold under the three-fold real value calculation will spend more rapidly; the acceleration of velocity forces up prices until the stock of dollars bears the correct proportion to "total money work to be done".

If at any given absolute price level the "supply" of money is greater than the "demand" expenditures on goods and services will increase until prices rise sufficiently to eliminate the excess supply. This would be a very good description of the Patinkinian real-balance effect were it not for the fact that Ellis does not think it is legitimate to speak about the demand for money.

The view of the nominalists that the marginal utility explanation of the value of money is circular cannot be attributed to their failure to distinguish between "individual experiments" and "market experiments". They knew that the demand for wheat determines the value of wheat and that the quantity demanded depends on that value, and that consequently it makes sense to speak about the demand for wheat. But they insisted that money is different and that the same argument, though unexceptionable when applied to ordinary commodities, becomes circular when applied to money. In discussing the value-determination of

[52]Kuhn (52, p. 3).
[53]Ellis (13, p. 68).
[54]Ellis (13, pp. 193–194).

ordinary commodities they would have started their analysis by postulating a price and then seeing whether quantity demanded equalled the quantity supplied. In the case of an ordinary commodity a certain amount is demanded at any given price to satisfy real wants. But money only yields circulatory satisfaction and as circulatory satisfaction is obtained only after money is spent on the purchase of goods it cannot set or cause the value of money. Real satisfaction does not depend on the price of commodities. Hence it can cause or explain value. Circulatory satisfaction depends on the price of money. Hence it cannot explain that price.

Whereas a given value or price upon coal divides the potential users into the intra-marginal portion who actually buy and whose wants are satisfied and the extra-marginal or excluded portion, with money no such separation is evident. There are no excluded or extra-marginal buyers. . . people who cannot afford to use money. *Everybody already uses money. . . .* What Helferrich fails to deduce however is that if marginal utility loses its meaning, so does marginal demand by the same token and if the margin disappears, the supposed demand schedule loses its causative significance, since marginal demand sets value (emphasis added).[55]

Karl Helferrich had argued that although marginal utility cannot explain the value of money because it itself depends on that value, supply and demand can explain the value of money. But any rigorous concept of demand must be derived from subjective value considerations. Hence Ellis has no difficulty in disposing of Helferrich's argument.

In value theory a price does not divide consumers into an intra-marginal and an extra-marginal portion. To say that marginal demand sets value does not mean that when the price of the commodity rises above the equilibrium level some consumers become non-consumers. It only means that at the higher price fewer units of the commodity are demanded. It is tempting, therefore, to dismiss Ellis' reasoning as being based on an error. From an historiographical point of view, however, nothing is to

[55]Ellis (13, p. 65).

be gained by decrying arguments based on the old paradigm. Whether or no Ellis' reasoning is "false" is not so important. What is important is to understand the sort of world these theorists lived in, and the way in which they solved the puzzles that arose within their paradigm. Ellis says that people do not demand money that they simply have it. The significance of such a conception of money will become apparent in a later section where it will be demonstrated that it is congruous with the orientation of the quantity theory of money which is an integral part of the classical paradigm.

Ludwig Mises made an ingenious attempt to rescue the marginal utility approach. For Mises the marginal utility of money is the marginal utility of the goods on which it is spent.

It is true that the subjective valuation of money presupposes an existing objective exchange-value; but the value that has to be presupposed is not the same as the value to be explained; what has to be presupposed is *yesterday's* exchange-value.... If in this way we continually go farther and farther back we must eventually arrive at a point...where the value of money is nothing other than the value of an object that is useful in some other way than money.[56]

It is a consequence of Knapp's theory of money that the "demand" for money is not a derived demand, i.e. the lytric demand cannot be derived from the platic demand for money. Mises argues that the demand for money is *ultimately* a derived demand. Today's demand for money cannot indeed derive from the platic use of money in the arts and industry as follows from the nominalist theory to which Mises subscribed. But as the problem of the value of money cannot be solved until it is derived from subjective value considerations the only way out of the difficulty is to resort to an historical regression. But this is tantamount to admitting that one does not have an adequate theory of the value of money.

According to Ellis the Cambridge cash-balance theorists had succeeded in deriving the value of money from subjective value considerations. In England monetary theorists in the Marshallian

[56]L. Mises (63, pp. 120–121).

tradition did say that the value of money is determined by demand and supply. But demand in this theory is not a demand for money but a demand for "resources in the form of money", to use Marshall's expression.[57]

Similar problems arise with the concept of the "supply" of money. First, there is the difficulty in connection with the velocity of money. Money, unlike ordinary commodities, performs its functions by circulating from person to person. Hence, in a sense the "supply" of money should mean not only the existing stock of money but the rate at which it circulates, i.e. MV rather than M should denote supply. Second, as Ellis has argued, although the expression "supply of money" can be used, no additional information is conveyed which would not be given by "stock" or "quantity". Take the case of paper money. "The patent fact under inflation is that the 'supply' of notes is neither fixed nor a function of the exchange value of the issue."[58] In the case of a metallic money the amount of the metal produced varies inversely with the purchasing power of money. Hence one can speak of a supply schedule for gold. Even here there are difficulties. As long as gold production retains its aleatory nature part of the quantity produced will not depend on variations in the purchasing power of money. Also, the annual "supply" of gold is such a minute proportion of the existing stock or existing "supply" that changes in the value of money do not have appreciable effects on the "supply" of gold.

[57]The fundamental problem for the post-Knappian nominalists was to explain the peculiar property of money which enables it to yield circulatory satisfaction. In other words, the question was the sense in which money has "value". From the circulatory argument monetary theorists concluded that money does not have "value" in the sense in which commodities have "value". But there are other senses in which money may be said to have "value" or "utility". There is for example the Marshallian concept of the marginal utility of income. But as the marginal utility of income presupposes prices it cannot be used to explain them. Money may be said to have "value" because it is superior to barter. But surely this "value" of money cannot explain the absolute price level.

In authylic theory these problems do not arise. In authylic monetary systems the demand for money *qua* money seems to arise from the platic demand for money regarded as a commodity. It is only because the nominalist claims that the lytric properties of money cannot be deduced from the platic that these difficulties arise.

[58]Ellis (13, p. 69).

CONCLUSIONS

Although the majority of economists after Smith were quantity theorists they were not overly concerned with developing a sound theory of the essential nature of money. Knapp's theory of money was put forward in 1905. Although there is an element of hyperbole involved it may be said that Knapp axiomatized monetary theory. Knapp's nominalist theory was extended and refined by subsequent theosists. This nominalist theory found the "soul" of money in the property that enables it to yield circulatory satisfaction. Money was seen as an object that does not have the power to satisfy real wants but has the power to purchase things that do have that power. Thus the antimercantilist theory of money initially put forward by Smith was put on a sound basis.

Several puzzles arose in the articulation of this paradigm theory. Money seemed to elude the universally valid Marshallian supply and demand organon. The puzzles could not be solved on the basis of the concepts and theories supplied by the paradigm. Paradigm-based expectations were frustrated. But other paradigm-based expectations were fulfilled. The nominalist theory merely articulated the theories of Smith and Mill. Furthermore, it fulfilled the expectations that were based on the quantity theory of money. Quantity theorists had argued that as average prices are always proportional to money the amount of work done by money is independent of its quantity. The amount of real satisfaction afforded by a commodity is obviously an increasing function of the quantity of the commodity. Quantity theorists maintained that this is not true in the case of money. By demonstrating that money has the peculiar property of yielding circulatory satisfaction the nominalist theory of money fulfilled this expectation derived from the quantity theory of money.

## Section III

### THE QUANTITY THEORY OF MONEY

The quantity theory of money is one of the oldest theories in economic science. According to Professor Hegeland[59] the quantity theory of money was known to Confucious and Xenophon at least in an inchoate form. We may leave to the exponents of the individualistic approach the task of decrying, through the mists of hoary time, the lineaments of this seminal theory when it was first put forward. Fortunately, in a Kuhnian analysis one does not have to decide whether passages like the one given below state the quantity theory or not.

> A material was chosen, the value of which, being generally recognized and lasting, would remedy the difficulties at the bargaining by the equality of the quantities. And this material, coined by the state, is connecting the right to use and to own not so much on account of its substance (content) as on account of its quantity (number of coins) and so both are no longer called commodities, but one of them price.[60]

In the mercantilist system money is wealth. Consequently the welfare of a nation is not independent of the quantity of money. On the contrary the wealth of a country consists precisely of the precious metals it contains. In challenging this view Smith said that money is merely the instrument of commerce and a measure of value. As money is the instrument of commerce it is in great demand. Goods and services can be obtained only through the expenditure of money. Hence it may seem to the vulgar mind that money itself is valuable. But money cannot satisfy wants. It can only purchase other things that can satisfy wants. That being the case, does the work to be done by money depend in anyway on the *quantity* of money? The most authoritative answer to this question was given by Mill.

It often happens that the universal belief of one age of man-

---

[59] H. Hegeland (39).
[60] H. Hegeland (39, p. 11).

kind. . .a belief from which no one *was*, nor, without an extraordinary effort of genius and courage, *could* be at that time free. . .becomes to a subsequent age so palpable an absurdity, that the only difficulty then is to imagine how such a thing can ever have appeared credible.[61]

After reflecting on the mercantilist doctrine Mill continues:[62]

So soon as they as asked themselves what is really meant by money – what it is in its essential characters, and the precise nature of the functions it performs – they reflected that money, like other things, is only a desirable possession on account of its uses. . .Further consideration showed that the uses of money are in no respect promoted by increasing the quantity which exists and circulates; the service which it performs being as well rendered by a small as by a large amount. Two million quarters of corn will not feed so many persons as four millions; but two millions of pound sterling will carry on as much traffic. . .as four millions. *Money, as money, satisfies no want* (emphasis added).

There cannot, in short, be intrinsically a more insignificant thing, in the economy of society, than money; except in the character of a contrivance for sparing time and labour.[63]

Almost seventy years later Cambridge quantity theorists described the essential nature of money in almost the same terms. This is the real sense in which the quantity theory operated as a paradigm for classical monetary theory. The "quantity theory" is first a theory of the essential nature of money. In terms of Knapp's theory it states that the circulatory satisfaction yielded by money is independent of its quantity.

The influx of the precious metals from America in the fifteenth or sixteenth century and the concomitant rise in prices prompted theoretical speculation about the relationship between money and the level of prices. Although Copernicus had alluded to such a relationship it was Bodin who used it explicitly and syste-

[61]J. S. Mills (60, p. 3).
[62]J. S. Mill (60, pp. 5–6).
[63]J. S. Mill (60, p. 488).

matically to explain the rise of prices. This is why Bodin is regarded as the founder of the quantity theory of money. Bodin was the "first" to point out that it is the influx of metals from America that *caused* the rise in prices and the depreciation of the value of money.

We know that in the latter half of the eighteenth century the mercantilist paradigm had been replaced by the quantity theory paradigm. Smith was one of the main architects of this revolution. According to Hegeland, the first economist to state clearly this anti-mercantilist theory was the English philosopher John Locke. Bodin had formulated a quantity theory of the value of money, not the idea that the quantity of money did not affect the validity of money. Locke said that prices are always *proportional* to the quantity of money. Consequently the amount of work done by money is independent of its quantity. Bodin's proposition about causation and Locke's proposition about proportionality were later combined by Hume and others into the proposition that variations in the quantity of money would cause proportional variations in the value of money. This became the generally accepted version of the quantity theory until Cantillon pointed out that other things are not always equal. Thus the extended quantity theory, as Hegeland calls it, was formulated. This is Cantillon's statement of the extended quantity theory.[64]

Everybody agrees that the abundance of money or its increase in exchange raises the price of everything. The quantity of money brought from America to Europe for the last two centuries justifies this truth by experience. . .He (Locke) has clearly seen that the abundance of money makes every thing dear, but he has not considered how it does so. The great difficulty of this question consists in what way and in what proportion the increase of money raises prices. . . .I conceive that when a large surplus of money is brought into a State the new money gives a new turn to consumption and even a new speed to circulation. But it is not possible to say exactly to what extent.

This is the paradigmatic theory that held undisputed sway over

[64]E. Dean (8, pp. 3–8).

the minds of economists for another 200 years or so. Notice that the idea that velocity can vary is explicitly introduced. The problem that Cantillon poses for himself is not the discovery of a conceptual framework. He knows that he has one whose truth has been corroborated by "experience". The problem is merely to determine the exact extent of its applicability, to interpret the facts in terms of its categories and to articulate it so as to place it beyond the pale of dispute or controversy. This task was finally accomplished by Irving Fisher whose theory will be studied below.

The extended quantity theory states that the quantity theorem is true only when certain conditions are satisfied. Hence it is definitely an improvement on the naive quantity theory which states that an increase in the quantity of money always raises prices by the same proportion. Such an elaboration and articulation of the quantity theory must not be misconstrued. Schumpeter, for example, argues that as Fisher and Mill were aware of the fact that the velocity is variable they anticipated Keynes.[65] In the case of Fisher, Schumpeter says that "he (Fisher) explicitly recognised the variability of velocity" and that his theory "constitutes a stepping-stone between money and employment."[66] But a theory is never consistent with all the facts. In other words, there are dissonant elements within every scientist's cognitive field. A scientist's awareness to minor dissonant elements must not be taken to mean that he "anticipated" the correct theories that are to be developed in the future. The crucial point is that the quantity theorists were *committed* to the basic approach. The commitment enabled these scientists to achieve a considerable degree of consonance within their cognitive fields. The quantity theorists did not consider two alternative conceptual frameworks to decide "rationally" on their merits. Cantillon, for example, knows that the theory is correct. What he wants to show is how and why it is correct. He has implicit confidence that phenomena do behave in the way the theory predicts. All he wants to show is that particular phenomena behave in that fashion.

[65]Schumpeter (80, p. 705).
[66]Schumpeter (8, p. 234).

## FISHER'S THEORY

Fisher was one of the most famous exponents of the quantity theory of money. Fisher expressed his theory in the well-known equation of exchange MV—M'V'—PT. As Newcomb was the "first" to express the theory in this form the equation of exchange is often called the Newcomb – Fisher equation.

Fisher's theory was by no means "original". But Fisher carefully stated the theory and specified the conditions under which it is true. He was impelled to do this "because it seems nothing less than a scandal in economic Science that there should be any ground for dispute on so fundamental a proposition".[67]

Fisher's theory is that except during transition periods the effect of a change in the quantity of money is a proportional change in money prices. This theory is not the same thing as the equation of exchange. The equation of exchange is merely a convenient way of expressing the theory, and demonstrating its validity when duly supplemented by specific data.

The equation of exchange has often been referred to as a truism or a tautology. The implication is that as the equation of exchange expresses an analytic proposition, it does not give any information about experience. Economists operating on a crude positivist theory of knowledge have been satisfied with such a view of the matter. Recently, however, Harrod has stated that he calls the equation of exchange a tautology only with some misgiving. Harrod says that he is "profoundly dissatisfied with the existing state of deductive logic".[68] If all analytic propositions are mere manipulations of symbols that give us no "information" about experience, how is it that some analytic propositions (such as the propositions of mathematics) are more useful than the infinitely many utterly useless tautologies?[69] Of course, Harrod is not the first to criticize the analytic – synthetic distinction. Anti-empiricists such as Blanshard and Polanyi have made similar criticisms of the positivist theory.

---

[67]I. Fisher (17, p. 158).

[68]R. Harrod (33, p. 155).

[69]The classic statement of the positivist theory of mathematics is to be found in the article by C. Hempel, "Geometry and Empirical Science" in W. Schaaf (79). For particularly incisive criticisms of this theory, see M. Polanyi (69).

Fisher's view about the equation of exchange is very interesting.[70]

"Truisms" should never be neglected. The greatest generalizations of physical science such as that forces are proportional to mass and acceleration, are truisms...these truisms are the most fruitful sources of useful mechanical knowledge. To throw away the equation of exchange because it is so obviously true is to neglect the chance to formulate for economic science some of the most important and exact laws of which it is capable.

The equation of exchange should be regarded as a shared exemplar of the classical paradigm. In Kuhn's theory a shared exemplar is a particular solution of a puzzle that is used by scientists in a tacit way to see different situations as like another. For example, the "truism" $F=MA$ is a shared exemplar in physics. This equation tells the student what to look for. It signals "the gestalt in which the situation is to be seen".[71] A student learning physics has to study the laws of motion of a pendulum. He has already learnt that problems of motion have to be studied in terms of the relationships among the three entities, namely force, mass, and acceleration. (In the time of Aristotle a student would learn that problems of motion have to be studied in terms of the natural faculties or powers within bodies which move them to their "natural" places.) The law $F=MA$ signals the gestalt in which the problem of the motion of pendulum is to be seen.

The equation of exchange fulfilled a similar function in economics. Although the equation was developed only by Newcomb and Fisher, earlier economists made tacit use of it. A student learning classical monetary theory would be told that money must always be studied in relation to the price level. In 1935 when Hicks called for a marginal revolution in money the fundamental problem was not the relation between money and prices. According to Hicks the fundamental problem of the theory of money was the relationship between the holding of money and the interest rate. Monetary theory had to answer the question why people hold money even when interest rates are positive. Such a problem could not be formulated within the classical paradigm.

---

[70]Fisher (17, p. 159).
[71]Kuhn (52, p. 189).

Classical monetary theory laid special emphasis on the special relationship between the quantity of money and the price level. Virtually all the major theorists from Smith to Dennis Robertson took special care to point out that other things being equal a change in the quantity of money leads to a proportional change in money prices.

Fisher was careful to point out that the quantity theory does not treat velocity and the volume of trade as constants. From the point of view of the relation between money and prices they should be regarded as exogenous variables. In other words when the quantity of money is increased the volume of trade and the velocity of money may change due to the operation of *other causes*. If they change they may offset or neutralize the effect of money on prices. What the quantity theorist says is that "so far as M *by itself* is concerned, its effect on the p's is strictly proportional".[72] Fisher has been criticized by Tobin and others for not having a theory of velocity and trade. What this criticism amounts to is that Fisher did not have a "correct" theory of these variables. In his article in the encyclopaedia of the social sciences on liquidity preference Modigliani thinks that it is very surprising that in his theory of money Fisher does not once talk about interest rates. These criticisms stem from the use of a faulty historiographical framework. The task of the historian is not to seek the permanent contributions of an older science to our present knowledge. His task is to understand the world in which the older scientists lived, the kinds of puzzles they solved and the gestalt in which they were wont to perceive situations that we may now be looking at differently.

Fisher made tacit use of the classical theory of output and employment that has been described in the first section. It is for this reason that he can say that the stream of business depends not on the quantity of money, but on the natural resources of the country and the productivity of the labour force. Similarly his theory of velocity stressed institutional considerations such as the frequency of payments and so forth. The idea here was to show that as far as the relationship between money and prices is concerned velocity, of money is not so important.

[72]Fisher (17, p. 158).

Fisher stated explicitly that the quantity theory of money is valid only under "normal" conditions. In "transition periods" phenomena behave differently. Fisher's theory of the "transition period" is the following.[73] Suppose that an opportunity for a very profitable investment is opened up for a group of Schumpeterian innovating entrepreneurs. As these entrepreneurs borrow money from the banks to finance their projects, the quantity of money, particularly in the form of bank-deposits, rises. This means that the total volume of debts rises. From the equation of exchange we infer that prices rise. The rise of the price-level is accelerated due to the increase of velocity (particularly of $V'$). Velocity increases because of the greater optimism in the business community and the fear of depreciation of money balances. On the other hand, the rise in prices is mitigated by an increase in production. The appreciation of goods in terms of money is not fully taken account of by the banks. As a result the real rate of interest lags behind the money rate. As prices rise faster than costs businessmen increase their borrowing. Over-indebtedness ensues. Liquidation begins. Businessmen try to reduce their debts. The quantum of bank-deposits falls. From the equation of exchange we infer that prices fall. The fall of prices increases the real burden of debts. Banks at last raise the money rate of interest. As a result of all these factors there are many bankruptcies and the downward process begins.

It will be recalled that Mill empirically articulated Say's theory of output (i.e. the theory signalled the gestalt in which the empirical phenomena were to be seen). Mill admitted that at times there may be an undersupply of money and he attributed it to an excess of speculative purchases. Fisher performed a similar empirical and theoretical articulation of the quantity theory of money. Fisher admitted that during "transition periods" the strict quantity theorem fails to hold. But he did not attach much importance to the transition periods. Whenever phenomena failed to conform exactly to the quantity theory, it could always be said that this was a "transition period" in which deviations from the predictions of the theory are to be expected. The important point is these qualifications and reservations did

[73]This theory was expanded in Fisher's *Booms and Depressions* (18, pp. 55–73).

not dilute or weaken Fisher's commitment to the quantity theory.

> The quantity theory has been one of the most bitterly contested theories in economics, largely because the recognition of its truth or falsity affected powerful interests in commerce and politics. It has been maintained – and the assertion is scarcely an exaggeration – that the theorems of Euclid would be bitterly controverted if financial or political interests were involved.[74]

If a theory is incontrovertibly correct, then it follows that it cannot be controverted and impugned on rational or intellectual grounds. Some other reasons have to be found.

## KNAPP'S THEORY OF MONEY AND FISHER'S QUANTITY THEORY

Although Fisher did not contribute significantly to the theoretical articulation of the money concept, he knew that in order to have a rigorous quantity theory of money it is necessary to have a sound theory of money. Fisher was aware of the work of Knapp.[75] He knew that Knapp's nominalist theory of money provides the rigorous foundation for the quantity theory of money.[76]

> It is the number (of dollars) and not the weight, that is essential. This fact needs great emphasis. It is a fact which differentiates money from all other goods and explains the peculiar manner in which its purchasing power is related to other goods. Sugar, for instance, has a specific desirability dependent on its quantity in pounds. *Money has no such quality* (emphasis added).

> The quantity theory of money thus rests, ultimately, upon the fundamental peculiarity which money alone of all goods

---

[74]Fisher (17, pp. 14–15).

[75]On page 32 of his book Fisher refers to the work of Knapp and the other German nominalists.

[76]Fisher (17, p. 32).

possesses, — the fact that it has no power to satisfy human wants except a power to purchase things that do have such power.

The essential point in the problem of the purchasing power of money is the *number* of dollars and not their weight. A change in the quantity of money will have a proportional effect on prices. Consequently the amount of work done by money is independent of its quantity. In the case of ordinary commodities which yield real satisfaction the amount of work done by them depends in a direct manner on the quantity of the commodity. Hence it follows that the satisfaction that money gives must be of a different sort. The question about the kind of satisfaction that money gives had been satisfactorily answered by Knapp and the German nominalists. Money yields circulatory satisfaction. The equation of exchange was a shared exemplar of the classical paradigm. It told the theorists to look for and emphasize a special relation between the quantity of money and the level of prices. As a result of the work of Knapp and the German nominalists it was seen that this peculiar relation between money and prices was ultimately due to the fact that money does not have the power to satisfy wants except the power to purchase things that do have such power.

It must not be supposed that Fisher was the only one to see the relation between Knapp's theory and the quantity theory. This is what Keynes said.[77]

(The quantity theory) is fundamental. Its correspondence with fact is not open to question. . . .The Theory flows from the fact that money as such has no utility except what is derived from its exchange-value, that is to say from the utility of the things which it can buy. Valuable articles other than money have a utility in themselves.

Robertson also adverts to the two peculiarities of money: the relation between the quantity of money and its value is of a very special sort, and the fact that because money yields only circu-

[77]J. M. Keynes (49, pp. 81–82).

latory satisfaction the work done by money does not depend on its quantity.[78]

## Section IV

### NORMAL RESEARCH RELATING TO ABSOLUTE PRICES AND VELOCITY

The equation of exchange states that money and prices are connected in a certain way. The influence of money on prices depends upon the two other terms of the equation, V and T. The classical theory relating to T has already been described in the first section.

An important focus of normal monetary research had to do with the P term. In this area, perhaps more than in any other, Fisher made the most signal contribution. The concept of the absolute price level is by no means one that naturally comes to the mind. Its formulation requires a definite amount of analytic effort. Relative prices are more concrete and more familiar. A large part of Fisher's writings is devoted to the elucidation of the distinction between these two concepts. We are not sure but it is likely that the concept of money-illusion is his brain-child. It is easy to understand why he was so interested in the concept of absolute prices. It played an important part in his monetary theory, cycle theory, banking theory, and in his practical proposals. But most important of all is the fact that the concept of the absolute price level made it possible to develop a rigorous quantity theory of money. Of course other quantity theorists had talked about "prices" and the influence of money on them. But their ideas on the matter were not very clear. Fisher saw the problem of absolute prices was intimately connected with the problem of index-numbers. Consequently he

---

[78]Robertson (71, pp. 5–6). Similar views were expressed by other economists. For an account of Walras' views the reader is referred to Schumpeter, *History* p. 1100. Ellis, *op. cit.*, pp. 4–6, also tells us about the extremely close connections between the quantity theory and the nominalist theory of money. The entire argument is to be found in J. S. Mill's chapter on the value of money, *op. cit.*, pp. 489–498.

devoted a lot of attention to them. In his *Purchasing Power of Money* he compiled a list of 44 index-numbers and commented on their merits and defects. All this work had significance and value because there was a theory which guaranteed that it would be useful.

While Fisher primarily contributed to the empirical articulation of the concept of the price level, work on its theoretical properties was being done by Kunt Wicksell of Sweden. The question that intrigued Wicksell was the nature of the forces that stabilized the absolute prices at a given level. In studying this question Wicksell came to the conclusion that the principles governing relative prices are fundamentally different from the principles governing absolute prices. The principle governing relative prices is the marginal utility principle. In equilibrium, the relative prices of commodities must be equal to the ratios of their marginal utilities. If the price is different from the equilibrium price corrective forces will be brought into play to drive it back to the equilibrium level.

With money and its price the case is different.

No theorist can today lend his support to the traditional conception that money possesses in itself an independent, and more or less invariable, intrinsic value .... Money as such, i.e. so long as it fulfils the functions of money, is of significance in the economic world only as an intermediary. *It is its purchasing power over commodities that determines its utility and marginal utility, and it is not determined by them.*[79]

The marginal utility of money does not determine the price of money as in the case of ordinary commodities. The marginal utility of money itself depends on the price of money. But then what is the principle that governs absolute prices? Wicksell considers and rejects the suggestion that the force governing absolute prices is to be found in the commodity market. If all prices are changed in the same proportion, ratios of marginal utilities are still equal to the ratios of relative prices and no excess demand appears anywhere.

[79]K. Wicksell (92, p. 29).

If there is any reaction whatever away from a *general* level of prices that is too high or low, it must originate somehow or other from *outside* the commodity market.[80]

Wicksell's search for the principle governing absolute prices is conducted openly in the pages of his book. First, Wicksell considers a view that was popular in his time. According to this "theory" movements in absolute prices can be attributed to changes taking place on "the side of goods". The price of each good tends to equality with its cost of production. Hence if there is technical progress in the production of a group of important commodities, can we not attribute a fall in the price level to the change in the cost conditions of such industries? Wicksell has little difficulty in disposing of this argument. The fallacy lies in assuming that because the relative price of commodity A has fallen as compared with other commodities the average price-level has also fallen. But the average price level need not fall. It may even rise.

The second theory is Nassau Senior's cost of production theory. The shortcomings of this theory are well known. It does not apply to papyroplatic money. Even when gold (chrysoplatic money) or silver (argyroplatic money) is used as means of payment, the theory has limited applicability because the annual supply of such metals is only a tiny fraction of the existing stock and the price of money depends on the existing stock.

According to Wicksell the correct explanation is provided by the quantity theory of money. If for some reason the level of prices rises and the stock of cash is unchanged "the cash balances will gradually appear to be *too small in relation to the* new level of prices".[81] Relative to the *flow* of money expenditures the *stock* of cash balances will be too small. This is precisely what Patinkin means by the real-balance effect.

(The Quantity Theory) consists of more than a mere "truism"... The Theory provides a real explanation of its subject matter, and in a manner that is logically incontestable....The quantity theory is *theoretically* valid as long as the assumption of *ceteris*

[80]K. Wicksell (92, p. 24).
[81]Wicksell (92, p. 39).

*paribus* is firmly adhered to. But among the "things" that have to be supposed to remain "equal" ... is the velocity of circulation.[82]

But the velocity of circulation of *cash* cannot be supposed to be equal in an economy in which *bank credit* is used. Credit increases the "virtual velocity" of cash.[83] In other words, Wicksell treats credit as a rate of flow. A payment made by cheque increases the virtual velocity of cash. According to Wicksell's first condition of monetary equilibrium an upward cumulative process will be initiated if the banks lower their money rate of interest below the natural rate. Myrdal showed that such an interest-differential creates the opportunity for entrepreneurs to reap an investment gain.[84] Consequently, entrepreneurs will increase their *borrowing* from the banks and increase their *demand* in the higher stages of production. Thus prices will rise and the upward cumulative process will be initiated. The important point to note is that the increase of bank credit increases the virtual velocity of cash. Wicksell's interest-differential theory is designed to throw light on the forces that maintain prices at a certain level. From the quantity equation it follows that the price level depends upon the quantity of money and its velocity of circulation. Of course, it also depends upon T but Wicksell using the classical theory of output did not think that its influence on prices was appreciable. According to Wicksell earlier quantity theorists had not provided a rigorous theory of velocity. Wicksell's theory was intended to fill this lacuna. His theory also showed that whereas the marginal utility principle governed relative prices, the rate of interest governed absolute prices.

Eariler quantity theorists were aware that the level of prices depends not only on the stock of money but also on the rapidity with which it circulates. But the idea of the rapidity or velocity with which money circulates was never fully explored by them. Even J. S. Mill was very confused about the matter. Mill says that the phrase rapidity of circulation "must not be understood to mean the number of purchases made by each piece of money in a given time". "The essential point is, not how often the same

[82]Wicksell (92, pp. 39–43).
[83]Wicksell (92, chapter 6). Also see Ellis *op. cit.*, 154–159.
[84]Myrdal's reformulation of Wicksell's theory will be considered later.

money changes hands in a given time, but how often it changes hands in order to perform a given amount of traffic."[85]

In order to determine the amount of traffic to be done by money one must already know its "velocity". The problem is that Mill is using two different concepts of velocity: the velocity of money and the velocity of circulation of goods.[86]

Both Fisher and Wicksell did much towards devoloping a satisfactory theory of velocity. They distinguished between the coin-transfer concept and the person-turnover concept of velocity. In the person-turnover approach one considers the average number of coins that pass through one man's hands and divide it by the average amount of money held by him. In the coin-transfer approach one considers the average number of times a coin circulates in a given period of time. Care must be exercised in the use of the second method. The V that is relevant to the quantity equation refers only to the net circulation of money against goods and not the gross circulation. Furthermore, the term V in the quantity equation is a weighted average of velocities of different coins.[87] In addition to these concepts there is the concept of the "average time of turnover". This concept measures the amount of time taken by all the money in being turned over once.

In addition to the development of these concepts of velocity, economists also tried to give velocity a psychological grounding. They did this to assimilate this part of monetary theory with the theory of value, which, after the subjective-value revolution, had emphasized the psychological elements of decision-making. The Fisher approach was regarded as very "mechanistic".

The claim that I make on behalf of mine is merely that it is a somewhat more effective engine of analysis. It focuses attention on the proportion of their resources that people choose to keep in the form of titles to legal tender instead of

[85]*Principles*, p. 494. Wicksell chides Mill for his confused statement and deplores the unsatisfactory state of velocity theory.

[86]Much work was done in the twenties and thirties on esoteric aspects of the theory of velocity. This highly technical and difficult material cannot be considered here. The interested reader should consult A. Marget (58, Vol. 1, pp. 548–564) and the references cited there.

[87]For details, see Fisher (17, pp. 349–366).

focusing it on "velocity of circulation". This fact gives it, as I think, a real advantage, because it brings us at once into relation with volition.[88]

I am not in any sense an "opponent" of the "quantity theory" or a hostile critic of Professor Fisher's lucid analysis.[89]

This psychologizing of velocity theory by the post-Marshallian Cambridge theorists, such as Pigou, Hawtrey, Robertson, and Keynes was undertaken within the quantity-theory framework as Pigou himself points out.[90] Although Pigou insists that the cash-balance theory represents merely a different approach to the quantity theory of money, the difference between the Fisherine and Cambridge approaches is not inconsiderable. First, Fisher, unlike the Cambridge theorists, did not think that a supply and demand explanation is a real explanation. Second, the Cambridge theorists gave "demand" a volitional connotation that is not to be found in Fisher's theory. Third, none of these Cambridge theorists attached exclusive importance to money as the factor influencing prices. They were more inclined to think in terms of Marshak's concept of the "relative elasticities" of the factors in the quantity equation. According to Marshak velocity and trade in the quantity equation have a low elasticity. This is an improvement over saying that they are constants or always "equal". Fisher had a more rigid theory.

Nevertheless all these theories had a "family resemblance". It is this concept of Wittgenstein that is of fundamental importance in Kuhn's analysis. Just as there is no property common to all games, there is no property common to the theories based on one paradigm. Consequently, historians studying the structure of an older science should not be surprised to find a great diversity of views. Indeed, economists have demonstrated that if by "classical normal science" is meant a monolithic body of doctrines, no such thing ever existed. But lacking appropriate *philosophical* tools economists have floundered, so to speak, in a sea of anticipators and adumbrators.

---

[88]A. Pigou in E. Dean (8, p. 40).

[89]E. Dean (8, p. 30).

[90]For an account of the different quantity equations developed by these post-Marshallians, see Eshag (14, chapter 1).

## Chapter III

# "Speculative" Solutions of the Crisis Problem

The classical theory of output that was developed by Smith, Ricardo, Say, and Mill held a dominant position in the thinking of economists for about one hundred years. It is only in the ten or fifteen years before the publication of the *Treatise on Money* by Keynes that serious attacks were made on the classical paradigm. "Facts" were discovered that, at least in the eyes of the proponents of the new approach, could not be aligned with paradigm-based expectations. These intractable "facts" created a crisis in economic theory. The crisis elicited a great number of solutions from economists, businessmen and others who claimed to know what was wrong in the classical approach.

The crisis situation of the twenties has three fundamental characteristics. First, the attack on the classical paradigm was not undertaken exclusively by people with the economics profession. In fact, as shall be seen later on, most of those who initiated the attack on the classical paradigm were definitely from outside the economics profession.[1] Second, there was a great increase in the amount of attention devoted to the problem area. No doubt this was the work of individuals who were strongly affected by the anomalous situation of economic theory. However, their perception of the anomaly was strongly conditioned by an inchoate *group consensus* that legitimated and sanctioned these new ways of regarding the economic cosmos. Social psychologists[2] have studied the way in which individuals, when faced with an ambiguous situation, take cues from other persons or the group about the way in which this ambiguity is to be resolved. Individuals resolve this ambiguity and structure their environment by adopting or internalizing group-licensed perceptual styles. Furthermore, the classic experiments of Asch

---

[1]This is what Marget (58) is referring to when in chapter one of his *Theory of Prices* he talks about the "invasion of economic theory by babarians".

[2]See H. Lindgren (57).

and Crutchfield show that when there is a conflict between the habitual way of looking at objects or events and the way of looking at them which is based on a group consensus, the individual is more inclined to yield to social pressure (without always being aware of the social influence) when the degree of unanimity or social agreement is high. Those who were interested in economic phenomena in the twenties faced a highly anomalous and ambiguous situation. As traditional explanations had obviously broken down, depressions and unemployment presented a highly unstructured set of events. Perception of the anomaly was greatly facilitated by the rapid formation and development of group-licensed perceptual styles. The work of Foster and Catchings, Hobson, Douglas, Martin, Frederick Soddy and others was partly based on, and stimulated, by this group consensus. Their work, in turn, made its influence felt within the economics profession, on Keynes in particular.

This circumstance of the rapid formation of a group consensus explains in part the failure of the Malthusian approach during the time of James Mill and Ricardo. Even at that time some individuals had perceived the anomaly. For various reasons, however, a group consensus on the Malthusian approach could not be obtained.

The rapid formation of a group consensus in the crisis situation of the twenties brings us to the third aspect of the state of economic theory at the time. Once agreement on the fundamentals of their position was obtained, these men were able to devote themselves to more esoteric research. In a crisis situation this means that negative criticism of the old paradigm is not sufficient. It is also necessary to develop a new explanation of the problem that has evoked the crisis, and to show that the new theories give rise to puzzles that could guide future research. As we shall see, these "underworld" economists had a great variety of solutions.

From a Kuhnian point of view, it is essential to see the crisis as a *social response* to an anomalous and ambiguous situation. Once this has been seen it becomes much less meaningful to ask the following question that suggests itself naturally to one who is wont to employ an individualistic method. Did any of these "speculative" economists anticipate or adumbrate any of the ideas of Keynes and if so when was that idea first put forward?

We contend that the development of economic theory during the twenties can be understood much better in terms of the social dynamics of the community structure of economics and the process by which group consensus was obtained. In fact, as will be seen in the sequel, it is often impossible to determine the originator of an idea because the development of knowledge is a social process, and the dynamics of a social process cannot be understood on the basis of the individualistic categories used by economists.

This chapter shall study only the so-called "unscientific" solutions offered by men such as Hobson and Foster and Catchings to the crisis problem of depression and unemployment.[3] The individualistic historian who views the development of science as a linear unidirectional movement towards the "true" view of reality, naturally adopts, what Agassi[4] has called, the black-and-white approach to history. According to this view history consists of the "black" men who, because of their obscurantism, impeded the development of science towards its true goal, and the "white" men who held views very similar to the ones we believe in today. Thus, Haberler[5] stigmatizes the writings of the underconsumptionists as "unsystematic" and "unscientific"; whereas Klein[6] asserts that the underconsumptionists were more "scientific" than their contemporaries. As scientific work is necessarily based on paradigms, and as the paradigm determines the kinds of problems that the scientist should tackle and the kinds of explanations that are to be regarded as scientific, it is clear that men who believe in different paradigms will never be able to resolve their differences except by persuasion.

Kuhn's thesis does not require that the crisis should be produced by the work of normal scientists working on the basis of the old paradigm.[7] Consequently, the fact that the attacks on the

---

[3]It should be noted that depressions and unemployment are not necessarily anomalous phenomena. Those who were wedded to the old paradigms regarded them merely as puzzles that could be solved on the basis of the old paradigm. See, for example, Robertson's article "The monetary doctrines of Foster and Catchings (Q.J.E. May 1929).

[4]J. Agassi (3).

[5]G. Haberler (26, p. 119).

[6]L. Klein (50, chapter 2).

[7]T. Kuhn (52, p. 181).

classical theory of employment and output were first made by men who could not be regarded as normal scientists does not attenuate the force of Kuhn's arguments. The important fact is that the normal work of economists was affected once these doctrines began to make their influence felt. Nor on the basis of Kuhn's theory would we expect those who first experienced the anomaly acutely to work out a completely satisfactory theory of the problem that evokes the crisis. Hence the tendency, apparent in the economic literature, to ridicule the efforts and theories of Major Douglas and so forth is to be deprecated.

## THE THEORY OF FOSTER AND CATCHINGS

In the first section we shall present the essential features of the theory of Foster and Catchings. Then this interpretation will be supported by detailed quotations from their four books. In the second section we shall present the views of other economists and subject them to criticism. In the third section, their theory will be compared and contrasted with those that offered similar solutions to the crisis problem.

The first point to note about the writings of Foster and Catchings is that even a cursory reading makes it evident that they were actuated by a sharp sense of anomaly. The classical theory of output, which was based on Say's Law, predicted that there cannot be any unemployment that is not frictional. This proposition was buttressed by the apparently unassailable argument that goods are only bought with goods and that, consequently, production automatically creates an equivalent amount of demand. But the fact that there was unemployment was equally indubitable to Foster and Catchings.

Out of this conflict or anomaly there arose the idea that money is not merely a veil and that a monetary system is not merely a system of complex or indirect barter. Combined with the proposition that the sole end of economic activity is consumption, it follows that one of the fundamental relationships of a *money* economy is that between the flow of consumption goods and the flow of money that is used to purchase these goods. This relationship is christened the "annual production–consumption relation". The flow of consumers' goods today depends not only on the amount and quality of the original factors of production that is used to produce consumption goods, but also on the savings that have been done in the *past*. The amount of savings done in the past will determine the amount of capital equipment that is available today to produce consumers' goods. The amount of income available today depends on two things; the amount of money that is disbursed in producing today's consumers' goods. Hence, investment is double-edged. On the one hand it increases the money supply in the year in which it is undertaken and on the other it increases capacity in the future. It increases demand *immediately*. It increases supply *in the future*.[8]

Hence, there arises the "dilemma of thrift". Saving is necessary because otherwise the production of goods and services cannot be increased in the long run. But saving inevitably brings on a crisis; then a fall in prices and employment, and finally a depressed state of industry. Why does it have this effect? To answer this question consider what happens when savings increase and bring about an equivalent amount of new investment.[9] When investment increases more money is paid to the factors of production to spend on consumer goods. As the supply of goods has not changed, the production – consumption equation is upset in favour of consumption and prices rise. The demand for stocks increases and more orders are placed. As more orders are placed, more goods are produced and this means that more income is distributed. This constitutes the prosperity phase of the cycle. But the investment has increased capacity and entrepreneurs under the spur of higher prices and hope of higher profits increase their output of consumer goods. Inventories increase and there is an increase of speculative buying. Before long the output of consumer goods has increased considerably, and an excess supply is threatened. The excess supply and falling prices of consumer goods will supervene *unless* more money is pumped into the economy to enable consumers to purchase the now greatly increased supply at current prices, and this can be done by increasing investment which

[8]It is this part of their theory which leads Alan Gleason (24) to conclude that Foster and Catchings strikingly anticipated the ideas of Keynes and modern post-Keynesian growth economics.

[9]Foster and Catchings always envisage an expansionary process in this way. This fact is significant and will be dealt with later.

increases demand immediately. But this increased investment is bound to cause trouble in the future unless it, in turn, is offset by further investment. But for various reasons connected with the gold-standard and the banking system, the money supply cannot be increased beyond a certain point, making a crisis inevitable.[10]

How strong the influence of the classical paradigm was can be inferred from the following passage by Foster and Catchings:

> Fore more than a century, orthodox economists, dominant in the universities, prescribers of the only system of economics that most men ever studied, have been absolutely and inexcusably wrong on this crucial issue . . . . First, they assumed, merely assumed, mind you, these lords of economic theory merely assumed, without even an attempt at proof, that the financing of production itself provides people with means of purchase. . . . Led by Smith and Mill, blinded by their own errors, intolerant of all opposing views, as hidebound in their own field as their forefathers were in religion, these orthodox economists forced upon the world a system of economics. . . that is of no practical use whatever.[11]

Foster and Catchings insisted that general overproduction is a purely monetary phenomenon that could not arise in a barter economy.

> We have seen that overproduction – a supply in excess of demand – is a purely monetary phenomenon, an unbalancing that could not occur in a barter economy. In barter trading the annual equation is and always must be perfect, for the measure of demand *is* the supply; demand and supply are, in fact, one and the same thing, looked at from different viewpoints.[12]

[10]It is interesting to compare this part of their theory with that of Hayek. According to Hayek an involuntary increase in saving inevitably leads to a crisis because the subsequent increase of consumption expenditures decreases the flow of money in the higher stages of production, preventing the lengthened structure of production from being completed. In the Foster and Catchings system saving leads to a *completed* investment structure and hence brings about a crisis.

[11]Foster and Catchings (22, pp. 127–129).
[12]Foster and Catchings (21, p. 320).

But what about the traditional argument that money is just a complex form of barter?

The traditional argument against the possibility of over-production does not err in using the term with reference to human desires. It makes an error which is more serious because more subtle. How absurd it is – so runs the argument – to imagine that the supply of goods can possibly be greater than the demand for goods. As a matter of fact demand and supply are one and the same thing. Is it not clear that, when I drive to town with a load of hay, the hay is my demand for goods and at the same time another man's supply? To be sure, I may sell the hay for money and then the money at the harness shop; but I must not allow the fundamental nature of the transaction to be obscured by a mere medium of exchange. I have only to imagine a state of barter to see clearly that nothing really matters in this transaction except its two commodity ends. . . .This is the classical argument, typical of economic theory in overlooking the effects of money.[13]

It, therefore, follows that general overproduction is possible in a monetary economy. According to Foster and Catchings, however, not only is it possible to have general overproduction, but there are certain features inherent in a money and profit economy that ordinarily have that effect.

It appears, however, that there are two main reasons why people *cannot long* continue to buy things as rapidly as they can make them. The first reason is that the processes whereby goods are produced for sale at a money profits do not yield con-sumers enough money to buy the goods. As industry increases its output, its does not, *for any length of time*, proportionately increase its payments to the people. The second reason for a deficiency in consumer buying is that the people, under the impelling necessity of saving, cannot spend even as much money as they receive.[14]

The importance that Foster and Catchings attach to the time.

[13]Foster and Catchings (20, pp. 324–325).
[14]Foster and Catchings (19, pp. 20–21, emphasis added).

element in production (investment increases demand today; it increases supply in the future) is clear from the following passage in *profits* where they summarize their arguments:

> According to our theory, the most important factor in this entire cyclical movement, without which all other factors could neither cause a severe business depression, nor lift business out of a depression, is a changing volume of money flowing through various channels in such a way that the flow of money to consumers, which at first exceeds the flow of finished goods, presently fails even to keep pace with the flow of goods.[15]

In the *The Road to Plenty* Foster and Catchings expound their theories in the form of a debate between the professor (who is a stout defender of the classical paradigm) and the businessman who speaks for Foster and Catchings. When the businessman declares that he is now going to put forward for discussion an important law that was completely overlooked by the classical economists, the professor objects that economists have always insisted that we must save, and invest our savings in improved facilities, in order that we may be better off in the future. The Congressman says:

> In the *future*, yes; nothing new about that. It is possible to shell corn with the bare hands; but it is easier to use machines, and machines are the result of past savings. Unless somebody, sometime, had used up less than he produced, we should all have to shell corn now and defend ourselves from wild beasts with our bare hands. That, of course, as the Professor says, is old-line economics. It means that we must create better machines today in order that we may be better off tomorrow. But it never occurred to me that it is only by getting ready to do better in the *future*, and getting ready at the right rate, that we can do well in the *present*.[16]

The fundamental law of progress is the core of their theory. In a barter economy there can be no general overproduction,

[15]Foster and Catchings (20, p. 375).
[16]Foster and Catchings (22, pp. 88–89).

because demand is the supply. In a money economy it is possible, because in a monetary system there can be demand without supply or supply without demand. Saving is necessary for the society because otherwise it cannot provide for an increased standard of living for its people. But saving almost always leads to crisis and depressions. It does this because when savings get invested, they first increase the demand for consumer goods because of the new money that is distributed to labourers and so forth. But the investment, although it does not increase supply in the present, will increase it in the future. This increased supply of goods cannot be sold in the future at the prices prevailing in the future unless at that time new investment is being undertaken which adds to the demand and not the supply. Furthermore, the amount of investment that is undertaken in the future has to be at the right rate (i.e. the rate which does not disturb the production – consumption equation). If there is too much investment in the future, the prices of consumer goods will continue to rise; if there is insufficient investment, prices will fall and depression will ensue.

It follows that it is money that is the ultimate cause of business fluctuations. Money is suspended purchasing power. The owner of money has to decide when, where, and on what goods it is to be spent. The fact that it may ultimately be spent is irrelevant because *time is of the essence of the problem.* Foster and Catchings are emphatic about this.[17] Money makes it possible to create demand without supply or supply without demand. It is this peculiarity of money that is ultimately responsible for cyclical fluctuations.

## OTHER INTERPRETATIONS OF THEIR THEORY

The best account of the work of Foster and Catchings is to be found in the article by Alan Gleason that has already been referred to. Gleason notes that the theory of Foster and Catchings has been subjected to extensive discussion and criticism since the twenties. We agree with Gleason's main contention that Foster and Catchings deserve more credit for their keen insights into

---

[17]Foster and Catchings (21, p. 275).

cyclical processes than has been accorded to them. From the
quotations that have been given so far it is also clear that Foster and Catchings strikingly anticipated the ideas of modern
growth Faster economics. Once the Gestalt switch is made and the
work of Foster and Catchings is regarded in this light, it is hard
to believe that their work can be so grossly misinterpreted by men
like Nemmers and Robertson whose interpretations will be considered presently. Hence, Gleason is right that they anticipated or
adumbrated the ideas of Domar.

It is Gleason's view that they anticipated the ideas of Keynes
regarding the independence of the decisions to save and to invest,
the importance of offsets to saving and the great variability of
investment. But there is a difficulty with this interpretation. It
was stated earlier that Foster and Catchings always start out by
assuming that an increase of saving is initially *beneficial* to the
consumer industries. So savings always get invested. Investment
increases demand for consumer goods but does not increase the
supply of consumer goods. After the new capital goods have
been built and are used in production, the total output of consumer goods increases. *It is only at this stage* that enterpreneurs
in the consumer industries have to fear insufficient demand,
because the new capital goods have increased the output of consumer goods to a very great extent.

> Every dollar saved and invested, we say, causes one dollar
> of deficiency in consumer buying *unless that deficiency is made
> up in some way*. At times it is more than made up, and that
> causes trouble; at times it is not made up, and that causes
> trouble. At all times, it is largely a matter of chance.[18]

In the Keynesian system the cause of the trouble is the fact
that savings do not get invested. If savings ex ante are equal to
investment ex ante there is equilibrium. In the passage just quo-
ted, however, a different idea is expressed. It is said that even
the saving which is invested can cause trouble. In fact, it almost
always causes trouble. Hence the deficiency that Foster and
Catchings refer to is the deficiency that is likely to arise in the
future when the output of consumer goods is increased.

---

[18]Foster and Catchings (19, p. 50).

Nevertheless, if Foster and Catchings had been asked about the effects of saving that is not invested, they would probably have said that the effect is deflationary as in the Keynesian system. But the fact is that they never considered the matter in this light. All these ambiguities and inconsistencies are found because their analysis is not rigorous enough. Terms such as "saving", "investment", "income", or "equilibrium" that are crucial to the argument are not even defined rigorously. Furthermore they lacked the notion of a saving function. All this made it very hard for them to work out a theory of the complex interrelationships among these variables.

Gleason fails to mention what we regard as the essential part of their theory. According to the interpretation presented in this paper Foster and Catchings attributed business cycles and depressions to the fact that in a *money economy* demand and supply are independent. Demand can be increased without increasing supply and vice versa. This makes it possible to *advance* money in production. Investment increases demand today without increasing supply. In the future, the supply is increased. An excess supply is threatened in the future. It will materialize unless more investment is undertaken in the future.

In the second edition of his book Kuhn has added a postscript in which he further articulates his theory and considers some of the animadversions upon his book made by Popperians and empiricists. Kuhn asserts that the most original and least understood part of his work is his notion that the knowledge embodied in *shared exemplars* is a tacit form of knowledge in Polanyi's sense.[19] In Polanyi's terminology it may be said that the scientist's knowledge of the real world is *from* the knowledge embedded in shared exemplars *to* the external world. This means that the scientist's knowledge of the real world is assimilable more to the act of perception than to the act of interpretation.[20] Interpretation involves a weighing and comparison of alternatives from a neutral standpoint. According to Kuhn this is just something that the scientist does not do.

This idea will enable us to understand the crisis situation in economic theory. It is submitted that the quantity theory of

[19] M. Polanyi (68).
[20] See Norwood Russell Hanson (31) for an excellent discussion of the subject.

money, particularly in the form of equation of exchange, was a shared exemplar of the classical paradigm. This means that the knowledge embedded in this exemplar was tacit in the sense of Kuhn. Consider what Robertson had to say about the theory of Foster and Catchings:

> In focussing attention on the subtle interrelations between the supply of money and the phenomena of saving, Messrs Foster and Catchings have hit upon a fruitful theme.... Their failure to achieve convincing results is due, perhaps, to two main causes. In the first place I can feel little doubt that they were born with a double dose of the inflation-bacillus in their composition.... Secondly, the tools with which they work are not sharp enough.... Is it too much to hope that in the interests of *truth* they will throw over the whole of their *pseudo-scientific* apparatus?[21]

Robertson's adjuration to Foster and Catchings to abandon their "pseudo-scientific apparatus" in the interests of "truth" is a good example of tacit knowledge in operation. Scientists do not study the external world or other theories about that world with a Lockean "tabula rasa". Group-licensed and time-tested perceptual styles are built into the mind through the habitual use of shared exemplars to apprehend reality. Robertson studied and assimilated the monetary theory of Marshall. He used this exemplar in his book *Money* published in the early twenties to articulate Marshall's monetary theory as presented in his *Money, Credit and Commerce*. Robertson's main conclusion is that money is like ordinary commodities as far as value-determination is concerned and that money is not as important as it seems to be.[22] The main exemplar of the neo-classical paradigm, namely the supply and demand apparatus, is used to apprehend two different objects as being alike in an essential manner. The argument that money is not as important as it appears to be and that it is important for the student to pierce the money veil to see the real nature of economic transactions as consisting of the exchange of goods against goods is, of course, the argument that

[21]The monetary doctrines of Foster and Catchings, pp. 497–99, (emphasis added).

[22]Robertson (71).

follows from the classical paradigm. But it is precisely this proposition that Foster and Catchings deny and, as we have seen, the essence of their theory can only be understood on the basis of the negation of that classical proposition. Is it any wonder then that Robertson concludes that Foster and Catchings would not have arrived at some of their results had they proceeded on the truly scientific bedrock of the Marshallian quantity theory of money?[23]

Erwin Nemmers has presented another interpretation of their theory:

> Foster and Catchings' theory strikes at profits as the unbalancing factor of the economy. Insufficient purchasing power is distributed in production for the repurchase of goods at cost *plus a profit*, which is collected *before* it is spent, and hence the only possible adjustment is a falling of prices.... It is submitted that there is no necessary conflict between the Foster–Catchings and the Hobsonian theories except in so far as each claims to have the *sole* causal factor. The monetary element and the real element in underconsumption may conceivably exist side by side.[24]

Nemmers' interpretation is as follows: Foster and Catchings think that industry periodically suffers from depression and unemployment because of the fact that profits are not distributed as dividends but retained within the firm, thus preventing consumers from obtaining enough purchasing power to buy the product of industry at constant prices. Hobson thinks that industry

[23]According to the Popperian philosophy of science scientists *adopt* a theory and then try assiduously to falsify it. They devise most stringent tests to falsify their theory. This is a strange argument. How could economists test the modern theory of employment, say, in the twenties when it took another fifteen or twenty years and a strong degree of commitment on the part of economists even to establish what that theory of employment is? As "evidence" bearing on the theory of employment was unavailable in the twenties, it was impossible for Robertson to carry out the Popperian "programme of falsification". The critique of Foster–Catchings could not be used in a Popperian way to "test" the classical paradigm. Robertson used tacit knowledge, in the sense of Kuhn, to apprehend reality and the unscientific" approaches of others to that reality.

[24]E. Nemmers (65, pp. 108–109).

suffers from depression because of an unequal distribution of income which results in oversaving. After all the lag of wages behind profits during the upswing of the cycle makes income distribution more equal. Hence there is no difference between their theories except in emphasis.

It is contended that Nemmers' interpretation is untenable. First of all, it is simply not true that the Hobson and Foster and Catchings approaches are essentially the same. In the Foster and Catchings theory money is ultimately responsible for cyclical fluctuations. Nemmers himself states that Hobson accepts Say's Law even for a money economy.[25] This means that their theories cannot be the same. Second, there is no reason to single out profits as the unbalancing factor in the Foster–Catchings theory. Personal saving has the same effect on the annual production-consumption equation as profits. Third, Nemmers does not mention the crucial importance that time has in the theory of Foster and Catchings. Fourth, Nemmers is right in saying that Foster and Catchings wrongly accuse Hobson of neglecting to consider the effects of savings when they are invested in new capital facilities.[26] But even Nemmers will agree that the analysis presented by Foster and Catchings is far more rigorous and exhaustive than the one given by Hobson. Fifth, Nemmers fails to see the two important senses in which Foster and Catchings were "oversaving" theorists. In the Hobsonian sense "oversaving" means too much saving relative to consumption. In the Keynesian sense "oversaving" means too much saving relative to investment. According to the interpretation presented in this paper Foster and Catchings felt that as the expansion gets under way there is Hobsonian oversaving. As a result of this Hobsonian oversaving there may be Keynesian oversaving in the later phases of the cycle. In the *Treatise* Keynes suggests that such a view is plausible, though different, and not irreconcilable with his own view.[27] Lastly, Nemmers fails to see the extent to which they anticipated the ideas of Harrod and Domar.[28]

[25]Nemmers (65, p. 98).

[26]Nemmers (65, p. 108).

[27]Keynes (48, Vol. 1, pp. 178–179).

[28]The interpretation of their theory presented in this paper is also different from that of Hansen (28) given in his book *Business-cycle Theory.* Hansen says that it follows from the argument of Foster and Catchings that "it

## ABBATI'S SOLUTION

The reader will probably be surprised by the title of this section. After the basic results of the Keynesian theory had been assimilated, and their importance recognized, individualistic historians, employing the "plotting on a straight line approach" to the development of science, have discovered a great number of anticipators and adumbrators of the ideas of Keynes. But the name of Abbati is not to be found among them. This fact is not a little surprising when we consider that Abbati strikingly anticipated the ideas of Keynes.[29]

As the work of Abbati is almost completely unknown it is desirable to start by summarizing the central features of his theory. Abbati states in the beginning of his book that he is primarily interested in finding the cause of general trade depressions. At any given point of time there is a certain quantity of the various resources that can be used to produce goods and services. The total money volume of the goods and services that can be produced with those resources is the "ready productive capacity" of the economy. Income is in equilibrium when the total quantum of final buying (consumption plus investment demand) is equal to the ready productive capacity of the economy.

Saving consists of the passive act of refraining from final buying. Investment consists of the active act of creating commodity capital. There can be saving without investment and investment without saving. Saving and investment are independent. When saving exceeds investment actual production is below the ready productive capacity of the economy. This, in brief, is Abbati's theory of employment and output.

is impossible for society to save without producing price fluctuations, prosperity and depression" (p. 56). This is not correct. When society saves, the first effect is that the savings are invested and demand for consumer goods increases immediately, but not the supply which increases only in the future. Because of the saving propensities of individuals and corporations "Hobsonian oversaving" is threatened in the future. The excess supply will not materialize if investment in the right amount is undertaken. Foster and Catchings argue that investment of the right amount will not, in general, be undertaken.

[29]Keynes acknowledges his debt to Abbati in the *Treatise* (Volume 1, p. 172).

Let us consider the theory in greater detail. Abbati begins by examining the theories of business depression that were most widely accepted at that time.[30] He divides these theories into three classes. In the first class there are two theories which find the cause of depressions on the productive side of business. There is the theory that attributes depression to the inadequate amount of money that is available for financing production. Second, there is the theory that regards the depression as caused by the disproportionate production of particular kinds of goods in relation to each other.

The theories in the second class find the cause of the depression in the market mechanism. One theory asserts that not enough purchasing power is distributed to consumers to enable them to buy the product at prices that cover costs and profits; the other theory asserts that even when sufficient purchasing power is distributed to the consumers they may not, for one reason or another, choose to exercise their purchasing power.

There is one other theory and it attributes depressions to the fact that a money economy is fundamentally different from a barter economy.

It must be emphasized that under-consumption and insufficient general final buying do not "induce the production of more goods", but cause decreased production, together with both a decrease in the volume of bank loans for financing production and a decrease in the quantity of money distributed to final buyers by producers.... In effect, then we cannot be satisfied with all that is said about (1) shortage of money for production, (2) disproportionate production of different kinds of goods, (3) failure of the process of production to distribute enough money to final buyers, (4) overproduction of productive equipment and stocks of goods in relation to consumption and (5) the special merits of a barter economy as regards the relationship of final-buying to production.[31]

After rejecting these theories of depression and unemployment Abbati states what he regards as the true theory:

[30]Abbati (1, p. 2).
[31]Abbati (1, pp. 10–11).

In a word, if it is a fact that final buyers can at any time – and frequently do, voluntarily and deliberately – decrease the velocity of final buying in relation to the velocity of production, and if it is a fact that such a decrease in the velocity of final-buying sooner or later entails a corresponding decrease in the velocity of production, this would account for general trade depression at a time when materials, equipment and labor are plentiful.[32]

It is important to note that by the term "final-buyers" Abbati means the buyers of consumer goods and new capital goods. Hence the volume of "final-buying" determines the effective demand for output. Abbati's theory of effective demand is stated clearly in the following passage:

However, whereas variations in the velocity of production, other than those warranted by variations in the velocity of final-buying cause final buyers slowly and with difficulty to alter their behaviour and, incidentally, the velocity of final buying, producers and distributors are continuously and anxiously seeking to adjust the velocity of production to the velocity of final-buying....Variations in the velocity of productions are therefore dominated by variations in the velocity of final-buying or insufficient final-buying impede production.[33]

Abbati says that he does not seek to "estimate either maximum productive possibilities or maximum ready productive capacity. What we want to know exactly is why ready productive capacity, such as it is at any time, is not always fully engaged."[34] His answer to the question is a Hobsonian one. "Broadly speaking, the velocity of final-buying, is within the limits of ready productive capacity, dependent upon distribution of income, and upon the habits of people in relation to consumption, utilization of non-productive equipment, and abstinence."[35]

Abbati's theory of saving and investment is such a dramatic

[32]Abbati (1, pp. 11–12).
[33]Abbati (1, pp. 43–44).
[34]Abbati (1, p. 44).
[35]Abbati (1, p. 47).

anticipation of the Keynesian theory that it is worthwhile to quote Abbati's conclusions in detail:

> It is necessary to distinguish between, on the one hand, the passive part of abstinence or automatic frugality, and, on the other, the active part of producing commodity capital or ordering it to be produced. In the modern economic system the active part of producing commodity capital or ordering it to be produced is determined by the extent of final-buying of commodity capital. In the modern economic system the active part of producing commodity capital or ordering it to be produced is not dependent upon abstinence; for neither abstinence nor automatic frugality is required at a time when ready productive capacity is not fully engaged, and failing enough abstinence at a time when ready productive capacity is fully engaged, automatic frugality is imposed. When money income made available by abstinence is used without delay, directly or indirectly, for the final-buying of equipment, the velocity of final-buying is not decreased and the production of new equipment is ordered... When money income made available by abstinence...is held on deposit, should the sum of the different kinds of irregular final-buying be not great enough fully to neutralize the absent final-buying of the abstainers...the velocities of final-buying and production will decrease in relation to ready productive capacity.[36]

Abbati states very clearly that when the funds made available by saving are used to buy productive equipment final-buying is not decreased. On the other hand, if these funds are held on deposit and are not offset by the final-buying of productive equipment, the volocity of final-buying will be less than the velocity of production, causing the latter to fall.

Abbati states that there are different kinds of offsets to saving. Investment is the regular offset. By "irregular final-buying" Abbati means the final-buying of governments, residents of other countries and the purchase by traders and distributors of goods to add to their inventories. This last kind of irregular final-buying calls for a comment. What Abbati is

[36]Abbati (1, pp. 60–61).

trying to say is that when traders want to hold increased quantities of stocks of goods they increase their orders from the manufacturers. The additional income that is distributed makes it possible to increase final-buying by consumers.

Nowhere in the economic literature, so far as I am aware, has any reference (let alone description and analysis) been made to the work of Abbati with the notable exception of Keynes. It is interesting to ascertain Keynes' impression of Abbati's book. As was his wont, Keynes generously acknowledges his debt.

> But so far as I am concerned – and I think the same is true of most other economists of the English-speaking world – my indebtedness for clues which have set my mind working in the right direction is to Mr. D. Robertson's "Banking Policy and the Price Level" published in 1926. More recently Mr. Abbati's "The Final Buyer" (1928) has reached – independently I think – some substantially similar results. Mr. Abbati has probably failed to make his thought fully intelligible to those who have not already found the same clue themselves.... Moreover, by the aggregate of "final buying", Mr. Abbati means expenditure on consumption *plus* investment, and he attributes depressions to a failure of this aggregate to reach the aggregate of money-incomes.[37]

Assume for the nonce that the true solution to the problem of unemployment is expressed in the proposition that when ex ante saving at full employment exceeds ex ante investment at full employment income falls to a lower level. Which economist first discovered this idea? Was it Foster and Catchings or Abbati? It is extremely hard to answer this question. The question is meaningful only within the individualistic historiographical framework. But from the point of view of Kuhn the development of economic theory in the twenties is to be regarded as a social response to an anomalous and ambiguous situation. This implies that it is important to study the dynamics of consensus-formation.[38] This paper studies the theories of these

---

[37]Keynes (48, pp. 171–172).

[38]In the Asch experiment one naive subject and seven confederates of the experimenter are taken to a room with two blackboards. On one of the blackboards a vertical line segment of a certain length is drawn. On the other,

economists not with the view of determining which economist first thought of one of the Keynesian ideas, but to show the way in which a certain perceptual style or *a priori* framework was adopted by many economists. All these economists knew that the classical approach was regarded as the correct approach by the majority of economists since the time of Ricardo, and that even in the twenties most academic economists believed in it. Dissent from such an "objective" view of reality is always hard, and as the Asch experiment described below demonstrates, produces considerable discomfort or "dissonance". When he sees other dissenters, therefore, he is reassured.

From an individualistic point of view Abbati strikingly anticipated Keynes. From a Kuhnian point of view Abbati's work contributed to the formation of a group-consensus that made it easier for others to challenge the "objective" view of reality. As Keynes said, "Mr. Abbati has probably not succeeded in making intelligible his thought to those who have not found the clue themselves." Hence Abbati's work must also be seen in relation to those who espoused the objective view of reality.

## THE THEORY OF J. A. HOBSON

J. A. Hobson was the first major economist to controvert the classical paradigm. Born in Derby, England, in 1858, he studied classics at Oxford and turned to the study of economics at the age of thirty. Profoundly influenced by Ruskin, he took a much larger view of economic reality than is customary in economic

three parallel line segments are drawn and are numbered 1, 2 and 3. The subjects are asked to tell which line segment on the second board is equal in length to the one on the first board. The naive subject always gives his answer last, so that the influence of social consensus can be measured. It has been demonstrated that when the seven confederates are instructed to give wrong answers the naive subject yields to the social pressure. The naive subject is faced by a conflict between the objective view and the view that is sanctioned by a group consensus. When the degree of social consensus is high, the naive subject begins to believe that the objective view is not so objective after all. The experiment also showed that when one of the confederates is instructed to give the correct answer the naive subject was more inclined to resist the group pressure.

science. In his first major work "The Physiology of Industry", written with Mummery, the classical harmony of interest thesis is thrown over. He was chastized for this irreverent attitude to the basic truths of classical science. Edgeworth's animadversional review of that book and Marshall's hostile attitude prevented him from getting an important academic post in England.

A full-scale study of Hobson has been undertaken by Erwin Nemmers (65). This section is based in part on Nemmers' book.

In the preface to their book *The Physiology of Industry* published in 1889, Hobson and Mummery state:

> We are thus brought to the conclusion that the basis on which all economic teaching since Adam Smith has stood, viz., that the quantity annually produced is determined by the aggregates of Natural Agents, Capital and Labor available, is erroneous, and that, on the contrary, the quantity produced, while it can never exceed the limits imposed by these aggregates, may be, and actually is, reduced far below this maximum by the check that undue saving and the consequent accumulation of over-supply exerts on production; i.e., that in the normal state of modern industrial Communities consumption limits production and not production consumption. We illustrate the effect of this check, step by step, by the commercial phenomena of the years immediately succeeding 1870.[39]

In a sense it is true that the crisis in economic theory has its provenience in this book which impugns the validity of the classical paradigm by adducing facts that are inconsistent with it. Presumably the problems of overproduction and unemployment were not serious enough at that time. Partly because of this and partly because of other reasons a rapid group consensus could not be established and Hobson failed to make a dent in the classical theory.

But what is the theory that is espoused in this book? Hobson and Mummery contend that it is very important to study the quantitative relation of production to consumption. They felt

[39]Hobson and Mummery (45, Preface).

that because of the doctrine that supply creates its own demand this subject did not receive adequate attention from the classical economists. In the normal state of commerce with no technological progress "there is a definite relation between the total amount of commodities produced in the present, and the total amount of wealth in various shapes which has *usefully* existed in the past".[40]

> If increased thrift or caution induces people to save more in the present, they must consent to consume more in the future. If they refuse to assent to this condition, they may persist in heaping up new material forms of capital, but the real effective capital will be absolutely limited by the actual extent of their future consumption . . . the nominal capital is a mere body, the real capital the same body so far as it is animated by productive force in economical work.[41]

But did not Mill demonstrate the incontestable validity of the proposition that there can never be general overproduction by arguing that when production is increased not only the desire but also the power to consume is increased? No, say Hobson and Mummery.

> The desire to save may lead them to increase their rate of production indefinitely beyond the desire for present or immediately future consumption. Mill, then, has no right to conclude that the very fact of a thing being produced is a proof that the desire to consume it will be exercised.[42]

In the normal state of industry and commerce there is a definite relation between the consumption of commodities and the amount of capital goods and raw materials that are being used in the different stages of production. When individuals increase their savings these savings are invested in new capital goods. Overproduction will result unless in the future people increase their consumption. The new capital that is created will be

[40]Hobson and Mummery (45, p. 27, emphasis added).
[41]Hobson and Mummery (45, p. 51).
[42]Hobson and Mummery (45, p. 105).

"nominal" capital, i.e. it will lie idle unless consumer demand increases sufficiently.

But what determines the amount of saving?

If the interests of each individual in a community were always identical with the interest of the community there could be no such thing as over-supply. It is impossible to suppose that a company of men, producing in common for the common good, would at any time produce more than was required for consumption in the present or near future. It is, in fact, the clash of interests between the community as a whole and the individual members in respect to saving, that is the cause of Over-Supply.[43]

It is prudent for an individual to save. But what is prudence in the conduct of an individual's affairs may be folly for the community if the total savings of all the individuals in the community exceed the amount that is right for the community. Thus Adam Smith's famous maxim is jettisoned.

This is the basic theory that is contained in "The Physiology of Industry". The essentials of this theory are not changed in his later works but two or three new concepts are developed. One concept is that of a "surplus" which plays such an important role in Hobson's thinking.[44] There are two or three elements in Hobson's concept of a surplus. First, there is the idea that the return to various factors of production frequently exceeds the amount that is necessary to call forth their productive services. Price must be sufficient to compensate the marginal producer for the real cost incurred in the production of goods and services. But as price is uniform for all producers the intra-marginal producers gain a surplus. Part of this surplus is "productive surplus" in the sense that it adds to the productive efficiency of the factor of production. The remainder is "unproductive surplus" because it has no such effect. The second element in Hobson's concept of a surplus is that the unequal bargaining power that exists in various markets enables producers to restrict supply and to raise price and in this way to increase their surplus.

[43]Hobson and Mummery (45, p. 106).
[44]The reader is referred to chapter 5 of Nemmers' book for a fuller discussion of this concept.

After his initial work with Mummery, Hobson went through what Nemmers calls a quasi-orthodox period. He became interested in other questions such as imperialism, distribution and so forth. It is only in the tewenties when England was suffering from so much unemployment that he again became interested in the macroeconomic theory of income.

In its essentials the theory is unchanged but is sharpened in one or two respects. In the *Physiology of Industry* oversaving is attributed to excessive competition among individuals to save. As this competition is uncoordinated, too much saving results. In *The Economics of Unemployment* published in 1922 the surplus concept is used to explain the phenomenon of oversaving.

> It becomes too easy for a rich man, living on unearned income, to cause an excessive proportion of the labour which he commands, but does not himself perform, to be directed to the production of future goods which he, or someone else, may or may not consume.[45]

Furthermore the arts of consumption are conservative. "Though modern man, in his capacity of consumer, is far more progressive than his ancestors, his power of taki ng on new economic needs and of raising rapidly the quantity, variety and quality of his consumption, is limited by a narrowness or imagination and a servitude to habit which are far less dominant in production."[46]

Hobson did not think much of the so-called automatic checks that the classical economists felt would prevent general oversupply from materializing. In the earlier work with Mummery the argument that a fall in prices will check general overproduction by stimulating consumption is rejected on the ground that a fall in prices will reduce money income to the same extent without affecting consumption.[47] In the *Economics of Unemployment* on the other hand, two automatic checks are considered: the price mechanism and the interest rate mechanism. The price mechanism is said to be inoperative due to the conser-

---

[45] Hobson (44, p. 41).
[46] Hobson (44, p. 58).
[47] Hobson and Mummery (45, pp. 121–122).

vative nature of consumption.[48] When prices fall real income is increased. But this "transitory" increase of real income will not stimulate consumption. This "transitory" increase in real income is saved. This means that the short-run consumption function is flatter than the long-run consumption function. This is not to imply that Hobson thought in these terms.[49]

The automatic working of the interest-rate mechanism is also disallowed. It is asserted that to the extent that the fall in the rate of interest reduces savings the effect is indeed beneficial. But this method is extremely tardy and wasteful. Furthermore, the bulk of saving is "automatic", as Hobson calls it and does not depend on the interest rate.

## COMPARISON WITH FOSTER AND CATCHINGS AND ABBATI

Both Hobson and Foster and Catchings assailed the classical paradigm. Both regarded the phenomena of depression and unemployment as serious anomalies that could not be accommodated within the classical framework. Both attributed depressions to inadequate consumer buying. For Foster and Catchings money is the root cause of business cycles. According to Hobson it is not money but a maldistribution of incomes and the consequent creation of huge unproductive surpluses that is ultimately responsible for business cycles. As was pointed out earlier in the paper Hobson accepts Say's Law even for a monetary economy if the income distribution is equalitarian. Because of this Hobson's monetary theory is weak. Because Hobson did not realize the importance of money he failed to see the importance of the time element in production. Foster and Catchings laid great emphasis on the fact that investment can increase demand without increasing supply.

In contrast to Hobson and Foster and Catchings, Abbati be-

---

[48]Hobson (44, p. 55).

[49]Whether or not Hobson's thought can be given this interpretation is a moot question. The present writer is unsure. A similar interpretation has been proposed by Bronfenbrenner in the foreword to Nemmer's book that has already been referred to. Bronfenbrenner says that the Hobsonian idea that savings always get invested can be regarded as a precursor of the Keynesian equality of saving and investment ex post.

lieved that it is not consumer buying but "final-buying" that is important. Whether income is in equilibrium or not depends, in Abbati's system, on the relationship between the velocity of production and the velocity of final buying. But all three believed that demand determines supply and not supply demand.

## THE THEORY OF FREDERICK SODDY

Frederick Soddy, M.A., F.R.S., was a man of no mean talent. Winner of the Nobel prize in chemistry in 1921 and author of many books on the subject he was professor of chemistry at Oxford University. As a natural scientist he was very impressed by the principle of conservation of energy and matter. He was prompted by this to develop an ergosophical (his own neologism) view of wealth.

As the writings of Soddy have almost completely been ignored by economists, it is desirable, before we proceed to the details of his analysis, to get an overall picture of his ideas. Soddy felt that the technical problems of production had been solved as a result of the tremendous advance of the natural sciences. But if that is the case why is there so much unemployment of men and capital when consumers desire to purchase the products of capital and labour ? How is this peculiar situation to be explained ? Soddy averred that the fault lay in the distributory mechanism of society of which money is the main vehicle. It is not that industry cannot produce a vastly greater quantity of output. The problem is that that output cannot be distributed due to a lack of purchasing power. The insufficiency of purchasing power is due to certain peculiarities of a medium of exchange and the fact that banks create money. Soddy defines money as "the nothing which we get for something before we can get anything". But when banks create money they, or those who borrow money from them, get something for nothing. The producers who borrow money from the banks increase purchasing power without adding to the supply of goods. Thus the price of consumer goods rises and it is because the existing holders of money are deprived of a part of their purchasing power that those who borrow from the banks can get something for nothing. Sooner or later the supply of goods is going to rise. At

that time more money is needed to circulate the increased quantity of goods. But it is just at this time that the banks, because
of the gold-standard or for other reasons, contract their loans
thus bringing about a depression. Soddy claims that none of these
untoward consequences, will ensue if the original expansion is
financed by saving and not by the creation of new money.[50]

Soddy is aware that the classical theory cannot explain unemployment.

> Scientific men, having successfully solved the problem of wealth
> production, may be credited with having contributed some-
> thing to the understanding of the real nature of wealth, and to
> them, as indeed to anyone who thinks about it, the co-exis-
> tence of poverty and involuntary unemployment is a sufficient
> indication, that, for a long time past, the orthodox economist
> has been somewhere vitally at fault.[51]

Here is the most succint statement of Soddy's theory in his
own words:

> To issue money by fictitious loans to "stimulate production"
> is to increase immediately the consumption of goods, but the
> production only after the interval required to produce
> them.... There is a definite interval between initiation and
> achievement, *which is in fact the key of the whole problem*,
> and it has been hitherto completely ignored.

> Consumption during the time-lag, is increased without any
> increase of production of finished wealth. The results at once
> in a shortage of goods for sale, rise of prices, – so that the
> new quantity of money only buys as much as the smaller
> quantity did before, – and a drain of gold to pay for addition-
> al imports to make good the shortage. This is followed by
> reduction in the quantity of money again as the gold basis of
> "credit" is reduced.[52]

Thus the banks are ultimately responsible for depressions

[50]It must already be clear that Soddy's theory bears some resemblances to
the theories of Hayek and Foster and Catchings.
[51]Soddy (84, pp. 65–66).
[52] Soddy (84, p. 57, emphasis added).

because they reduce the supply of money just when it should be increased to circulate the increased quantity of goods that come into the market as a result of the production process that was started some time back. "Consumption *must* be increased as soon as the new rate of production is achieved, or the last state of the nation will be worse than the first. More money is needed to complete, not to start the process."[53]

The essence of Soddy's theory is contained in the proposition that "more money is needed to complete, not to start the process". If money is to perform its functions efficiently and industry is to be kept on an even keel it is necessary that the price level should be stabilized.[54] As a result of the savings of individuals new capital goods are created. This means that an increased output of consumer goods will be produced in the future. At that time the money supply has to be increased otherwise the price level will fall. This increased money that is needed by industry should be made available by the taxation or expenditure policies of the government.

Under an ideal[55] system more money is needed when the process is completed. But why is more money not needed at the beginning of the process?

The only answer to our problem is that those engaged in initiating the new scale of production must be paid for by others abstaining to the same extent from consumption over the period required for the new scale of production to mature.[56]

Soddy was an advocate of 100%–reserve banking. Under such a system an expansionary process can be started only when the individuals in the community are willing to abstain from present consumption and to transfer their command over the labour to the entrepreneurs. After the process has been completed and the output of consumption goods is increased the

[53]Soddy (84, pp. 60–61).
[54]For a good discussion of Soddy's practical proposals, see Gaitskell's article "Four Monetary Heretics" in G.D.H. Cole (7).
[55]See F. Soddy (87). Here Soddy advocates 100%-reserve banking or, as he puts it, pound for pound banking.
[56]Soddy (84, p. 64).

government can stabilize the price-level by appropriately increasing the quantity of money.

But under the present system of fractional-reserve banking more money is injected into the economy by the banks and to those who borrow this money from the banks this money "is the *something* for nothing before anyone can get anything."[57] But true or honest money is the nothing that one gets for something before one can get anything. Those who borrow money from the banks are able to get money without having to sacrifice the enjoyment of wealth, and as they can purchase goods and services with this money created by the banks they get something for nothing. But from an ergosophical view this is a violation of the law of nature "Ex nihilo nihil fit" (nothing comes from nothing).

With an almost religious indignation Soddy excoriates the "money magicians" for flouting the laws of nature; his intemperate denunciations of bankers and the banking system betray a simplicity that is characteristic of amateurs when discoursing upon complex economic questions.

Science achieves her triumphs by the patient unravelling of natural laws and by working with them, not setting out to defy and trick them. All her achievements are now being perverted by money magicians, out to get something for nothing. Banking has become the supreme example of the folly of the belief in the power of the human mind and will to ignore and override fact. Already it has cost the world a thousand times as much human misery, frustration and waste of life as all the criminal classes put together.[58]

Nevertheless, Soddy's work deserves more attention than has been accorded to it by economists. In fact, his work is almost completely unknown. Part of the explanation of this fact is that economists writing on the Keynesian Revolution employ an individualistic framework. The individualistic historian is not interested in describing the coherence of the work of scientists during a certain stage of its development. He is not interested in

[57]Soddy (86, p. 26).
[58]Soddy (87, p. 4).

describing the puzzles that face the scientists at various times. He does not think it is important to describe nascent perceptual styles and the group-consensus that is being based on them . Consequently, when an individualistic historian studies the state of economic theory in the twenties from the point of view of the Keynesian Revolution, he is only interested in some of the anticipators of Keynes. After commending these anticipators for their deep insights into economic processes he usually passes to other periods to find other anticipators of Keynes. Thus Klein, after a brief (and caustic) description of Major Douglas and his theory, proceeds to the early nineteenth century to find other anticipators such as Malthus and Sismondi.

In presenting the theory of Soddy the object is not to disinter another obscure anticipator of Keynes. On the contrary, the object is to relate the work of Soddy to the work of many other writers who contributed to the formation of a group-licensed perceptual style that made it possible for other economists to question the "objective" view of reality represented by the classical paradigm. Instead of saying that many of these writers anticipated Keynes it is more accurate to say that Keynes was influenced by them. This is not mere logomachy. The individualistic approach with its emphasis on anticipators implies that an individual scientist has a tete-a-tete with nature. If he is clever he will be able to penetrate her secrets. Keynes never had such an encounter with nature. He did not approach economic reality with a Lockean tabula rasa.[59] He studied economic theory in a definite social environment. He internalized group-licensed perceptual styles. As late as 1922 or 1923 Keynes had not made the Gestalt switch. During the twenties he read many of the writers that have been mentioned in this paper.[60] There is no doubt that it is the influence of all these writers that made him consider whether the "objective" view was so "objective"

[59]C. West Churchman calls such enquiring systems "Lockean enquiring systems". From an epistemological point of view Locke is an atomistic empiricist. Individualistic historians assume that scientists are Lockean enquiring system.

[60]In his article "Four Monetary Heretics", already referred to, Gaitskell informs us that the names of Soddy and Douglas were very well known in England during the twenties. The followers of Douglas were numerous and were fitted with uniforms. They were called the "greenshirts".

after all. Once economic theory in the twenties is seen as a *social response* to an anomalous and ambiguous situation all the questions about anticipators and adumbrators become much less important.

## THE DOUGLAS THEORY

Major Clifford Hugh Douglas, who was an engineer by profession, is well known to economists. Keynes gave him an honorable mention in the "General Theory". Keynes said that "it is better to see the truth imperfectly or obscurely than to maintain error". Ever since then his so-called A + B theorem has been subjected to some analysis and much ridicule.

No writer in economics has endeavoured so strenuously to make his thought opaque to the reader. His writings at some places are so obscure that even after prolonged study no sense can be attached to them. Only a tentative interpretation of his work is offered in this paper. Our purpose will be accomplished if it can be shown that a re-appraisal of his work is necessary.

On the basis of the interpretations given by other economists it is hard to make sense of or give coherence to his writings. But his thinking must have had some internal consistency and coherence. It is submitted that the most fruitful hypothesis on which to proceed is that the Douglas theory is very much like the theory of Foster and Catchings.

In chapter 8 of his "Economics of Unemployment" Hobson presents his criticism of the Douglas theory. Hobson says that he agrees with Douglas that the major cause of trade depressions is the fact that consumer buying is insufficient relative to production. But Hobson "traces this failure, not to any lack of the monetary power to purchase all the commodities that could be produced, but to the refusal of those in possession of this power of purchase to apply enough of it in buying consumables, because they prefer to apply it in buying non-consumables, in other words, to buying capital goods."[61]

In commenting on this passage Douglas says that "this represents a radical cleavage, the static versus dynamic cleavage

[61]J. Hobson (44. p. 119).

of attack on the problem."[62] What Douglas means by this is stated clearly in the following passage:[63]

> It is a physical impossibility for the wages of the current week to buy the production of the current week; it is not in the market to buy. It probably will not come into the market, on the average, for at least six months....To reiterate categorically, the theorem criticized by Mr. Hobson; the wages, salaries and dividends distributed during a given period do not, and cannot, buy the production of that period; *that production can only be bought, i.e., distributed, under present conditions by a draft, and an increasing draft, on the purchasing power distributed in respect of future production, and this latter is mainly and increasingly derived from financial credit created by the banks.*

Note that Douglas states very clearly that today's productions can be distributed not only by a draft on the purchasing power created in respect of future production *but an increasing draft* on the purchasing power created in respect of future production. Investment creates demand and increases supply. Investment creates demand and supply in such a way, however, that unless the absolute rate of increase of investment is increasing demand will be insufficient to maintain equilibrium. According to Domar equilibrium in a growing economy is maintained if investment increases at a constant percentage rate. But this means that investment in absolute terms increases at an increasing rate.[64]

In his debate with Hawtrey here is what Douglas said:

> Quite obviously, if you save 50 pounds, that 50 pounds of goods which are represented by the savings cannot be bought at that moment. Now then supposing you apply that 50 pounds, not to buying more consumable goods, but to create

---

[62]C. Douglas (12, p. 3).

[63]C. Douglas (12, p. 5, emphasis added).

[64]The evidence on which Gleason concludes that Foster and Catchings anticipated Domar is not more substantial than this. But whether or not Douglas anticipated Domar it is certainly true that his theory bears strong resemblances to that of Foster and Catchings.

some more capital goods, in making those capital goods the 50 pounds will undoubtedly go out again into the consumer's market, as you yourself explained and the consumers' goods, the original consumers' goods, can now be bought. The *deficiency has been restored* but you have more capital goods to the extent of 50 pounds against which there is no distribution of purchasing power.[65]

It must be clear by now that Douglas' theory is not a "nonsensical theory" as Klein puts it.[66] The "naive underconsumptionist" was not so naive after all. But what in Douglas' view explains the fact that, as Douglas might put it, "purchasing power is not equal to prices".

Now this theorem that bank loans create bank deposits, and the deduction from it that the repayment of bank loans destroys deposits, is vital to an understanding of the process we have been discussing. The deficiency between purchasing-power, and goods with money prices attached to them can be made up...by this process of creating bank money. This enables the business cycle to be carried through. And conversely, the refusal to create fresh money by banking methods or otherwise, whatever the cause of this refusal may be, is sufficient to paralyse production and consumption... This is surely plain enough; but it has also to be remembered that this process of repayment of bank loans, is a "chain" process.[67]

Anyone who has read Fisher's "Booms and Depressions" knows that Fisher describes a cumulative downward movement in similar terms. Towards the end of the prosperity phase wages and interest rise faster than prices. This together with the fact that the debt-asset ratio is high induces businessman to repay loans. As the rising costs create bankruptcies and as there has been a drain of cash into circulation banks start calling in loans. This means that the money supply falls and then prices

---

[65]C. Cole (7, p. 289, emphasis added).
[66]Klein (50, p. 141).
[67]Douglas (10, pp. 88–89).

fall and there are more bankruptcies and so on. But this is far from being a "nonsensical theory".

Many critics have felt that Douglas' theory proves too much. If Douglas maintains that "purchasing power is always less than prices" then how can he explain the fact industry still continues to produce and that sometimes industry experiences prosperity.[68]

But Douglas never said that industrial production must decline monotonically to zero; nor is it true that the Douglas theory implies that never faces boom conditions. In the quotations that we have given Douglas states clearly that when saving increases by fifty dollars this does not mean that there is a deficiency in purchasing power. If these savings are used to produce new capital goods these fifty dollars are returned to consumers. This means that prices rise because investment has increased demand without increasing supply. Douglas' theory is that there is no guarantee that consumer purchasing power will be adequate in the future just because it is adequate today.

To put it another way, the rate at which money can be spent this week does not depend at all on the goods which can be, and are, supplied this week, and is not part of the cost of the goods which can be supplied this week. An increase in the money paid this week is identical with any other form of money inflation under present circumstances – it widens effective demand, stimulates production and raises prices – There is nothing in the arrangement which guarantees that a larger amount of *consumable* goods per head can be bought in the future as a result of a larger amount of money distributed this week.[69]

The criticism of Foster and Catchings of the theory of Douglas is unacceptable.[70] They raise two objections. First, they argue that the wages paid to a worker who assists in the production of a machine can be spent just as readily on consumer goods as the wages of an opera-singer or dentist. This is true but Douglas

---

[68] See, for example, James Estey (15, p. 255).

[69] Douglas (12, pp. 6–7).

[70] Foster and Catchings (21, pp. 338–339).

certainly did not deny it. Second, they contend that the normal course of business requires that money be *advanced* in production. This again is true but Douglas certainly did not deny it. In fact, Major Douglas regards this as one of his most important discoveries.

But the views of Foster and Catchings or Estey have not been as influential as those of Klein.

> But the colorful crank, Major C. H. Douglas, in England, has done much to lower the scientific achievement of this school. Hobson, for example, was anxious to dissociate his beliefs from those of Douglas. The latter is one of the best examples of an amateur economist supporting a reasonable economic policy on the basis of a *nonsensical theory*.
>
> Douglas had no underconsumption theory of business cycles. His theory was one of permanent stagnation and more particularly inefficiency.
>
> The entire theoretical basis for the Douglas underconsumption situation was the famous $A + B$ theorem, *an all-time high in economic unscience*.[71]

These statements of Klein are a cavalier and gross misrepresentation of the facts. Crass assertions like these stultify themselves.

## CONCLUSIONS

The period we have studied is surely one of the most remarkable in the history of economic doctrine. About two hundred years ago the perspicacious investigations of the "astute" Mr. Hume (as Kant used to call him) awakened Kant from his dogmatic slumber. When Kant awakened he conducted some of the most profound investigations into the nature of human knowledge. Economists in the twenties were in the process of awakening from their Marshallian and Ricardian slumbers, and it is the process of awakening that we have studied in this chapter.

All the writers studied in this chapter came from different

---

[71]Klein (50, pp. 140–141, emphasis added).

backgrounds. They had different interests and orientations. The details of their theory were as varied as the men themselves. But one thing they had in common: their perception of an anomalous and ambiguous situation. They were aware that the existing doctrine that productions can only be bought by productions, that supply creates its own demand could not explain the breakdown of the financial or distributive mechanism of economics in which money is used. The fact that the distributive mechanism had broken down and that existing theory could not explain it, was, to them, indubitable.

According to Leon Festinger[72] whenever individuals are faced by such a "congnitive dissonance" they initiate attempts to reduce this dissonance. Economic theory in the twenties can best be regarded as a social attempt to remove this congnitive dissonance and to move towards congnitive consonance. Classical writers resolved this dissonance in a different way. They did not think it was necessary to change their theory that general overproduction is impossible and that money is only a complex form of barter. In other words they simply changed their cognition of commercial facts to make them consistent with their theory. Mill said that "I am convinced that there is no fact in commercial affairs which, in order to its explanation, stands in need of that chimerical supposition (of general overproduction)".[73] Keynesianism resolved the dissonance by changing the theory in order to make it consistent with its cognition of the facts.

[72]L. Festinger (16).
[73]J. Mill (60).

# Chapter IV

# Myrdal and Robertson

## INTRODUCTION

The object of this chapter is to elucidate another aspect of the crisis in economic theory during the twenties and thirties. In the previous chapter it was demonstrated that the work of men such as Foster and Catchings and Hobson contributed to the formation of new paradigms. But these men were not normal economists. In fact, some of them were from outside the economics profession. In contrast, the men to be considered in this chapter were normal economists.

Neither Robertson nor Myrdal claimed that a radically new orientation was needed for economic theory. Both felt that with suitable amplifications and modifications of the traditional theory it is possible to account for the phenomena of the business cycle. Consequently, the sense of anomaly and ambiguity, that is so palpable in the writings of say Hobson, is absent in their writings.

Nevertheless, their work intensified the crisis in economic theory. Kuhn's thesis does not require that the crisis should originate in the work of normal economists. But in most of revolutions that Kuhn studied the crisis did, in fact, originate in this way. This paradoxical result can be explained in the following way. Scientific theories are not able to account for all the empirical phenomena that come within their range. In fact, it is this very fact that explains the existence and fruitfulness of normal science. If paradigms were not open-ended there would be no puzzles for the normal scientists to solve. This means that all scientific theories have counter-instances. The task of the normal scientist is to show that such putative counter-instances can be subsumed under the theory. Normal articulating activity is usually successful in doing this. Some counter-instances, however, flagrantly contradict the predictions of the paradigm and are resistant to normal articulating activity. Scientists, however, are rarely dismayed by such initial failures. They devote an increasing amount of attention to the problem-area confident that their paradigm can handle such cases, if it is suitably extended. Hence there arises, what Kuhn calls "a proliferation of articulations". The proliferation of articulations means that the old paradigm has been changed. These articulations contain the seeds of the new paradigm. In trying to confirm their old paradigm scientists actually disconfirm it.

The work of Myrdal and Robertson examplifies this aspect of Kuhn's argument and it is the object of this chapter to see how the theories of Robertson and Myrdal accentuated the crisis.

## MYRDAL'S MONETARY EQUILIBRIUM

Myrdal's *Monetary Equilibrium* was published in Swedish in 1931, translated into German in 1933, and into English only in 1939. Although Myrdal was familiar with Keynes' *Treatise* no reference is made by Keynes to the work of Myrdal, in the *General Theory*. Linguistic inaccessibility seems to be the only explanation for this fact inasmuch as, of all the European writers in the Wicksellian tradition, Myrdal reached results that accord most closely with the theory of employment presented in the *General Theory*.

The method employed by Myrdal is that of "immanent criticism", or criticism from within. This means that Myrdal does not start out by giving a systematic presentation of his own theory. Instead he introduces his views within the framework of Wicksell's ideas. His book is in no way a mere exposition of Wicksell's ideas. Myrdal tries to determine what Wicksell would have said had he pursued his basic insight to its logical conclusion.

Before proceeding to the details of his analysis it is desirable to give the essential features of his theory. Myrdal is concerned with the elucidation of Wicksell's concept of monetary equilibrium and his theory of the cumulative process. According to Wicksell for monetary equilibrium to obtain three equivalent conditions have to be fulfilled: the first condition is that the money rate of interest has to equal the natural rate of interest, the second condition is that the demand and supply of savings have to be equal, and the third condition is that the money rate is "normal" if and only if the price level has no tendency to change. Wicksell felt that these three conditions are equivalent. If one of them is satisfied the other two are also satisfied. The cumulative process arises when these conditions are not fulfilled.

According to Myrdal monetary equilibrium in the sense of Wicksell has two characteristics that distinguish it from equilibrium in the ordinary sense. Unlike equilibrium for ordinary commodities, monetary equilibrium is labile. This means that when a disturbance impinges on the system there are no equilibrating forces which return the system to equilibrium. Monetary disequilibrium is cumulative and self-reinforcing. Secondly, when monetary equilibrium obtains some economic variables have to have a certain relationship to each other, for example, the natural and money rates of interest have to be equal. From these equilibrium relationships, however, nothing can be inferred about the behaviour of other variables in the system. It may be that these other variables have to change in order to preserve equilibrium. For example, in a dynamic economy in which productivity is increasing the demand for savings may be equal to the supply of savings. In such an economy monetary equilibrium implies a falling price level.

Myrdal's main conclusion is that Wicksell's second condition is the true condition for monetary equilibrium. The third condition is invalid, as the example just given illustrates. The first condition is not an independent condition of monetary equilibrium. The first equilibrium formula merely demonstrates the *casual* factors at work behind the second formula. It states the condition that must be fulfilled not for *monetary* equilibrium but for *investment* equilibrium.

To see why this is the case consider Wicksell's conception of the natural rate of interest.[1] Let us suppose that there is an economy with no capital. All its land and labour resources are uninvested. Let us suppose that in a given year resource-owners decide to *devote* their resources to future production. This means that they reduce their consumption in the current year and advance liquid capital to entrepreneurs who use this liquid capital to hire the services of land and labour. The labourers may be supposed to build capital goods with a maturation term

[1] K. Wicksell (92, pp. 102–104).

of one year. If the value of consumption goods is C units before
the formation of capital, it will increase to C + iK units due to
the superior productivity of roundabout production, where K
is the amount of capital lent. The natural rate of interest is i. It
measures the marginal productivity of waiting. In such an
economy loan transactions are made *in natura*.

It is to this "technical" conception of the natural rate of
interest that Myrdal objects. The yield of capital goods depends
not only on what they can produce in the future but the prices
at which this output can be sold. Hence a concept of exchange-
value productivity is needed.

> We had to replace the concept of physical productivity of
> waiting by one of exchange value productivity because pro-
> ductivity depends on relative prices which cannot be assumed
> to be stable. But the conditions on which credit is given
> and taken . . . themselves influence these relative prices and
> through the relative prices the exchange value productivity of
> real capital. Our conclusion, therefore, must be that credit
> and the money rate of interest must be included even in the
> formula by which the natural rate of interest is defined.[2]

Furthermore, Myrdal maintains that Wicksell's own monetary theory makes it impossible to hold a purely "technical"
conception of the natural rate of interest. The explanation for
this seems to be the following. Fisher had demonstrated that
the Austrian theory of capital and interest implies that the
interest rate enters into the explanation of the price formation
of all commodities. The price of any commodity today is the
discounted value of the services that it will render in the
future. Thus if land is expected to yield an income of $105 in
the next year and the money rate of interest is 5% the price of
land today will be $100. The own-rate of interest on land is
equal to the money rate of interest. Suppose that the price of
land today is less than $100. Equilibrium has been disturbed
since the "natural rate" of interest on land exceeds the money
rate of interest. The demand for land will increase and the price
of land today relative to the price tomorrow will be increased.

[2]G. Myrdal (64, pp. 52–53).

In central price theory Wicksell was a Bohm-Bawerkian. According to Myrdal the great importance of Wicksell's work lies in the fact that he contributed, without being fully aware of it, to the integration of monetary theory with the central theory of price formation.[3] When the money rate of interest is below the natural rate of interest an upward Wicksellian process is initiated. The essential characteristic of an upward Wicksellian process is not only that the absolute level of prices rises. Of equal importance is the *order* in which particular prices within the price level rise. The price of raw materials and capital goods rises before the price of consumption goods. Hence in the Wicksellian system the interest rate is connected not only with the movement of the absolute price level but also with changes in relative values.

Myrdal feels that from such a monetary theory Wicksell should have concluded that a purely physical definition of the natural rate of interest cannot be given, for the very definition of the natural rate involves reference to the money rate of interest, as in the example given above. Thus by using the method of "immanent criticism" Myrdal shows what Wicksell would have believed had he followed his train of thought to its logical conclusion.

Myrdal defines the yield of existing real capital as the ratio of the net return to the value of existing capital.

The net return e′ for an individual firm for a unit period, calculated ex ante, at a given point of time is:

The discounted sum of all anticipations of gross returns in the next unit period, b′; *minus* the discounted sum of anticipations of gross cost in the form of operating cost of the co-operating means of production in the same period, m; *minus* the anticipations of value-change, d′, calculated for the period by taking into consideration all expectations of income and cost for the *whole* remaining life of the capital goods and also the interest rates which actually rule in the existing situation and are expected to rule in the future .... (The anticipated value-change) is then defined as the difference between the present value of the real capital and the expected capital value at the

[3] Myrdal (64, p. 24).

end of the unit period. This net change of value has also to be discounted to the present.[4]

Note first that the net return calculated in this fashion refers to the return obtainable from *existing* capital goods. Note secondly that Myrdal's formulation is similar to that of Keynes. The difference arises because Myrdal divides the life of existing equipment into two parts corresponding to operation during the next unit period and depreciation which depends on the profitability of the equipment during succeeding periods. But this difference in formulation is not really significant because in either case the present value of the equipment depends not only on the anticipations of incomes and costs during the next period but on anticipations of incomes and costs for all succeeding periods. Myrdal states explicitly that the anticipated value-change is not determined only by "technical" wear and tear but by expectations of prices in the future.[5]

Now the yield of existing real capital is the ratio of the net return so calculated to the value of existing capital. But the value of existing capital is the discounted sum of all future goods incomes minus operating costs. Hence the yield of real capital must always be equal to the money interest rate. Now Myrdal's concept of the yield of real capital is designed to measure the exchange value productivity of capital. In other words, Myrdal's yield of real capital is like the "natural rate" of interest in Wicksell's system. But if the yield of real capital is always equal to the money rate of interest how can a Wicksellian cumulative process ever arise? This difficulty can be resolved if we distinguish between the yield of real existing capital and the *yield of planned investments*. When Wicksell said that a lowering of the money rate of interest increases the profitability of investment, he meant that the investments that the entrepreneurs were planning to undertake, but which they had not actually undertaken, would increase in profitability.

The result of our analysis so far is that, if the yield of real capital is to fit into Wicksell's monetary theory, it has to be defined in such a way that it always by definition equal the

[4] G. Myrdal (64, p. 58).
[5] G. Myrdal (64, p. 57).

market rate of interest. At first sight this result seems to be quite dangerous to his whole train of thought. . . . But it is to be noticed that the argument so far relates only to the real capital *already existing*. And the effect of the difference between the money and natural rate of interest, according to Wicksell, is precisely that it stimulates *investment*, i.e., construction of new capital . . . . Henceforth we shall mean by yield the *yield of planned investments*. It would evidently have to be defined as *the ratio between the net return on the projected real investments and the cost of their production*.[6]

But this "yield of planned investments" is just another name for Keynes' concept of the marginal efficiency of capital. Keynes defined the marginal efficiency of capital as that rate of discount which makes the present value of the prospective yield (in Keynes' sense of a series of annuities) equal to the supply price of capital. Furthermore, Keynes makes it clear that the concept applies to investment that the entrepreneurs plan to undertake.

The reader should note that the marginal efficiency of capital is here defined in terms of the *expectation* of yield and of the *current* supply price of the capital-asset. It depends on the rate of return expected to be obtainable on money if it were invested in a *newly* produced asset.[7]

Using the concept of the yield of planned investments Myrdal is able to make precise Wicksell's notion of the stimulus given to new investment when the money rate is below the natural rate. When the money rate of interest is below the yield of planned investments entrepreneurs are able to realize *invest-ment gains* on their new investment projects. More accurately, it is the anticipation of investment gains that provides the real stimulus to investment.[8]

---

[6] Myrdal (64, pp. 64–65).

[7] J.M. Keynes (47, p. 136).

[8] One of Myrdal's great contributions to economics is his introduction of the ex-ante ex post schema. Using this organon Myrdal distinguishes among three kinds of gains and losses. First, there are capital gains and losses. Capital gains and losses arise when anticipation about future

There are two versions of the inducement to invest in the *General Theory*: the relation between the marginal efficiency of capital and the rate of interest and the relationship between the demand and supply price of a capital-asset. It has already been seen that Myrdal's concept of the yield of planned investments is essentially the same as Keynes' concept of the marginal efficiency of capital. But Myrdal, for a variety of reasons, is unhappy with the equilibrium condition that the yield of planned investments should be equal to the money rate of interest.

First, the net return on planned investments is replaced by the net return on existing capital and the cost of production of the planned investment by the cost of reproduction of the existing capital. These substitutions are made in order to increase the empirical applicability of the theory. Thus re-formulated the first equilibrium condition is that the money rate of interest must equal the yield on real capital. But even in this form the formula cannot be applied easily to reality.

The equilibrium condition can, however, be put in another form which means the same but which does not encounter the same difficulties if applied in the analysis of an actual situation. . . . If restated in terms of existing real capital (and not in terms of planned investments) – which means an approximation – the condition for monetary equilibrium could be formulated as the condition of *equality between the capital value and the cost of reproduction of existing real capital*. This equilibrium formula – expressed as a relation between capital value and cost of production instead of between the rate of interest and the yield – has essential advantages from the

revenues and costs change. When anticipations change the value of existing capital also changes. As these gains and losses refer to the value of existing capital they do not enter into the ex-ante calculations of entrepreneurs. Secondly, there are the revenue gains and losses. These gains and losses arise when the actual revenues and costs are different from the expected revenue and costs. Such gains and losses obviously do not enter into ex-ante calculations of entrepreneurs. Finally, there are the investment gains and losses. The ex-ante calculations of entrepreneurs are essentially concerned with these gains and losses inasmuch as they refer to the profitability of investment projects that entrepreneurs are considering whether to undertake or not.

standpoint of practical application. First of all, the magnitude "money rate" is not explicitly contained in the equilibrium formula thus reformulated.[9]

The original formula is the hardest to apply to reality because it requires information about entrepreneurs' expectation of the yield of planned investments which exists only "in their minds" and even there they are not very clearly formulated. The second formulation is objectionable because "the" money rate of interest enters into the formula, while in reality there is not one rate but a complex of rates. The formulation in terms of demand and supply price advocated by Myrdal by virtue of its greater empirical applicability is identical with the formulation of Keynes in the *General Theory*.[10]

Now we are in a position to explain why Myrdal thinks that the first equilibrium formula is not an independent condition of monetary equilibrium. For what the first equilibrium formula tells the entrepreneurs is whether it is profitable to change the amount of investment that they at present are undertaking. If the yield of planned investments exceeds the money rate of interest it will be profitable to purchase one more unit of capital and to continue to do so until the yield is equal to the rate of interest. Consequently, the first equilibrium formula is a condition not of *monetary* but of *investment* equilibrium. The reason for this is that the absence of net saving is not a necessary condition of monetary equilibrium. In other words, monetary equilibrium may obtain even with positive amounts of net investment. The second equilibrium condition is the true condition for monetary equilibrium. This condition states that there is monetary equilibrium if the demand for savings is equal to the supply

[9] Myrdal (64, pp. 69–70).

[10] Other refinements of the first equilibrium formula are also discussed by Myrdal (pp. 76–82). For example, Wicksell's assumption that all firms are alike, can be dropped. If this assumption is dropped each firm will have a different demand and supply price for a given capital-asset. In Myrdal's notation "c" (value of capital) and "r" (cost of reproduction) will be different for different firms. Furthermore, if the assumption of rationality is dropped, a given excess of "c" over "r" will not call forth from different firms the same volume of new investment. Hence each firm has a coefficient of investment reaction which measures the amount of new investment undertaken as a function of $c - r$.

of savings. Given that a certain amount of saving is being undertaken the first equilibrium formula tells us what the relationship between the yield of planned investments and the money rate of interest must be in order to bring forth such a level of investment as to create a demand for savings which is equal to the supply.

The zero-profit margin cannot be the criterion of monetary equilibrium under dynamic conditions but the criterion is instead that profit margin which stimulates enough investment to bring about equilibrium according to the second equilibrium formula... The conclusion is that Wicksell's first equilibrium formula is inadequate. To be determinate it must be related to the second formula.[11]

The second equilibrium formula states the true condition for monetary equilibrium because "that part of total national income which is not saved is always equal to the amount of consumption goods sold, multiplied by their price level".[12] This means that in the ex post calculus saving and investment are always equal. But this ex post equality of saving and investment is utterly useless for purposes of defining monetary equilibrium. Monetary equilibrium has to be defined in terms of ex-ante equality of savings and investment. Much of Myrdal's analysis in chapter 5 has to do with the relationships between the ex-ante and ex post calculi.

Myrdal clearly recognizes the independence of decisions to save and to invest :

This idea of the non-identity of investment and saving is so fundamental to Wicksell's whole theory... Now it must be obvious that, if saving is to be distinguished from real investment, monetary analysis is precisely where a "real" definition of saving *cannot* be used. The distinction *has* to be made since Wicksell's theory deals with an agreement or discrepancy between the two.[13]

[11] Myrdal (64, p. 84).
[12] Myrdal (64, p. 22).
[13] Myrdal (64, p. 89).

It is true that a "real" definition of saving would be useless for Wicksellian monetary analysis. The very question that the theory is designed to answer is whether at any given point of time there are forces in the economy which make for a cumulative and self-reinforcing change of the price level from its equilibrium level. The ex-ante equality of savings and investment is the condition for the absence of such cumulative and labile price changes. Yet investment and saving are always equal ex post no matter what happens in the economy.

However, it is not this meaningless balance in the subsequent bookkeeping for an expired period which is of interest to monetary analysis. Rather it is *the very changes during the period which are required to bring about this ex post balance.*[14]

Let us illustrate some of these ideas by describing Myrdal's conception of a Wicksellian cumulative process. Myrdal writes the second equilibrium condition in the following form: monetary equilibrium obtains when gross investment is equal to total capital disposal (p. 96). Total capital disposal is equal to saving plus the total anticipated value-change of existing real capital. Or putting it the other way saving has to be equal to gross real investment plus appreciation minus depreciation of existing real capital due to changes in anticipations.

Suppose that gross investment is equal to capital disposal and that the economy is in equilibrium. Assume that the equilibrium is disturbed by expectation of higher yield in the future. Before the disturbance impinged on the system the yield of planned investments was equal to the market rate of interest. But now as entrepreneurs expect higher yields in the future the yield of new investments become greater than the market rate of interest. Alternatively, the expectation of higher yield raises the capital value of planned investments above their cost of production. The anticipation of investment gain provides a stimulus to entrepreneurs to increase investment. But what happens to the other term of the equilibrium equation, namely the total capital disposal? As the money rate of interest is unchanged and the capital values of existing capital have risen due to the

[14]Myrdal (64, p. 121).

more optimistic expectations, the *ex-ante income* of the community has increased. Assume now that ex-ante consumption is not changed by the new expectations. This means that saving ex-ante has increased by as much as ex-ante income has increased. But although the increase of saving has augmented the total capital disposal the anticipated value-change has to be subtracted from capital disposal. In other words, ex-ante income has increased by an amount that is equal to the apprecation or smaller depreciation of capital expected in the future due to the more optimistic expectations of entrepreneurs.

The upshot is that expectation of higher yield in the future increases investment ex-ante and does not affect planned or ex-ante capital disposal.

Equilibrium therefore is disturbed, and the tendency to increased investment, as there is no corresponding tendency as regards free capital disposal, must be met by a creation of purchasing power to which no capital disposal corresponds. The increase of investment signifies, therefore, a tendency towards the typical shift of production in the upswing of Wicksell's cumulative process.[15]

It must be remembered that it has been assumed that the more optimistic expectations have not affected ex-ante consumption. As there is no reason for the supply of consumption goods to change there is equilibrium on the market for consumption goods. But the anticipation of investment gain induces entrepreneurs to increase their demand for producers' goods and raw materials. Thus prices rise *first* in the higher stages of production. As a result of the greater money incomes distributed in the higher stages of production and the decreased supply of consumption goods due to the transference of resources from the lower to the higher stages of production the prices of consumption goods increase.

We have here a race of different "price levels": Of prices of real capital, factors of production, and consumption goods. In

[15]Myrdal (64, p. 103). In this passage, Myrdal hints at the independence of investment decisions.

the theory is implied not only certain causal relations between them but also a *given order of sequence in their* movements.[16]

But why is the process cumulative? The answer is that entrepreneurial expectations partly depend upon the course of prices of consumer goods. Increased investment and the transference of factors of production to the higher stages result in a decreased supply and a higher price level of consumer goods. But when prices of consumer goods rise entrepreneurs' expectations of the future yield of capital rise again, thereby giving further impetus to the upward Wicksellian process.

The *speed* of the Wicksellian process depends on the response of consumption demand to the ex-ante increase in income caused by the more optimistic expectations. Hitherto we have assumed that consumption demand increases only after resources have been transferred to the higher stages of production. But the original increase of ex-ante income may itself lead to a higher consumption demand. In this case the free capital disposal which is the sum of saving and the anticipated value-change of capital *decreases* as a result of the more optimistic expectations. The reason for this is that the effect on capital disposal of the anticipated value-change (in this case a smaller depreciation) is partly dissipated in increased consumption demand. Hence the Wicksellian process is accelerated.[17]

The case where equilibrium is disturbed by a lowering of the money rate of interest should be briefly considered. A lowering of the money rate of interest, assuming fixed expectations, creates anticipations of investment gain in the minds of entrepreneurs by raising the value of existing capital above the cost of its reproduction. Thus ex-ante investment increases. So far the analysis is the same. But unlike the first case, a lowering of the money rate of interest leads to a fall of ex-ante income. The reason is that depreciation is a function of the money rate of

[16] Myrdal (64, p. 27).

[17] The relation between the ex ante and ex post calculi during a cumulative Wicksellian process is very complicated (pp. 116–122). Only simple case is considered here. Assume that an upward process is initiated by an excess of investment over saving. Entrepreneurs will then experience revenue gains. The ex-ante excess of investment is partly offset by the ex post increase in saving due to revenue gains.

interest. At a lower money rate more has to be set aside every year for the entrepreneur to recover the original cost of the capital asset at the end of its economic life. Hence the net return of the entrepreneur or the discounted difference between gross returns and operating costs is decreased. Again, if it is assumed that ex-ante consumption demand remains the same the result is that capital disposal is unaffected by the lowering of the interest rate. But ex-ante investment increases and the monetary equilibrium is ruptured.

In the Wicksell– Hayek system an increase of voluntary saving necessarily leads to a fall in the rate of interest and an increased circulation of money in the higher stages of production. Hayek believes that the crisis occurs not because of excessive saving, but because of inadequate saving. The second equilibrium formula leads to a very different result in the Wicksell–Myrdal system. In all the cases considered up till now it has been supposed that ex-ante investment exceeds ex-ante capital disposal. Instead if we suppose that expected saving exceeds expected investment a downward Wicksellian process is generated in an exactly analogous manner.

An increased saving does not in itself imply or cause a change in production in a more capitalistic direction–generally just the contrary. The ex post balance comes about not by a corresponding increase in investment but by losses destroying part of incomes to be accounted for ex post.[18]

According to Wicksell's third equilibrium formula the money rate is "normal" or equal to the natural rate if the absolute price level has no tendency to change. Davidson showed that this formula is invalid in a dynamic economy in which productivity is increasing. For in such an economy if the money rate of interest is kept at a level such that the second equilibrium condition is satisfied monetary equilibrium will be associated with a lower price level.

Myrdal's argument is that monetary equilibrium requires that a certain relationship should hold among the prices of varibles relevant to monetary equilibrium. A uniform movement of all

[18]Myrdal (64, p. 89).

prices will not disturb these price relationships.[19] Hence monetary equilibrium is independent of the absolute price level, *if* the price movements are always uniform. But in practice this condition is rarely satisfied. Some prices are sticky and others are more flexible. This implies that only those changes of absolute prices are consistent with monetary equilibrium that do not require changes in the sticky prices. Thus monetary equilibrium, in practice, does impose some restrictions on the value of the absolute level.

The idea that monetary equilibrium only fixes certain price relationships can be used to test Davidson's criticism of Wicksell. In an economy in which the productivity of factors is increasing the yield (in physical terms) of planned investments rises. Monetary equilibrium will be preserved if the price level of consumption goods declines because then the total yield of planned investments would not change. But monetary equilibrium could also be preserved with the same price level for consumption goods but a higher level of wages because in this case the higher capital values due to productivity gains will be offset by greater costs of production of capital.

## COMPARISON WITH KEYNES

Comparison of his theory with the Keynesian theory is made difficult by Myrdal's use of the method of "immanent criticism". By immanently criticizing Wicksell, Myrdal intends to convey the impression that he is saying nothing new or "original" and that it is all to be found in Wicksell's work. If Myrdal were an Aristotelian he might have said that although the theory of *Monetary Equilibrium* is not actually to be found in Wicksell's work, it is "potentially" there just as a tree is "potentially" in the seed from which it grows.

Let us grant to Myrdal that his theory existed "potentially" in Wicksell's work. But it cannot be said that Myrdal's theory follows logically from Wicksell's theory because Hayek and Mises, who obtained their inspiration from the same source, developed a rather different theory. One decisive example,

[19]Myrdal (64, p. 132).

referring to the effects of saving, has already been given to prove this assertion.

The problem becomes transparent if it is realized that normal scientists regard science as a cumulative and gradualistic affair. Their confidence in the existing paradigm is so strong that they find it hard to believe that any novel orientation to reality can be valid. They think that the puzzles of science can be solved by normal means. Myrdal's use of the method of the immanent criticism shows that he regarded economic science from the point of view of a normal scientist. The problem of industrial fluctuations had obviously become very important in the twenties. Men such as Foster and Catchings, who were not normal economists, felt that the events of the twenties had made the classical paradigm effete. They regarded the counter-instance as an anomaly that falsified the classical theory. Normal economists such as Robertson and Myrdal felt that these same events were mere puzzles that could be accommodated within the classical paradigm if it is suitably extended. It is remarkable that their normal articulating activity led to a theory (or concepts) that was similar to the one espoused by the more "speculative" scientists and which provided a basis for a new orientation for economic theory after the Keynesian theory was put forward.

Despite his disavowals of originality, Myrdal had succeeded in making considerable advances over the older way of looking at things. His account of the inducement to invest is almost the same as the one given by Keynes in the *General Theory*. He clearly recognized that saving and investment are independent. He showed how the ex-ante difference between saving and investment becomes an ex post equality. He showed that an increase of voluntary saving leads, not to increased investment as in the Wicksell-Hayek system, but to losses for entrepreneurs due to the fall in prices. He systematically introduced expectations into economic analysis.

But Myrdal's theory is still very different from the theory of the *Treatise*. In *Monetary Equilibrium* the money interest rate is an *exogenous* variable, something that is determined by the banks. In the *Treatise* the construct corresponding to it is an *endogenous* variable determined by the bearishness theory of the demand for holding money. The *Treatise* contains a theory of the comparative-statics multiplier. In Myrdal's theory quantity adjustments play no role. Nevertheless, as must be apparent from the preceding discussion, quantity adjustments can be built into Myrdal's model.

## OTHER INTERPRETATIONS OF MYRDAL'S WORK

This is Klein's view:

> Among economists *who have been far* from the Keynesian doctrines there grew up a very popular business-cycle theory in the early thirties called the neo-Wicksellian theory.... Swedish economists have been true to the "favourite son" and worked closely along Wicksellian lines, one of their best expositions being Myrdal's *Monetary Equilibrium*. But the Swedish economists were not the only ones who dressed up and elaborated upon Wicksell's theory; Mises and then Hayek developed a popular business-cycle theory...which started its analysis from the relation between the market rate and the natural rate.[20]

It is certainly misleading to say that Myrdal, Mises, and Hayek belonged to that group of economists who "have been far from" the Keynesian doctrines. The crucial difference between Hayek and Myrdal regarding the effects of saving has already been adverted to. Another important difference relates to the role of the banking system in the cyclical process. Hayek's view was that as long as the banks maintain a neutral money policy saving and investment can never get out of line. But Myrdal's view is different. If investment ex-ante exceeds planned capital disposal this excess will be met by a creation of purchasing power to which no capital disposal corresponds.[21] In other words, saving and investment can get out of line without any departure of the banks from a neutral money policy. This question was a main bone of contention in the Keynes–Hayek

[20]L. Klein (50, p. 49, emphasis added).
[21]See footnote 15, p. 111.

debate of the early thirties. So Myrdal's theory was much closer
to that of Keynes than Klein thinks.

This is Shackle's view:[22]

This rather flat and formal statement gives little hint of the
radical novelty of Myrdal's venture. For the first time, an
economic theory was to be based on men's imaginative construction of an unknown future. Myrdal himself did not thus
express it, being content to refer to anticipations and their
uncertainty. But the dramatic, uncompromising shift of ground
ought to be seen in its full meaning. The view of economics as
a human counterpart of celestial mechanics was being abandoned.... In all but its assignments of emphasis, *Monetary
Equilibrium* anticipated Keynes' *General Theory*, though not
conveying Keynes' sense of revolutionary achievement and
conviction of power.[23]

Little need be said about the first part of the passage. It
is true that Myrdal's great contribution was his introduction of
the ex-ante ex post schema into economic analysis.[24] But Shackle
overstates his case. The implication that the presence of uncertainty in economic affairs makes it impossible to use "exact
methods" is mistaken. The fallacy of such "rationalist" objections to the use of mathematics in economic science is too well-
known to need extended comment here.

More interesting is the assertion that "in all but his assignments of emphasis, Myrdal anticipated Keynes". The exact
nature of Shackle's view is hard to determine. For example,
Shackle says that Myrdal's theory is "as remarkable and in
some respects as successful an explanation of the variations of
general output as Keynes' own".[25] On the other hand, Shackle
says that "Wicksell and Myrdal were not really concerned with
unemployment of productive resources in the sense in which

[22]G. Shackle (82, chapter 10 contains an excellent discussion of Myrdal's
work).

[23]G. Shackle (82, p. 98).

[24]It is not clear if Myrdal was the "first" to do this. See *Treatise*, Vol. 1,
pp. 159–161.

[25]G. Shackle (82, p. 89).

Keynes treats it".[26] What Shackle seems to mean is that "had the *General Theory* never been written, Myrdal's work would eventually have supplied almost the same theory".[27]

According to the interpretation presented in this chapter Myrdal did not build a quantity adjustment mechanism into his model. From Shackle's inconsistent statements it appears that he does not disagree with this interpretation. All that he is saying is that Myrdal's work would eventually have supplied the same theory. But then can't the same thing be said about Abbati, Foster and Catchings, or Keynes' *Treatise*? Can't we say that had the *General Theory* never been written, Keyne's *Treatise* would eventually have supplied the same theory. Shackle's answer is an emphatic no. The theoretical framework of the *Treatise* is said to be "utterly different" from that of Myrdal or Keynes' *General Theory*.[28] This is another example of a *crass* misrepresentation of the theoretical structure of the *Treatise*.

Shackle's conception of Myrdal is that of "a radical innovator" who led economists into the "land of uncertainty". If he saw so much, is it not plausible to contend that he was even aware of the liquidity preference theory ? Yes, says Shackle. From the fact that Myrdal replaced Wicksell's technical conception of the natural rate of interest by the concept of exchange-value productivity, Shackle concludes that Myrdal had a dim awareness of the liquidity-preference theory.[29] It is submitted that the interpretation given in this paper is more consistent with the textual evidence. As in the case of the treatment of output Shackle has allowed himself to be led astray by his image of the man.

We are in agreement, however, with Shackle's explanation of the development of economic theory in the twenties and thirties:

The depression of the 1920s and its drastic worsening in the 1930s was not only a disaster in the real lives of millions but a profound intellectual shock. It exposed the

[26]G. Shackle (82, p. 124).
[27]G. Shackle (82, p. 124).
[28]G. Shackle (82, p. 89).
[29]G. Shackle (82, pp. 100–101).

established theoretical picture of the economic system as
fallacious and helpless. Out of a stunning intellectual crisis
there arose a sudden mental freedom to overturn all accepted
systems of thought.[30]

## THE THEORY OF D. ROBERTSON[31]

Central to the Robertsonian view of economic reality is the idea
that there are "appropriate" fluctuations and "inappropriate"
fluctuations. Appropriate fluctuations are those which have their
provenience in real demand and cost conditions. However, the
technical and psychological characteristics of industry are such
that the response of the economic system to such primary changes
is magnified beyond the level that is warranted by real demand
and cost conditions.

Fluctuations in output are justified if they arise in the following three ways. First, a change in the real cost (in the Marshallian sense) of producing the product will furnish a rational
inducement to entrepreneurs to change the level of their output.
Robertson believes that the revival of industry from a depression
is mainly due to a lowering of real cost, especially in the cons-
tructional trades.[32] Second, entrepreneurs of one group of industries have a rational incentive to alter the scale of their output if
there is a change in the intensity of their desire for the products
of other groups. For example, in a depression the intensity of
the demand of the non-instrument-making trades for instruments
increases and is an important factor contributing to the revival.
Third, fluctuations in output are justified if they are due to a
change in the real demand price of the products of one group.
The effect on output of a change in real demand price depends
on the effort-elasticity of demand for the products of the other
group. If the effort-elasticity is greater than one a rise in the
real demand price will induce entrepreneurs to expand their output; whereas a less than unit elasticity will induce them to

[30]G. Shackle (82, pp. 127–128).

[31]The following is not intended to be a complete discussion of Robertson's economics. For a fuller discussion the reader is referred to R. Saulnier (76).

[32]See D. Robertson (72, p. 239). The book was originally published in 1915.

reduce their output. As industry's demand in terms of effort for
the products of agriculture is usually greater than one increased
bountifulness of nature may well be an important cause of industrial revival, and the downturn may be the result of the terms
of trade becoming favourable for agriculture.[33]

If the demand for wheat rises relatively to the demand for
wine the price of wheat rises and resources are transferred from
the wine to the wheat industry. Such fluctuations are deemed not
only appropriate, but positively desirable in microeconomics.
Robertson's argument is that, in macroeconomics, fluctuations
that reflect real factors should be deemed appropriate.

But "the *actual* fluctuations in industrial output tend greatly
to exceed the rational or appropriate fluctuations" because "when
the instrument of production is very large, the process of investment in the trade concerned is imperfectly divisible". Then there
is the fact that "in many cases the durable instruments of production are *intractable*. The best rate of output, having regard
to the costs, immediate and deferred, of putting the instrument
out of commission, is greater than the rate of output which
would be best if no such costs existed."[34]

The main reason for which the actual expansions of industrial
output which occur are greater even than the *relatively* most
appropriate expansions, seems to be the stress of competition
aggravated by the length of time which is required to adjust
production to a changed demand.[35]

## CONCEPTS OF SAVING

A man "is lacking if during a given period he consumes less
than value of his current economic output."[36] A man dis-lacks if
he consumes more than the value of his current economic output. Lacking measures the extent by which *real* consumption
differs from *real* income. Thus a man may lack even if he spends

[33]Robertson attaches great importance to this explanation. See *Industrial
Fluctuations*, pp. 129–156 and pp. 239–241.
[34]D. Robertson (70, pp. 35–37).
[35]D. Robertson (70, p. 37).
[36]D. Robertson (70, p. 41).

his whole *money* income or even more than his money income. The things in the provision of which lacking eventuates are called capital.

Lacking is said to be unproductive if it consists in abstaining from present consumption in favour of those who use this lacking "unproductively" (in the classical sense). Lending money to governments for war purposes is the best example. Unproductive lacking must be distinguished from *abortive lacking*.

> If, however, he neither presents his money-claim himself nor hands it over to another, but simply adds it to his existing money stocks, he may be said to be Hoarding.. . .In this case he is from his own point of view saving, but is taking no steps to ensure the creation of Capital. Unless others take such steps, the effect of his action, assuming equilibrium of production and sale to be preserved, is that the consumption of other persons is increased, by as much as his own consumption is diminished.[37]

Keynes tells us that it is this concept of abortive lacking which gave him the clue and set his mind working in the right direction. Robertson informs us that Keynes' influence is most apparent in chapter 5 where all these saving concepts are introduced. If Kuhn's theory is right, Keynes must have experienced a Gestalt switch at some time. Using Schumpeter's theory that many writers have a *pre-analytic* vision which they try to express in their analytical constructs Leijonhufvud has argued that throughout his life Keynes attempted to implement his vision. The evidence, however, does not support this theory. Consider what Robertson says in his new introduction to his book on industrial fluctuations.

> Among the many things which at this time (*circa* 1915) I already owed to Keynes, I do not think my propensity to underconsumption was one. I have forgotten the details of his paper . . . but is seems pretty clear that his views at that date were of a more uncompromisingly "under-saving" type than my own.[38]

[37]D. Robertson (70, p. 46).
[38]Robertson (72).

In the debates on the nature of monetary theory which took place in the early thirties, as we shall see later on, Keynes stated explicitly that some time in the late twenties he did undergo a very significant Gestalt switch with respect to the nature of money, a switch, he thought, that it would be hard for a quantity theorist to make. There is no doubt that with respect to the theories he entertained about economic phenomena he did experience a significant switch. But that does not disprove Schumpeter's contention because he can still say that his "pre-analytic" vision (if that concept has any meaning) did not change. But as Kuhn's theory is not concerned with "visions" further comment is unnecessary.

To return to the main thread of the argument. Automatic stinting occurs "whenever an increase in the stream of money directed on to the market prevents certain persons from consuming goods which they would otherwise have consumed.[39] Automatic stinting involves automatic lacking only if the consumption of those who are affected by it is less than what they intended and below the value of the current economic output. Automatic stinting does not necessarily involve automatic lacking. For example, if all members of the community decide to dishoard, the intended dis-lacking of an individual may be cancelled by the automatic stinting which the spontaneous dishoarding of others imposes on him so that his consumption may equal the value of his current output. In this case there is no lacking. The opposite of automatic stinting is automatic splashing. If other individuals decide to increase their hoarding another individual will be able to indulge in automatic splashing as a given sum of money will buy more goods as a result of the fall of the price level. In this case automatic splashing implies automatic dis-lacking. But if all individuals decide to increase their hoards the intended lacking may be exactly cancelled by the automatic splashing which the intended hoarding of others makes possible. Lacking is said to be induced when people, realizing that automatic stinting has reduced the value of the *stock* of their money balances, decide to decrease their expenditure in order to bring actual stocks to the desired level. Both automatic lacking and induced lacking are a species of imposed lacking inasmuch as

[39]Robertson(70, p. 48).

they are the result of changes in the stream of money brought about by other persons. But induced lacking is voluntary; automatic lacking is not.

## ROBERTSON'S "FUNDAMENTAL" EQUATION

Much of Robertson's analysis is concerned with the relationships among banking policy, short lacking and the trade cycle. If the real-bills doctrine is correct, increases of the money supply by the banks for bona fide commercial purposes will not disturb equilibrium. The argument of the proponent of such a doctrine is that if traders borrow money from the banks on the strength of goods that they are going to sell within a short time, equilibrium is not disturbed because the increased money supply is met by an increased flow of goods.[40]

Robertson's fundamental equation is designed to show the exact conditions under which the real-bills doctrine is valid.[41] Let '$R$' denote the real annual income of a community. Let '$k$' denote the proportion of $R$ that people desire to hold in the form of money. Hence $kR = M/P$ is equal to the real value of the money supply. Let '$D$' denote the proportion that the period of production bears to a whole year. Hence $DR$ is equal to the real income produced during one period of production. Let '$a$' denote the proportion of $kR$ that is lent or created by banks for the purpose of creating circulating capital. Let '$b$' denote the proportion of circulating capital ($C$) that has been built up by traders with the aid of bank loans.

Assume first that all money consists of bank deposits. Assume also that value is added to circulating capital uniformly during a period of production. This implies that on the average the value of circulating capital $C$ is equal to half the income produced during one period of production. Hence $C = \frac{1}{2}DR$. But $akR = bC$. Substituting for $C$ we get $ak = \frac{1}{2}bD$ or $2\ a/b = D/k$. This is Robertson's fundamental equation.

To breathe some life into this formula consider a few cases. Assume that both $a$ and $b$ are equal to one. This means that all

[40]For an account of the evolution and discussion of the real-bills doctrine, the reader is referred to L. Mints (62).

[41]D. Robertson (71, pp. 70–89).

the money created by banks has been crystallized in circulating capital and that traders have built up their circulating capital only by borrowing from the banks. Suppose also that the period of production is half a year. This means that on the average it takes six months for the circulating capital to mature out in consumable goods. From the fundamental equation it may be inferred that the velocity of circulation of money for the purchase of final goods must be 4, if equilibrium is to be maintained, i.e., $k$ must be equal to $\frac{1}{4}$. Suppose that $k = \frac{1}{8}$. In this case $D/k$ is greater than $2a/b$ and there will be a tendency for prices to rise.

To see why equilibrium is disturbed in this case and, consequently, why the real-bills doctrine fails to be true, suppose that Smith borrows $100 from the bank all of which, by our assumption, he invests in circulating capital. Initially Smith's deposits at some bank are increased by $100. He uses this money to hire workers and to buy raw materials. The money is transferred to the accounts of others. Now, if the loan is made in January, say, the circulating capital will not mature out in consumable goods till July. But as the velocity of circulation of money is 8, each unit of money changes hands 8 times a year. This means that before Smith's goods reach the market in July, the money that was created on the strength of them is "perching" on various goods and services and raising prices in the process.[42]

> The longer the products take in coming to birth, the more damage will the money have time to do ... the validity of the claim of the "needs of trade" party is somehow bound up with two things – our old friend the velocity of circulation of

---

[42]The reader must have noticed that the "paradigm-confirming" research of Robertson led to the same results as the "paradigm-shattering" research of Foster and Catchings. The phenomena that Robertson thinks can be explained by "our old friend the velocity of circulation" Foster and Catchings regarded as subversive of the classical paradigm. In their theory the time element in production is emphasized. This together with the concept of the "circuit velocity" of money is used by them to enunciate a fundamental law of progress. The content of this fundamental law is the same as that of Robertson's fundamental equation: investment increases demand today; it increases supply only in the future.

money and something which we may call the *average period of production of goods.*[43]

What the fundamental equation states is that, given values of $a$ and $b$, equilibrium requires for any given value of the period of production a definite value for the velocity of circulation. The longer the period of production, the smaller must be the velocity of circulation if bank loans are not to disturb equilibrium. If traders decide to increase the proportion of their circulating capital which is built up with the aid of bank loans (i.e. if $b$ increases) expansion of bank loans will disturb equilibrium by raising prices since $D/k$ will then be greater than $2a/b$. The reason for this is clear. If $b$ increases and other things remain constant, before the circulating capital can mature out in consumable goods *more money* will circulate at the *same velocity* instead of the same amount of money circulating at a higher velocity of circulation as in the case previously considered. The effect on prices in either case will be the same.

Using the concepts and tools developed above it is possible to present Robertson's analysis of the relationship among banking policy, short lacking and the trade cycle. Assume that the economy is at the nadir of depression. Output is low and unemployment is high. Machines and equipment lie idle and are wasting away. Business is in the doldrums. Suppose that a new product or a new use for an old product is discovered and that the kindliness of nature results in abundant harvests. In such circumstances industry will experience a revival. The augmented agricultural output makes the terms of trade favourable for manufacturing industry vis-a-vis agricultural industry. The increase in the real demand price for their products will furnish a rational inducement to entrepreneurs in the consumptive trades to increase their output. Furthermore, these entrepreneurs who have discovered a new product will experience an increase in the intensity of their desire for machines. In addition entrepreneurs in all industries will experience a lowering of the real cost of producing output because in a depression costs are low and productivity is high.

For all these reasons industry will experience a revival. As a

[43]Robertson (71, p. 84).

consequence the demand for circulating capital on the part of entrepreneurs will increase. In order to provide this circulating capital entrepreneurs will turn to the banks. In addition the proportion of their circulating capital that they finance in this way will increase, i.e. $b$ will increase. As people's saving habits are more or less stable it is unlikely that this sharp increase in the demand for circulating capital can be met by an increase of the spontaneous short lacking of the public.

There seems no doubt that in fact the supply of short lacking is not sufficiently elastic to cope with such pronounced and discontinuous increase in demand, and that the responsibility for meeting them rests almost entirely upon the banking system. . . . Under such conditions it seems unreasonable to expect the banking system *both* to ensure that appropriate additions are made to the quantity of Circulating Capital *and* to preserve absolute stability in the price-level.[44]

If spontaneous short lacking cannot meet the demand for circulating capital the banking system has to provide it. The banks supply this short lacking by imposing automatic stinting on the people. By appropriately increasing the quantity of money lent to entrepreneurs, who are only too willing to make use of resources provided by the banks, the banking system is able to cause an increased stream of money to flow on the markets to compete with the ordinary stream of money. Thus by raising prices the banks impose automatic lacking on the public. A rise of the price-level in this case is an appropriate rise because it originated in changes in real demand and cost conditions.

The banks also perform an important role in transforming the spontaneous lacking of the public into applied lacking. An increase of spontaneous lacking, if unaccompanied by any action on the part of the banks, will become abortive inasmuch as the fall in the price level resulting from the spontaneous hoarding will permit others to indulge in automatic splashing. Thus banks by lending money entrusted to them to entrepreneurs impose automatic stinting and prevent the automatic splashing that would otherwise have occurred. In this case the banks have provided

[44]Robertson (70, p. 60).

short lacking to entrepreneurs by preventing a fall in the price-level; whereas in the other case they did this by raising prices by an appropriate amount.

During the revival of industry to the extent that productivity is increasing and real cost of producing the product is declining, the banks are able to provide the required amount of short lacking with smaller increases in the price-level.

## CONCLUSIONS

The remarkable thing about the men studied in this chapter is that both disclaimed originality for their theories. Both were normal economists in the sense that they were merely extending traditional models in order to account for cyclical phenomena. Myrdal believed that he was merely developing consequences that were implicit in Wicksell's extension of the Ricardian model. He sneers at the "unnecessary originality" of Anglo–Saxon economists. In his introduction to his book on industrial fluctuations Robertson has expressed a similar deprecating attitude.

> To begin with, I do not think I had been brought up with any exaggerated respect for Say's Law of Markets . . . . I had learnt from Marshall that "though men have the power to purchase they may not choose to use it". . . . But, to speak frankly, I think there is too great a disposition among the general public to believe that in the mid-'30s some revolutionary discovery was made about "effective demand" which has transformed the whole outlook.

What Robertson really means is that *he* did not undergo any Gestalt switch at the time. This is in accordance with Kuhn's theory. For there are some normal economists who are never able to make the switch. It has already been noted that Robertson was unperturbed by the very phenomenon that others regarded as providing conclusive evidence of the effeteness of the classical paradigm. And what is more remarkable is that the theory that Robertson developed for the phenomenon is similar to the theory that others, not wedded to the classical paradigm, had independently developed. This phenomenon is a rather striking confirmation of Kuhn's theory that, to put it paradoxically, paradigm-confirmation leads to paradigm-disconfirmation as a result of the loosening of the rules that bound normal research. The proliferation of normal articulating activity leads to the introduction of new concepts that arise naturally as a result of the attempts by normal economists to explain the crisis problem in terms of the old paradigm. But these new concepts ultimately provide a basis for a new orientation for science. It is submitted that this chapter provides striking evidence in favour of Kuhn's theory.

# Chapter V

# The Theories of J. M. Keynes

## INTRODUCTION

This chapter shall tell a story about a remarkable transformation. In the decade of the twenties the economic theory of Keynes underwent a considerable modification. In 1923 Keynes wrote *Monetary Reform*. The theory contained in that book was an empirical and theoretical articulation of Marshall's monetary theory. Keynes worked on the *Treatise on Money* in the late twenties. When the book was published in 1930 the *gestalt* in which the economic situation is to be seen had changed.

In this chapter a new interpretation of the basic theoretical structure of the *Treatise* shall be presented. On the basis of this new interpretation I shall argue that the decisive break with the classical theory occurred with the publication of the *Treatise*. The *General Theory* merely actualized the promise contained in the earlier book.

Of course, within Kuhn's framework the exact date at which a revolution occurs is not so important. Revolutions are *social processes*. Nevertheless it is important to know the Keynesian paradigm. If the interpretation presented in this and subsequent chapters is correct we will have to conclude that the *Treatise* is the paradigm for Keynesian normal science.

## KEYNES' MONETARY REFORM

In the early part of this century Marshall had expressed the view that the central corpus of economic theory is "well in hand".[1] Most of the fundamental theoretical work had already been done and the only problem was to attempt an empirical articulation of economy theory. According to Marshall the central organon

[1]Recently Solow said that macroeconomic theory is now "well-in-hand".

of monetary and value theory had to be used to elucidate particular problem-situations. This is what Keynes said in 1922.

> Before Adam Smith this apparatus of thought scarcely existed. Between his time and this it has been greatly enlarged and improved. Nor is there any branch of knowledge in the formation of which Englishmen can claim a more predominant part. It is not complete yet, but important improvements in its elements are becoming rare. The main task of the professional economist now consists, either in obtaining a wide knowledge of *relevant* facts and exercising skill in the application of economic principles to them or in expounding the elements of his method in a lucid way.[2]

Keynes' object in *Monetary Reform* was to undertake a theoretical and empirical articulation of Marshall's monetary theory. Now Marshall had originated the cash-balance approach to the value of money.[3] Marshall's approach is different from Fisher in that Marshall treated velocity from a subjective viewpoint. Subsequent English monetary theorists in the Marshallian tradition, like Pigou and Robertson, further explored this psychologistic approach to velocity. In addition, they developed algebraic equation to express Marshall's theory.

One of the most famous equations of this type is Keynes' quantity equation. Let '$k$' denote the *amount* of purchasing power that people in the aggregate want to hold in the form of money. Keynes says that "we can measure this definite amount of purchasing power in terms of a unit made up of a collection of specified quantities of their standard articles of consumption or other objects of expenditure."[4] If $n$ is the number of notes and $p$ the price of the "consumption unit", the quantity equation in its simplest form can be written as $n = pk$. The equation can be expanded to include bank deposits. Let $k'$ denote the amount of resources that people want to hold in the form of bank deposits. Then $pk'$ will be the value of their resources that people want to hold in the form of bank deposits. If the

[2]Introduction to H. Henderson (41).

[3]A. Marshall (59).

[4]J. M. Keynes (49, p. 76).

reserve-deposit ratio is $r$, the expanded quantity equation can be written as $n = p (k + rk')$.

In this book Keynes espoused a quantity theory of money. Keynes said that the quantity theory "is fundamental. Its correspondence with fact is *not* open to question."[5] Keynes stated that so long as $k$ remains unchanged $n$ and $p$ will move together. A change of $n$ will produce proportionate changes in the prices of goods in the consumption unit. Virtually every major monetary theorist since Cantillon was aware that during "transitional" periods the strict quantity theorem fails to hold. This is what Keynes had said.

But the Theory has often been expounded on the further assumption that a *mere* change in the quantity of currency cannot affect $k$, $r$, and $k'$. ... Now "in the long run" this is probably true. ... But this *long run* is a misleading guide to current affairs. In the *long run* we are all dead.[6]

Like many other monetary theorists in England Keynes thought in terms of Marshall's concept of "relative elasticities" of the factors in the equation of exchange. The most important effects of changes in money would be on the price level. But the precise proportional effect on prices would be upset by small changes in velocity. In other words, $M$ and $P$ have a high elasticity of variations; $V$ and $T$ have a low elasticity of variation.

On the empirical level Keynes used his own version of the Marshallian quantity theory to elucidate certain problems relating to the gold standard. The basic question facing Britain was whether to return to the gold standard on the old gold parity. Returning on the gold parity prevailing, before the war entailed raising the exchange rate of sterling vis-a-vis the other currencies. This would have necessitated a deflationary policy at home. On the other hand, equilibrium could have been restored by refraining from a deflationary policy and allowing the sterling parity to fall in terms of gold.

In order to answer this question satisfactorily it is necessary to have a theory of inflation and deflation. In *Monetary Reform*

[5]J. M. Keynes (49, p. 82).
[6]Keynes (49, p. 80).

Keynes made a powerful case for monetary stabilization. Society consists of three classes: the investor or "rentier" class, the business class, and the earning class. Inflation and deflation were shown to have different effects on these classes of society. Keynes argued that although both inflation and deflation affect favourably at least some of the classes, their overall effect is harmful.

We see therefore that rising prices and falling prices each have their characteristic disadvantage. The inflation which causes the former means injustice to individuals and to classes . . . particularly to investors; and is therefore unfavourable to saving. The Deflation which causes falling prices means Impoverishment to labor and to enterprise by leading entrepreneurs to restrict production, in their endeavour to avoid loss to themselves; and is therefore disastrous to employment . . . . Thus Inflation is unjust and Deflation is inexpedient. Of the two perhaps Deflation is, if we rule out exaggerated inflations such as that of Germany, the worse; because it is worse, in an impoverished world, to provoke unemployment than to disappoint the rentier.[7]

## CONCLUSIONS

In a previous chapter it was demonstrated that the quantity equation operated as a shared exemplar of the classical paradigm. This shared exemplar signalled the gestalt in which empirical phenomena were to be seen. The equation told the scientist that the most fundamental relationship was that between the quantity of money and the level of prices. In his book *Monetary Reform* Keynes conformed with this tradition.

In 1922 Keynes expressed the view that the most fundamental theoretical work had already been done in economics. The only task left for economists was to acquire a wide knowledge of relevant facts and to use basic theory to elucidate various problem-situations. A year later *Monetary Reform* was published. The theory contained in that book is a theoretical

[7]Keynes (49, p. 44).

and empirical articulation of the Marshallian version of the quantity theory of money.

## KEYNES' TREATISE ON MONEY[8]

The basic theory of the *Treatise* is presented in Books three and four. Book three begins with a discussion of the concepts of income, saving, and profits. In *Monetary Reform* Keynes was primarily interested in the relationship between the quantity of money and the level of prices and the small changes in velocity that disturb the proportional relationship between these two variables. Attention was directed to the terms of the quantity equation. In the *Treatise*, on the other hand, the spotlight is focussed on the relationship among the variables that are significantly different from those that appear in the quantity equation.

During any given period of time society utilizes its productive resources to create goods and services. This total output is made up of the available output and the non-available output. Available output consists of the output that is in a form that is available for consumption. The non-available output is not in a form available for consumption.[9]

The production of this output during any period of time gives rise to money-income. Keynes says that he proposes to mean the same thing by the following three expressions: (1) the community's money-income; (2) the earnings of the factors of production; and (3) the cost of production of the output.[10] Profits of entrepreneurs do not belong to the community's income. They constitute the difference between the value of the total output and its cost of production.

The earnings of entrepreneurs consist of their "normal

[8]Unless otherwise stated all subsequent references will be to the first volume.

[9]The available output is approximately equal to the production of consumer goods. Similarly, the non-available output is roughly equal to the production of investment-goods. For a full discussion of these concepts see Appendix 1.

[10]Keynes (48, p. 123).

remuneration" and their profits, i.e. profits constitute the difference between the actual remuneration of entrepreneurs and their normal remuneration. As the theory of profits is vital to Keynes' analysis the following passage should be studied carefully.

> For my present purpose I propose to define the "normal" remuneration of entrepreneurs at any time as that rate of remuneration which, if they were open to make new bargains with all the factors of production at the currently prevailing rates of earnings, would leave them under no motive either to increase or decrease their scale of operations.[11]

Note that the quantity-adjustment mechanism is explicitly built into the model. The existence of profits implies that entrepreneurs are endeavouring to either increase or decrease the volume of employment they offer to the factors of production.

Keynes defines saving as "the sum of the differences between the money-incomes of individuals and their money-expenditure on current consumption".[12] As profits do not belong to the income of the community the expenditure of a part of these profits by entrepreneurs on consumer goods is equivalent to negative saving.

Keynes' object in the *Treatise* was to examine the forces that determine the level of output and employment.[13] It is for this reason that he felt that he had to "break away from the traditional method of setting out from the total quantity of money",[14] and to focus attention on the relationship between the proportion of the community's income that has been earned in the investment and consumption industries and the proportion in which it is divided between saving and expenditures on consumer goods. The volume of employment that entrepreneurs offer to the factors of production at the existing rates of remuneration depends upon whether they are making profits. The profits of entrepreneurs depend upon the relationship between

[11]Keynes (48, pp. 124–125).

[12]Keynes (48, p. 126).

[13]Many readers will summarily reject this interpretation. By adducing sufficient evidence it is hoped that the reader will be induced to abandon his position.

[14]Keynes (48, p. 134).

investment and saving. Keynes' fundamental equations are designed to express these ideas in a precise form.

## THE FUNDAMENTAL EQUATIONS

The following symbols will be used in the sequel:

$E$ = community's money income = cost of production of output = earnings of the factors of production.

$V$ = value of output.

$P$ = the price level of consumer goods.

$P'$ = the price level of investment goods.

$Z$ = the price level of output as a whole.

$R$ = the volume of consumer goods.

$C$ = the volume of new investment goods.

$O$ = $R+C$ = volume of total output.

$S$ = savings.

$E_R$ = earnings in consumer industries = cost of production of consumer goods.

$E_C$ = $I'$ = earnings in investment industries = cost of production of investment goods.

$Q_1$ = profits in consumer industries.

$Q_2$ = profits in investment industries.

$Q$ = $Q_1+Q_2$ = total profits.

$I$ = value of investment.

$W_1$ = $E/O$ = the rate of efficiency earnings or rate of earnings per unit of output.

$W$ = the rate of effort earnings. $W$ corresponds to the wage unit in the *General Theory*.

$e$ = $W/W_1$ = is the ratio of the rate of effort earnings to the rate of efficiency earnings. It is a coefficient of efficiency.

Now the two fundamental equations can be derived. Keynes chooses the units of quantities of goods in such a way that a unit of each has the same cost of production at the base date. This means that output is defined in cost units.[15]

[15]Hansen argued that the definition of output in cost units makes the first fundamental equation invalid. For a full discussion of this point see Appendix 2.

Saving is defined by Keynes to be equal to the money income of the community minus the money expenditure on consumption. $S = E - P.R.$ This implies that $P.R. = E - S$. But the total income $E$ has been earned in the investment industries and the consumption industries, i.e. $PR = E_C + E_R - S$. Since $E_C = I'$ we have $P = E_R/R + I' - S/R$.

Now since output is defined in cost units $E_R = E. R/O$. Hence $E_R/R = E/O$. Now the fundamental equation can be written in the following form. $P = E/O + (I' - S)/R$. This is the first fundamental equation. It says that the price level of consumer goods is equal to the rate of earnings per unit of output plus the excess of the cost of investment over the volume of savings divided by the volume of consumer goods. It is easily seen that the term $I' - S$ measures profits.

$$Q_1 = P.R - E_R = E - S - E_R = E_R + E_C - S - E_R = I' - S.$$

Hence the first fundamental equation can also be written in the following form: $P = E/O + Q_1/R$.

In order to derive the second fundamental equation the price-level of new investment goods must be assumed to be known. The theory of the forces determining the prices of investment goods shall be considered in a later section. But assume for the nonce that the value of $P'$ is already known. Then $OZ = P.R + P'. C = P.R + I$ since $I$ denotes the value of investment. Hence we have $OZ = E_C + E_R - S + I$. Hence $Z = E/O + (I - S)/O$. This is the second fundamental equation. Again the second term measures unit profits. $Q = P.R + P'C - E = E - S + I - E = I - S$. The second fundamental equation can now be written in the following form: $Z = E/O + Q/O$.

The fundamental equations are designed to state in a precise form the conditions that must be fulfilled if the price level of consumption goods and of output as a whole is to be in equilibrium with the cost of production. Thus the first equation states that if the cost of investment exceeds the volume of saving the actual price level will exceed the expected price-level $E/O$ by $(I' - S)/R$. When $I'$ exceeds $S$, $Q_1$ or profits in the consumer industries are greater than zero and entrepreneurs' actual remuneration exceeds their "normal" remuneration. In the case of output as a whole entrepreneurs will make profits if the value of investment I exceeds the volume of savings. When profits arise entrepreneurs will increase the offers they make to the factors of production at the existing rates of remuneration.

The role of the fundamental equations is made clear by Keynes.

> Our present conclusion is, in the first place, that profits (or losses) are an effect of the rest of the situation rather than a cause of it....But, in the second place, profits (or losses) having once come into existence become, as we shall see (for this will be the main topic of several succeeding chapters), a cause of what subsequently ensure; indeed, the mainspring of change in the existing economic system. This is the essential reason why it is useful to segregate them in our Fundamental Equations.[16]

The meaning of this is that the second terms of both fundamental equations measure (or are an index of) effective demand. For the sake of simplicity let us restrict ourselves to the second equation. Whether aggregate income is in equilibrium or not depends on whether entrepreneurs as a whole are making profits, i.e., it depends on whether the value of investment is greater than the volume of saving. But during any period of time entrepreneurs have to make decisions about the amounts of the consumption and investment goods that they are going to put on the market. Their decision to continue the same level of output or to change it depends on their anticipations of effective demand.

> In so far as entrepreneurs are able at the beginning of a production period to forecast the relationship between saving and investment in its effect on the demand for their product at the end of this production-period, it is obviously anticipated profit or loss...which influences them in deciding the scale on which to produce and the offers it is worthwhile to make to the factors of production.[17]

Hence the first term of the fundamental equation measures

[16]Keynes (48, p. 140).
[17]Keynes (48, p. 159).

the supply price of output as a whole. It denotes the price level, which if it actually materializes, will leave entrepreneurs under no inducement either to increase or decrease their offers to the factors of production at the existing rates of remuneration. The value of the second term of the equation measures the degree by which the actual remuneration of entrepreneurs differs from their normal remuneration.

## THE FUNDAMENTAL EQUATIONS AND THE WAGE SYSTEM

The first term of both the fundamental equations is $E/O$. Now $E/O = W_1$ is the money rate of efficiency earnings of the factors of production. An excess of $I'$ over $S$ (or $I$ over $S$ in the case of output as a whole) Keynes calls "profit inflation". An increase of $E/O$ Keynes calls "income inflation".

The wage system is closely connected with income inflation. If $e$ is the coefficient of efficiency we can write $e = W/W_1$. Suppose that the productivity of labour is increased so that with the same expenditure of labour a greater output can be produced. Assume that wages are time-wages and not piece-wages. In this case $W_1$ or the rate of efficiency earnings will decrease and the price level will fall. As wages are time-wages the rate of effort-earnings $W$ does not vary with every change in the coefficient of efficiency and the price-level will vary inversely with changes in efficiency. On the other hand, if wages are piece-wages then any change in productivity will be neutralized by compensating changes in the rate of effort earnings $W$ and there will be no effect on the rate of earnings per unit of output $W_1$. Since $W_1 = W/e$ a wage increase not accompanied by an increase of productivity due to the pressure of truculent trade unions will raise $W_1$ and the price-level as necessarily follows from the fundamental equations.

According to Keynes such "spontaneous" changes in the rate of efficiency earnings are not likely to occur. The induced changes are much more important.

In existing circumstances, however, the most usual and important occasion of changes will be the action of entrepreneurs, under the influence of the actual enjoyment of positive or negative profits, in increasing or diminishing the volume of employment which they offer at the existing rates of remuneration.[18]

When the value of investment is greater than saving entrepreneurs as a whole will be earning profits. This profit inflation will induce them to increase their offers to the factors of production. As a result of this increased demand it will cost more to produce a given unit of output, i.e. $E/O$ will rise. Hence prices will rise.

In the *General Theory* Keynes assumed that industry operates on a U-shaped cost curve. As more and more labourers are used with the fixed capital equipment output does not increase as fast as employment. Marginal costs increase even when there is no increase in the wage unit. In such conditions the elasticity of prices with respect to effective demand is small. In conditions of full employment, on the other hand, this elasticity is high because the wage unit rises.

In the *Treatise* this part of the theory is not satisfactorily developed. All that Keynes had to say is that "as a rule, the existence of profits will provoke a tendency towards a higher rate of employment and of remuneration for the factors of production, and vice versa".[19] Nevertheless Keynes was aware that income inflation is more likely to take place when full-employment is reached and that in conditions of less than full-employment the elasticity of output with respect to effective demand is high. Consider the following passage.

This secondary phase is even more likely than the primary phase to involve some measures of Income Inflation....For the attempt to increase still further the volume of employment will probably have the effect of stiffening the attitude of the factors of production and enabling them to obtain a higher rate of remuneration per unit of output.[20]

[18]Keynes (48, p. 157).
[19]Keynes (48, p. 182).
[20]Keynes (48, p. 288).

## THE FUNDAMENTAL EQUATIONS AND THE MONEY SYSTEM

While the wage system is primarily connected with the first term of the fundamental equations the money system is connected intimately with both the terms. The second fundamental equation states that $Z = E/O + (P'.C - S)/O$. The first problem is to consider the way in which the money system determines $P'$ or the price-level of new investment-goods. Keynes did not write an equation for the price-level of new investment-goods. Keynes advanced a new theory of the price of investment-goods.

When a man earns money-income the first decision he has to make concerns the proportion of his income that he will spend on consumer goods and the proportion that he will add to his wealth. With respect to the part of his income that he decides to add to his wealth he has to make a further decision. He has to decide the form in which he will hold his wealth. He may invest in securities or he may increase his holding of money. Keynes uses the term "securities" to cover both loan capital and real capital, i.e. bonds and shares. Consequently, an individual's decision about the form in which to hold his wealth "relates not only to the current increment to the wealth of individuals, but also to the whole block of their existing capital".[21]

Keynes first explains how the actual price-level of securities (or "investments" as he sometimes says) is determined.

Now when an individual is more disposed than before to hold his wealth in the form of savings–deposits and less disposed to hold it in other forms, this does not mean that he is determined to hold it in the form of savings–deposits *at all costs*. It means that he favours savings–deposits more than before at the existing price level of securities. But his distaste for securities is not absolute and depends upon his expectations of the future return to be obtained from savings–deposits and from other securities respectively. . . . If therefore the price-level of other securities falls sufficiently (i.e. the long rate of interest rises), he can be tempted back into them. If, how-

[21]Keynes (48, p. 141).

ever, the banking system operates in the opposite direction to that of the public and meets the preference of the latter for savings – deposits by buying the securities which the public is *less* anxious to hold . . . then there is no need for the price-level of investments to fall at all. . . . It follows that the actual price-level of investments is the resultant of the sentiment of the public and the behaviour of the banking system.[22]

The price of new investment-goods is determined by the price of existing investments.

The price-level of investments as a whole, and hence of new investments, is that price-level at which the desire of the public to hold savings – deposits is equal to the amount of savings – deposits which the banking system is willing and able to create.[23]

Keynes lumps together bonds, shares, and new investment goods in one category and assumes that they are subject to the same forces. Keynes assumes that all these are substitutable forms of wealth. Hence their prices are subject to the same set of forces.

The price-level of new investment-goods exercises an important influence on the profitability of the production of investment-goods. If $P'.C$ exceeds $I'$ entrepreneurs in the investment industries will be earning profits and they will increase their offers to the factors of production. In addition, if the price-level of securities or new investment goods is such that $P'.C$ (the value of investment) exceeds the volume of saving, then entrepreneurs as a whole will be making profits. This does not mean that entrepreneurs in the consumer industries must be making profits. It only means that the profits in the investment industries are not counterbalanced by losses in the consumer industries. But the effect of the capital inflation in the investment-goods market (i.e. $P'.C$ greater than $I'$) is to induce entrepreneurs to increase their production of capital goods. The effect of this is to increase $I'$ the cost of investment. Unless saving increases pari passu

[22]Keynes (48, p. 148).
[23]Keynes (48, p. 149).

$I'$ will become greater than S and the second term of the *first* fundamental equation will become positive.

Thus, in general, a capital inflation in the investment-goods will be followed by a commodity inflation in the commodity market. An expansion of the investment industries makes it profitable for the consumer industries to expand. According to the classical theory the two types of price-level should move in *opposite* directions.

> Movements in our two types of price-level are connected at one remove and are, generally speaking, in the *same* direction.[24]

The price-level of securities is determined by the behaviour of the banking system and the bearishness of the public. It is that price at which the desire to hold savings–deposits is equal to the total quantity of savings–deposits. A savings–deposit "is not required for the purpose of current payments and could, without inconvenience, be dispensed with if, for any reason, some other form of investment were to seem to the depositor to be preferable[25]."

The Industrial Circulation consists of the Income deposits and the Business deposits $A$. These are the transactions and precautionary balances of individuals and firms for the convenient and smooth transaction of the industrial activities associated with the production of goods and services. The interdependence between these two categories of deposits is clear, for the income deposits flow into the business deposits when businessmen receive money for their goods and services. These business deposits will either immediately flow into the income deposits reservoir, say, by the payment of wages and salaries, or to the business deposits of other entrepreneurs and then either to the business deposits $B$ (used by firms for financial purposes) or to the income deposits.

Generally speaking, one would expect the average value of $k$ (the ratio of $M_1$, the income deposits, to income $E$) in a given

---

[24]Keynes (48, p. 181).

[25]Keynes (48, p. 36). The savings–deposits $A$ are not so sensitive to the price of securities. The savings–deposits $B$ constitute the real bear funds.

economic society to be a fairly stable quantity from year to
year.[26]

Another important link has been forged between the quantity
of money and the variables in the fundamental equations. According to Keynes the income deposits bear a fairly stable relationship to the money income of the community. The savings–
deposits influence the price-level of securities and new investment-goods; and the price-level of securities influence the second
terms of both fundamental equations. The income-deposits are
closely connected with the income of the community.

The Financial Circulation is made up of the business deposits $B$ whose velocity is supposed to be highly variable and the
savings–deposits. Part of these savings–deposits (the $A$ deposits) are not really speculative because their holding is not
based on the "view" taken of the market, the differentiating
characteristic of the $B$ deposits.

The way in which the financial circulation interacts with the
fundamental variables in the fundamental equations can be
brought out if we consider the four types of speculative
markets.

1. A bear market with a consensus of opinion. In this market
   the price of securities (bonds and shares) has not fallen, or is
   not falling sufficiently to induce some of the bears to become
   bulls, and the bears are increasing their positions.
2. A bear market with a division of opinion. Because there are
   these two "views" some of the bears have joined the bull
   brigade and are closing their positions on a falling market.
   As the number of bulls is increasing the fall in security prices
   will be arrested as compared with the first type of market.
   What happens is that when a bear becomes a bull the bear
   funds will either be transferred to the income deposits directly,
   or indirectly, by first passing through the business-deposits
   via the new issue market. If the bear pressures were weaker
   these bulls would raise prices, but as the bear pressure is
   strong the fall of prices is compatible with some of the bears
   closing their positions.

[26]Keynes (48, p. 44).

Similarly there are two kinds of bull markets with and without a difference of opinion. A bear market with a consensus of opinion and a bull market with a division of opinion have the effect that they raise the requirements of the financial circulation and unless new money is created by the banking system such a financial state of affairs will put pressure on the industrial circulation. But their effect on the production of investment-goods will be different. A bear market with a consensus of opinion is unfavourable to investment because it raises the long rate of interest. A bull market with a division of opinion, on the other hand, is favourable for investment because it raises the prices of securities.

We conclude, therefore, that changes in the financial situation are capable of causing changes in the value of money in two ways. They have the effect of altering the quantity of money available for the Industrial Circulation; and they may have the effect of altering the attractiveness of investment.[27]

A clear picture of the way in which the money system interacts with the fundamental variables in the fundamental equations has now been obtained. A part of the money supply is needed in the industrial sector for the commodious and smooth financing of the production and sale of goods and services. The remainder of the money supply is left over to form the bear funds of those who take a dim view of the future price of securities. In equilibrium the total demand for money must be equal to the supply. Those who subscribe to the standard interpretation of the *Treatise* will find it hard to believe that the following astonishing view is expressed in that book.

If we assume that banking habits and practices are unchanged, the requirements of the Cash-Deposits are mainly determined by the magnitude of the earnings bill, i.e. by the product of the rate of earnings and the volume of output; and the requirements of the Savings–Deposits are mainly determined by the bearishness of the public's disposition taken in conjunction with the price-level of securities. Or putting it

27Keynes (48, p. 254).

the other way around, given the total quantity of money, only those combinations of the rate of earnings, the volume output and the price-level of securities are feasible which lead to the aggregate requirement of money being equal to the given total.[28]

## THE INDUCEMENT TO INVEST AND THE PROPENSITY TO SAVE

The fundamental equations state that the employment entrepreneurs offer to the factors of production depends upon the relationship between the value of investment and the volume of saving (between the cost of investment and the volume of saving in the case of employment in the consumer industries). Thus whether income $E$ is in equilibrium or not depends upon the relationship between saving and investment. Thus a theory of the forces that determine the behaviour of income $E$ must be a theory of investment and saving. It must explain how these magnitudes are determined.

The following is Keynes' theory of saving:

The business of saving is essentially a steady process. If there are disturbances in the economic world, these by affecting prosperity may react on saving. But a disturbance will seldom or never be initiated by a sudden change in the proportion of current income which is being saved.[29]

What Keynes wants to bring about is that the *proportion* of current income that is saved does not undergo violent changes. This passage must not be interpreted to mean that the *amount* of saving does not change. Thus in the second sentence when Keynes says that "these by affecting prosperity may react on saving", he does not mean that prosperity does not react on the *amount* of savings. What he means is that prosperity does not significantly influence the "business of saving", i.e. the proportion of income that is saved. On any other interpretation much of the theoretical analysis of the *Treatise* does not make sense as will be demonstrated in the sequel.

[28]Keynes (48, p. 146).
[29]Keynes (48, p. 280).

The essentials of Keynes' theory of investment are presented in the following passage.

> The attractiveness of investment depends on the prospective income which the entrepreneur anticipates from current investment relatively to the rate of interest which he has to pay in order to be able to finance its production; or putting it the other way round, the value of capital goods depends on the rate of interest at which the prospective income from them is capitalized. That is to say the higher the rate of interest, the lower, other things being equal, will be the value of capital-goods. Therefore, if the rate of interest rises $P^1$ will tend to fall, which will lower the rate of profit on the production of capital-goods, which will be deterrent to new investment.[30]

By "investment" Keynes means investment in working capital, liquid capital, or fixed capital.[31] The interest rate that is taken into account by entrepreneurs in considering investment in these different types of capital is not the same. Thus Keynes says that when "it is a question of controlling the rate of investment, not in working capital but in fixed capital, it is the long-term rate of interest which chiefly matters".[32] Investment, therefore, is not a function of "the" rate of interest. The entire spectrum of interest rates, (from the discount rate of the Central Bank to the rate on long-term bonds) is relevant. Nevertheless, Keynes often speaks of "the rate of interest (e.g. in the quotation given above) influencing the attractiveness of investment. The reason is that at that time Keynes believed in Riefler's "fluidity theory" of the term structure of interest rates.[33]

## THE STANDARD INTERPRETATION OF THE *TREATISE*

In the previous section an account was given of the conceptual

[30]Keynes (48, p. 154).
[31]For a full discussion of these concepts, see Appendix 1.
[32]Keynes (48, Vol. 2, p. 352).
[33]Keynes (48, Vol. 2, pp. 352–362).

and theoretical "building blocks" that Keynes used in the *Treatise*. In this section an attempt shall be made to put these building blocks together in order to obtain a clear picture of the basic theory of the *Treatise*. Before embarking on that task it is necessary to examine the traditional interpretations of the *Treatise*. It is submitted that the traditional interpretations do not do justice to Keynes' thought as it is expressed in the *Treatise*.

Anyone who has even a cursory acquaintance with the Keynesian literature cannot help being struck by the scanty attention given to the *Treatise* in a description of the Keynesian Revolution. Ordinarily when one talks about the Keynesian Revolution one refers to the ideas expressed in the *General Theory* and the effects they have had on the subsequent development of economic theory and policy. One does not refer to the *Treatise* except as one of the many books Keynes wrote in his unregenerate "classical" days. Many specialized works have appeared in the literature which deal with the development of the ideas of Keynes since the publication of his book on Indian currency and finance.[34] Even here one finds that the *Treatise* is scarcely given the attention it deserves.

In the comparatively brief space that is devoted to the *Treatise* it is usually pointed out that it was a "transitional" work which contained some brilliant ideas. Reference is made to the bearishness theory of the price of securities and the importance that Keynes attached to saving and investment. The proponent of the standard interpretation hastens to point out that although the *Treatise* adumbrates many of the ideas of the *General Theory* its theoretical structure is utterly different from that of the later book. Klein's book *The Keynesian Revolution* is regarded as the most authoritative work on the development of the ideas of Keynes. The interpretation of the *Treatise* theory presented therein, which in its essentials is supported by the majority of economists, will be designated the "standard interpretation". It is necessary, therefore, to examine Klein's views in great detail.

We can describe the *Treatise* as a book in classical economics based on two important and well-known theories. These two

---

[34]See for example L. Klein (50) and R. Harrod (34).

theories are the business-cycle theory which makes investment fluctuations the prime mover of the capitalistic system and the theory that the rate of interest is determined in equilibrium by the equality of savings and investment. With these two theories superimposed upon a classical model, it is possible to develop the important arguments of the *Treatise*. . . .It may seem odd that the liquidity preference doctrines should come out of a work based on the interest theory of the *Treatise*; however this only illustrates the confused state of Keynes' ideas at the time.[35]

This passage deserves careful study. Klein makes three important points. First, the *Treatise* contains a theory of the business-cycle based on the volatility of investment expenditures. Second, it contains a saving–investment theory of interest, by which we mean a theory which states that the intersection of the saving and investment schedules (as functions of the interest rate) determines a price for capital at which the demand is equal to the supply. This means that if saving increases the rate of interest will fall, there will be more investment and of the fixed given volume of output more will be invested and less consumed. The fact that the *Treatise* contains the bearishness theory of the price of securities poses a problem for Klein. According to Klein, Keynes had not "seen the light", when he wrote the *Treatise*. But then it becomes hard to explain the presence of that theory. The problem is "solved" by attributing it to the "confused state" of Keynes' thinking at the time.

Klein thinks that the principal fault of the *Treatise* was that it did not contain any theory of effective demand.

The variable *E* which represents income paid out to the factors of production was never adequately accounted for by Keynes, this being the principal fault of the *Treatise*. This variable represents effective demand, and the lack of any theory of effective demand was precisely the fault which prevented Keynes from producing a satisfactory result at this time.[36]

[35]Klein (50, pp. 15–16).
[36]Klein (50, pp. 20–21).

The principal defect of the theoretical side of the *Treatise* was, as has been shown, the failure to explain how the level of effective demand gets determined. Keynes wanted to explain an equilibrium situation in which prices would be stable. The main criterion of this equilibrium situation was pictured by him as the equality of the flows of saving and investment.... This exposition may seem to be nothing more than a statement of the Wicksell theory, from which the terminology was certainly borrowed.[37]

Even Klein hesitates to state categorically that the *Treatise* contains a saving–investment theory of the interest rate. In the last line of the quotation a doubt seems to be expressed when he asserts that the terminology was certainly borrowed from Wicksell. A similar doubt is expressed in a footnote on page 16 when it is stated that "the interest theory presented in the *Treatise* is somewhat Wicksellian".

Klein explains Keynes' policy prescriptions during the years 1930–36 in a manner that is entirely consistent with his views about the *Treatise*.

Economists can sometimes go very far in the advocacy of proper sound policy measures based on an inadequate formal theory.... His early analysis in the beginning of the depression was based entirely on the classical model of the *Treatise*. It was not his theory which led him to practical policies, but practical policies devised to cure hones-to-goodness economic ills which finally led him to his theory....He had not yet dropped the condition of a given output level....He was still working under the assumption that increased consumption must be at the expense of investment and vice versa.... We must admit that Keynes advocated certain policies in the early thirties in spite of, rather than because of, his theoretical background.[38]

But what according to Klein was the theoretical innovation needed to effectuate a revolution in economic science? His answer is given in the following two passages:

[37]Klein (50, pp. 18–26).
[38]Klein (50, pp. 31–32).

And at the same time Mr. R. F. Kahn was formulating the theory of the multiplier, the missing link between what Keynes was saying in policy and what he wanted to say in theory. The theory as Kahn formulated it was just the step needed to show that savings and investment determine in equilibrium the level of output and *not the rate of interest.*[39]

If we take Joan Robinson as a reliable sounding board of opinion within the Keynesian group, we find a great change of ideas during 1933....In "Economica" of February 1933, Mrs. Robinson wrote an article...(which was) a perfectly clear exposition of Keynes of the *Treatise*....But when we came to the second article which appeared in the "Review of Economic Studies" (Oct. 1933) we get material which is infinitely more interesting and powerful....In this later article Mrs. Robinson again claimed to be giving an exposition of the "Treatise", but such was not the case... Mrs. Robinson was overgenerous to the master and was actually writing the essential parts of *General Theory*.... She first assumed a disequilibrium and then showed the conceptual process by which the level of real income would adjust to bring saving and investment into equality.[40]

Joan Robinson claimed that the *Treatise* model showed how income changes to bring saving and investment into equality. But the *Treatise* according to Klein does not even contain a theory of effective demand. Consequently, this "puzzle" is resolved by saying that Robinson was being overgenerous to the master. Schumpeter is proponent of the standard interpretation.

The *Treatise* was not a failure in any ordinary sense of the word. Everybody saw its points and, with whatever qualifications paid his respects to Keynes' great effort...But from Keynes' own standpoint it was a failure.... He had entangled himself in the meshes of an apparatus that broke down each time he attempted to make it grind out his own meanings.... There was nothing for it but to abandon the whole thing, hull

[39]Klein (50, p. 36).
[40]Klein (50, pp.39–40).

and cargo, to renounce allegiances and start afresh.[41]

One thing is clear and that is that Schumpeter's view must be abandoned "hull and cargo". When Schumpeter tells us that "everybody" saw its "points" it is not clean who is encompassed in the term "everybody". Schumpeter's interpretation *is* a failure in the *ordinary* sense of the term.

Leijonhufvud's view is much more reasonable, even though his interpretation regarding the multiplier theory has to be rejected. The contrasts between the two works are dramatized by the switch from the Fundamental Equations of the *Treatise* to the investment multiplier of the *General Theory* as the expository device whereby Keynes sought to compress a complicated and sophisticated theory in a nutshell. The switch is theoretically significant, yet it must not be misinterpreted. The multiplier does indeed summarize the *two* major changes in the model, i.e. (1) the idea that the system responds to disturbances by quantity adjustments and not simply by price-level adjustments (while remaining at full employment) and (2) the idea that initial disturbances are amplified through the consumption income relation.[42]

By the "multiplier" Leijonhufvud seems to mean the idea that the system responds to disturbances *not only* by price-level adjustments and the idea that the consumption income relation amplifies any disturbance that impinges on the system. By the "multiplier" Leijonhufvud does not mean any fixed ratio between investment and income, or the "timeless multiplier".

Shackle agrees with the proponents of the standard interpretation regarding the multiplier theory. Shackle says that the theoretical framework of the *Treatise* is "utterly different" from that of the *General Theory*.[43] With respect to the multiplier theory Shackle says that although Keynes "was aware of the question whose answer is the Multiplier, he did not, in the *Treatise*, perceive this answer."[44]

[41]S. Harris (32, pp. 89–90).
[42]Leijonhufvud (54).
[43]G. Shackle (82, p. 89).
[44]G. Shackle (82, p. 201).

Shackle's interpretation is based on his theory of the role of uncertainty in economic affairs. The following quotations give an idea of Shackle's semi-metaphysical views on the subject.

The possibility of massive general unemployment thus springs from the bearing of a human institution, that of money, upon the ultimate nature of human existence, the human being's endless journey into the void of time... .A theory of unemployment is, necessarily, inescapably, a theory of disorder. The disorder in question is the basic disorder of uncertain expectation, the essential disorder of the real, as contrasted with the conventionally pretended, human condition.[45]

Not much can be said about Shackle's expatiations on the "real human condition" or about his views regarding the unformulable complexity and ineluctable uncertainty of the future. What is important here is that his interpretation of the fundamental equations is vitiated by his philosophical views about time. For according to Shackle the fundamental equations have that incisive quality because they show that the entrepreneurs' calculations are based on an unknown future. The magnitude of the second term measures the extent to which these expectations have been fulfilled. This is correct. But the story does not end here. Shackle merely concentrates on the fact that at the *threshold* of an interval the entrepreneurs make certain decisions and that at the end of that interval they learn whether or not their expectations were fulfilled. But Keynes' theory of profits says that when entrepreneurial expectations are not fulfilled they will change the scale of their offers to the factors of production and that this will have effects on the industrial and financial circulations and saving. In fact, Keynes stated explicitly that he segregated profits in the fundamental equations because they are the mainspring of change in the existing economic system. According to Shackle the great merit of the fundamental equations is that they show that profits can occur. But profits are also a *cause of what happens subsequently*. And this is what Shackle ignores because what happens subsequently has the nature of a "mechanism". For example, when profits increase

[45]G. Shackle (82, pp. 133–149).

and entrepreneurs increase their offers to the factors of production, income $E$ increases. When income increases the requirements of the Industrial Circulation increase, and so forth. The subsequent movement of the system towards equilibrium does not depend so much on man's immitigable uncertainty about the future. This is why Shackle ignores it.[46]

Leijonhufvud and Shackle cannot be regarded as proponents of the standard interpretation. Both have done much to revive interest in the *Treatise* and have challenged the view that it is not an important book. But their view of the multiplier theory in the *Treatise* is similar to the views. This is the reason for their inclusion here.[47]

## A NEW INTERPRETATION

The new interpretation to be presented in this paper is as follows: The *Treatise* describes a process of contraction or expansion of money income and real income. The saving-investment tool is used to describe this process. If the amount of saving is equal to the investment that is being undertaken, income is in equilibrium. Suppose now that saving exceeds investment. The first effect of this is that the price of investment goods and consumption goods falls. Initially the system responds to a disturbance by a price adjustment. When prices fall, entrepreneurs make losses. As a result of their losses, they will reduce the offers they make to the factors of production, and output and employment fall. In the second stage the system responds by quantity adjustments. When output falls income also falls. If at this reduced level of income saving still exceeds the cost and value of investment, entrepreneurs will continue to make losses and will reduce their offers to the factors of production.

At this stage of the analysis, as we shall see presently, Keynes is inconsistent, or more accurately, seems to be inconsistent.

[46]It is hard to give brief quotations to support our interpretation of Shackle. But see chapter 13 of his book. For other expressions of the standard interpretation see S. Harris (32), E.A.G. Robinson's obituary article (74) on Keynes and M. Stewart (90). This list is not meant to be exhaustive.

[47]For more discussion about the views on the *Treatise*, see the Postscript.

On the one hand he says that equilibrium cannot be restored, if as a consequence of the losses and the fall in output, entrepreneurs seek to reduce the rate of remuneration of the factors of production. Each entrepreneur feels that his situation can be improved if he lowers his cost of production, but if all entrepreneurs follow this course of action there will be no relief, unless the all round lowering of costs has the effect of reducing saving and making it equal to the value of investment, because no matter how much the entrepreneurs reduce cost of production they will continue in the aggregate to make losses as long as saving exceeds the value of investment.

On the other hand Keynes maintains, somewhat inconsistently with the above views, that true equilibrium can only be restored when as a result of the fall in prices and output, the money rate of remuneration of the factors of production has fallen. In these passages, it seems to us, that Keynes was assuming that the fall in the money rate of efficiency earnings reduces saving and makes it equal to the cost of investment. If it did not have this effect *we could not have a position of equilibrium*.

We shall now give detailed quotations from the book to support this interpretation.

> For my present purpose I propose to define the "normal" remuneration of entrepreneurs at any time as that rate of remuneration which, if they were open to make new bargains with all the factors of production at the currently prevailing rates of earning, would leave them under no motive either to increase or to decrease their scale of operations. Thus when the actual remuneration of entrepreneurs exceeds (or falls short of) the normal as thus defined, so that profits are positive (or negative) entrepreneurs will... seek to expand (or curtail) their scale of operations at the existing costs of production.[48]

Note that the quantity adjustment mechanism is built into the very structure of Keynes' model, a fact which has been ignored by Klein and others. Thus when Klein tells us "that the fundamental equations represented an attempt to improve upon the classical quantity equations" (*op. cit.*, p. 17) he fails to see the

[48]Keynes (48, pp. 124–125).

crucial role played by Keynes' theory of profits in a process of income expansion and contraction. It is true that the fundamental equations tell us how the level of prices of consumption goods, for example, is determined. But the fundamental equations also tell us what will happen as a result of the price change, how money income will change until the discrepancy between saving and the cost of investment is eliminated. Consider this passage, for example:

> But in the second place, profits (or losses) having once come into existence become, as we shall see (for this will be the main topic of several succeeding chapters), a cause of what subsequently ensues; indeed the mainspring of change in the existing economic system.[49]

Keynes says (48, pp. 155-156) that 'it will be convenient to call the rate of interest which would cause the second term of our second Fundamental Equation to be zero the *natural-rate* of interest and the rate which actually prevails the *market-rate* of interest", and on page 201 the market rate of interest is regarded as a sort of average of short and long rates. Suppose that at any moment of time saving exceeds both the cost and value of investment. This is the same as saying that the natural rate is below the market rate; and to say that income will change to bring the market and natural rates into equality is equivalent to saying that income will change to bring saving and investment into equality.

With these things in mind let us see how Keynes describes a process of income change:

> Now, from the point of view of individual entrepreneurs, there will be no occasion for a reduction in the output of (investment) goods, unless their price is falling relatively to their cost of production, or unless the demand is falling off at the existing price. In what way can a rise in bank-rate tend to bring this about?. . . (The demand price for capital goods) depends on *two* things—on the estimated net prospective yield from fixed capital. . . measured in money and on the rate of interest at which this future yield is capitalized.[50]

[49]Keynes (48, p. 140).
[50]Keynes (48, pp. 201-202).

Thus, generally speaking, we may expect the direct and *primary* effects of a rise of bank-rate to be a fall in the price of fixed capital and, therefore, in $P'$, the price-level of investment goods. The fall in the attractiveness of fixed capital at the existing price will make it impossible for producers of capital-goods to market their output on terms as satisfactory as before in relation to their cost of production and will, therefore, be followed by a fall in the output of such goods.[51]

It may be assumed that initially the economy is in equilibrium. This means that saving is equal to investment or, in other words, the market rate is equal to the natural rate. Then the market rate is raised. The primary effect of this is a fall in the price of investment goods which in turn leads to a fall in the output of such goods. Up till now the first fundamental equation relating to consumer goods has not been affected.

But if the change in the market rate does *not* exactly correspond to a change in the natural rate, what will be the *tertiary* effects of the rise of bank-rate which we have been considering? The decline in the natural rate of investment will cause a fall in $P$ (the price-level of consumer goods) additional to any fall caused by the increase of savings, since there will be a reduction in the incomes of the producers of investment-goods available for the purchase of liquid consumption-goods, as necessarily follows from the Fundamental Equation.[52]

At this stage the second term of the first fundamental equation has become negative due to the amplifying effects of the consumption-income relation.

At this stage, therefore, we have a fall both in $P$ and in $P'$, consequent losses to all classes of entrepreneurs, and a resulting diminution in the volume of employment they offer to the factors of production at the existing rates of earnings. Thus a state of unemployment may be expected to ensue, and to continue until the risk in bank-rate is reserved or, by chances,

[51]Keynes (48, pp. 204–205).
[52]Keynes (48, p. 206).

something happens to alter the natural-rate of interest so as to bring it back to equality with the new market-rate.[53]

Keynes clearly demonstrates how an excess of saving over investment leads to a fall in effective demand. This fall in effective demand of investment-goods is amplified by the consumer-income relation. The fall in the effective demand for consumer goods induces entrepreneurs to reduce their offers to the factors of production. Unemployment of the factors of production is clearly shown to be the effect of an excess of saving over investment. The Keynesian analysis does not stop there. During the process of income deflation there is an excess of saving over investment or, in other words, a natural rate below the market rate. Keynes states clearly that equilibrium cannot be restored unless the excess of saving is eliminated.

But how is this excess of saving to be eliminated? To a modern student the answer is obvious: a fall in income will reduce the quantum of saving. It turns out that Keynes' answer in the thirties is the same. It has been shown that the effect of the excess of saving is unemployment.

Moreover, the longer this state of affairs continues, the greater is the volume of unemployment likely to be....Finally, under the pressure of growing unemployment, the rate of earnings—though perhaps only at long last—will fall. This is the consummation of the whole process of pressure. Thus it is only when what I have called the consummation of the process has been achieved...that a true equilibrium will be re-established.[54]

The fall in the effective demand for goods results in a lower price for these goods and losses for the entrepreneurs. To protect themselves entrepreneurs reduce their output and reduce their costs of production by offering lower rates of remuneration to the factors of production. But the fall in the costs of production is not necessarily a good thing for entrepreneurs because even costs have a demand aspect.

[53]Keynes (48, p. 206)
[54]Keynes (48, pp. 207–208).

When for any reason an entrepreneur feels discouraged about the prospects one or both of two courses may be open to him—he can reduce his output or he can reduce his costs by lowering his offers to the factors of production. Neither course, if adopted by entrepreneurs as a whole, will relieve in the least their losses as a whole, except in so far as they have the indirect effect of reducing savings or of allowing (or causing) the banking system to relax the terms of credit and so increase investment...whilst, on the other hand, both courses are likely to aggravate their losses by reducing the cost of investment.[55]

The consummation of the whole process takes place when the reduction in the rate of efficiency earnings and the reduction in the offers of entrepreneurs to the factors of production have reduced income to such a low level that two equilibrating forces are able to restore equilibrium. First, the fall in the rate of efficiency earnings and the fall in output work to raise the natural rate of interest or, in other words, reduce the excess of saving over investment. It may be that even after this cost reduction saving exceeds investment; this means that entrepreneurs will continue to make losses, and income will fall further, until saving has become equal to investment. The other equilibrating factor is the effect of the fall in the costs of production on the money market. This is the Keynes effect. The reduction in the costs of production will reduce the requirements of the Industrial Circulation and release resources to the financial sector. Interest rates will fall and investment may be stimulated. Both these equilibrating factors will tend to raise the natural rate of interest, that is to say, they will reduce the excess of saving over investment which started off the whole deflationary process. The consumption-income relation will reduce the quantum of saving when income falls. The Keynes effect on the other hand, will tend to raise the level of investment. The extent to which investment is stimulated depends upon what happens to the price of securities. In a depression when income is low and unemployment is high, it is likely that the financial market is a *bear* market with a consensus of

[55]Keynes (48, pp. 160–61).

opinion. Now a bear market with a consensus of opinion increases the requirements of the Financial Circulation. Hence the resources released from the Industrial Circulation due to the income deflation in the commodity market will be needed in the financial sector to prevent a fall in the price of securities. This situation is analogous to the liquidity trap situation of the *General Theory* where a fall in the wage-bill cannot increase investment appreciably due to the high elasticity of the liquidity-preference schedule.

It is clear from the above discussion that Keynes described the working of the multiplier in the downward direction. But it is even more important to find out if Keynes was aware of the upward multiplier. It is Shackle's view that "the upward Multiplier, working in a 'fixprice' situation, was in 1931 an idea more alien to accepted thought than a downward Multiplier where no inflationary tendency could be in question".[56]

This is Llewellyn Wright's view.

It is Professor Kahn's analysis alone which clearly sets out the implications of the fact that consumption and investment might expand *together*. Here is the originality which makes his article the pioneering work in the field.[57]

Keynes begins his analysis by assuming that certain new investments have become profitable. The cause of this may be a new technical discovery, a shortage of houses due to a growth of population or a Capital inflation due to psychological causes.

Type 2, however, is the more usual, namely that in which the increased investment is accompanied by an increase in the total volume of production.... This assumes, of course, that the factors of production are not fully employed at the moment when the Cycle begins its upward course; but then that generally is the case.[58]

The capital inflation, let us suppose, has increased the price

[56]Shackle (82, p. 202).
[57]L. Wright (94).
[58]Keynes (48, p. 284).

of securities and new investment-goods. As a result of the profits in these industries entrepreneurs will increase the production of investment-goods and will offer more employment to the factors of production. But as the cost of investment is increased the second term of the first fundamental equation will become positive and entrepreneurs in the consumer industries make profits.

But the almost inevitable result of profits on current output and the visible depletion of stocks is to encourage manufacturers of consumption-goods to strain their efforts to increase their output. We thus have, under the influence of the windfall profits accruing from the price-rise consequent on the Primary Phase of the Credit-Cycle, *a secondary stimulus to an increased volume of production*—which, this time, is of an all-round character and affects all types of goods which are the object of general consumption.[59]

Furthermore, Keynes is aware that the concomitant expansion of the investment and the consumer industries takes place in a relatively 'fixprice' situation. Keynes points out that the secondary phase is much more likely to involve income inflation "due to the stiffening of the attitude of the factors of production (which) enables them to obtain a higher rate of remuneration per unit of output".[60] In the primary phase the elasticity of output with respect to effective demand is high.

Recall that there is a stable relationship between income and the industrial circulation. This means that the expansion cannot get under way unless the requirements of the industrial circulation are met. But it is precisely at such times when business confidence is high that the financial market is likely to be a bull market with a consensus of opinion. Such a market is not only favourable to investment. It releases resources which are needed in the industrial sector to finance a larger earnings bill.

The whole process started because investment increased relatively to saving and "so long as any element of over-invest-

[59]Keynes (48, p. 288).
[60]Keynes (48, p. 288).

ment continues some degree of profit will remain."[61] This implies that income rises up to the point at which saving is equal to investment.

The second element of the new interpretation is that the theory of money contained in the *Treatise* is integrated with the theory of the process of income change.

> Given the total quantity of money, only those combinations of the rate of earnings, the volume of output and the price-level of securities are feasible which lead to the aggregate requirements of money being equal to the given total.[62]

The usual IS-LM reasoning is the same. For each level of income a certain amount of money is demanded for transactions purposes. If the total quantity of money is constant, the amount left over for speculative purposes determines a price-level for bonds. Equilibrium is possible only if income, the price of bonds and the quantity of money are in the right relation to one another.

Once it is seen that the *Treatise* model contains a saving-investment theory of income it becomes supererogatory to prove that it does not contain a saving-investment theory of interest. But the notion that the *Treatise* is thoroughly Wicksellian in this respect is so deeply entrenched that it is worthwhile to give evidence for the opposite view.

> Thus whether the producers of investment-goods make a profit or loss depends on whether the expectations of the market about future prices and the prevailing rate of interest are changing favourably or adversely to such producers. It does *not* depend on whether the producers of consumable goods are making a profit or loss. For if the value of the new investment-goods is less than the volume of current savings, entrepreneurs as a whole must be making losses exactly equal to the difference.... These losses must be financed.... The bank-deposits thus released and the securities thus sold (by entrepreneurs) are available for, and exactly equal to, the

[61]Keynes (48, p. 289).
[62]Keynes (48, p. 146).

excess of current savings over the value of new investment.[63]

When entrepreneurs in the consumer industries make losses they will finance these losses by selling securities. This excess supply of securities will be exactly matched by the excess demand for securities on the part of the savers. Hence the price of securities will not change and investment will be unaffected.[64]

## MULTIPLIER ANALYSIS IN THE *TREATISE*

Hegeland's book contains much valuable information about the theory of the multiplier.[65] A plethora of multiplier concepts have been developed in the literature.[66] For our purposes it is only necessary to use the following multiplier concepts. First, there is the "logical multiplier" or the instantaneous multiplier. This multiplier holds without any time lag. It is used in moving equilibrium analysis. Second, there is the idea of a fixed relationship between investment (or increments of investment) and income (or increments of income). Third, there is the period or dynamic multiplier. The dynamic multiplier is usually based on lags and traces the effect of a change in investment through successive periods of time and depicts the rise in income in the form of a convergent geometrical series. Finally, there is the concept of a comparative-statics multiplier. The comparative-statics multiplier is a timeless multiplier in that it focuses mainly on the next equilibrium position and does not pay much attention to the motion of a system from one equilibrium to another. The comparative-statics multiplier shows that the consumption income relation amplifies any disturbance that impinges on the system. Investment increases consumption demand

[63]Keynes (48, p. 145).

[64]In the next chapter we shall see that it is this theory of the *Treatise* that caused much bewilderment, especially among the neo-Wicksellians. Hayek, for example, started out by assuming that the *Treatise* is Wicksellian (just like the proponents of the standard interpretation). He then discovered that many of the *Treatise* propositions are incomprehensible within a Wicksellian framework.

[65]H. Hegeland (40).

[66]For example, matrix multipliers, geographical multipliers, direct timeless multipliers and so forth.

by raising income. As a result the consumption industries expand. The idea is to show that income changes in order to bring saving and investment into equality. When Leijonhufvud, Klein, Shackle deny that the *Treatise* contains the multiplier they are using the term in this sense.

Hanson argues correctly that although Keynes presents the comparative-statics multiplier in the *General Theory* the basic analysis was presented in terms of the logical multiplier.[67] For the most part Keynes assumes that the consumption industries expand pari passu with the investment industries. In other words, the increase in the demand for consumer goods is foreseen completely by entrepreneurs. If the increase in consumption demand is not foreseen the first effect of the increase in investment is a rise in the price of consumption goods *exactly as in the Treatise model*. This is what Keynes said in the *General Theory*.

Take the extreme case where the expansion of employment in the capital-goods industries is so entirely unforeseen that in the first instance there is no increase whatever in the output of consumption-goods. In this event the efforts of those newly employed in the capital-goods industries to consume a proportion of their increase incomes will raise the prices of consumption-goods. ...As time goes on, however, the consumption industries adjust themselves to the new demand. ... The fact that an unforeseen change only exercises its full effect on employment over a period of time is important in certain contexts ... (on lines such as I followed in my *Treatise on Money*). But it does not in any way affect the significance of the theory of the multiplier as set forth in this chapter.[68]

Keynes himself has stated the relationship between the two models very clearly. In the *General Theory* it is assumed that the consumption industries expand pari passu with the investment industries. As the increase in demand is fully anticipated there need be no "more disturbance to the price of consumption-goods than is consequential, in conditions of decreasing

[67]A. Hansen (27, p. 108).
[68]Keynes (47, pp. 122–124).

returns, on an increase in the quantity which is produced".[69]

Let us consider how the *Treatise* model works if it is assumed that the effects of the increased investment are fully foreseen by the entrepreneurs in the consumption industries. If entrepreneurs in the consumption know that $I'$ the cost of investment is going to exceed saving they will immediately increase their production of consumption-goods and there need be no more disturbance to the price of consumption-goods than is consequential on an increase in the money rate of efficiency earnings of the factors of production (i.e. an increase of $E/O$). Keynes was aware that it is *anticipated* profits and not actually realized profits, that strictly govern the volume of employment that entrepreneurs offer to the factors of production.[70] The bulk of the analysis in the *Treatise*, however, is conducted in terms of an indirect effect of investment on output. Investment raises output, but only by raising the prices of consumption goods.

Nowhere in the *Treatise* does Keynes say that the fundamental equations must be interpreted in terms of *actual* profits and not *anticipated* profits. If we interpret the fundamental equations in terms of anticipated profits a startling result follows. On this interpretation it turns out that the *fundamental equations describe the logical theory of the multiplier*.

If they are interpreted in terms of actual profits they describe the working of a comparative-statics multiplier. But it is certainly not true that the fundamental equations are a variant of the classical quantity equations as some proponents of the standard interpretation of the *Treatise* have maintained.

## COMPARISON OF THE *TREATISE* THEORY WITH OTHER THEORIES

In this section the theory presented in the *Treatise* will be compared with the other theories that were put forward in the twenties. Consider first the theory contained in *Monetary Reform*. In this book Keynes was interested in the movements of the absolute price-level. The theory that he used to explain these movements he expressed in the equation $n = pk$. This equation

[69]Keynes (47, p. 122).
[70]Keynes is emphatic on this point. (48, p. 159).

belongs to the "family" of equations that were used by classical economists to elucidate the important relationship between the quantity of money and the level of prices.

Now in the *Treatise* the most conspicuous departure from this practice consisted in the use of equations in which *the variable P occurs but M does not*. But why should that be disturbing? The answer is given by Marget.

It is fair to say that, prior to the publication of Mr. Keynes' *Treatise*, little objection would have been raised to the proposition that any attempt to explain the determination of general prices must start . . .with a formulation with respect to the forces determining "prices" in which the *quantity of money* was given an unmistakable place. . . For, in substance, we were being asked to turn our backs upon a type of reasoning which goes back at least as far as the time of Jean Bodin.[71]

Although this was the most conspicuous departure from the classical tradition it was not necessarily the most important one. The main reason why the *Treatise* created so much confusion and bewilderment is that it advanced a theory of the forces determining output and employment. The theory of prices was part of this theory. Both the price-level and output were shown to depend on the offers that the entrepreneurs felt it worthwhile to make to the factors of production. The scale of their offers was shown to be dependent on the relation between investment and saving. Investment was regarded primarily as a function of the price of securities and saving was considered to be a stable function of income. The price of securities or the long interest rate was shown to depend on the behaviour of the banking system and the bearishness of the public.

The idea that the relationship between saving and investment is important was hardly original with Keynes. Robertson had shown in 1926 that "abortive lacking" can occur if the banking system follows "inappropriate" policies. Other writers such as Foster and Catchings and Hobson had argued that depressions are caused by oversaving. Abbati had shown that if the "velocity" of "final buying" is less the "velocity" of "production

[71]A. Marget (58, Vol. 1, p. 9).

income" will fall. It has already been demonstrated that the development of economic theory in the nineteen twenties must be regarded as a social response to an anomalous and ambiguous situation. The question of the originator of the saving-investment analysis is not important. All that is important to note is that the proliferation of articulating activity led to the formation of a group-consensus on perceptual styles.

Although many contributed to the formation of a group-consensus no one was able to produce a work that could command the allegiance of the majority of the profession. In other words nobody produced a paradigm until Keynes published his *Treatise* in 1930. Keynes incorporated the idea of his contemporaries in his system. But he did what many others had failed to do. He incorporated quantity adjustments in his model and described the working of the comparative-statics multiplier. Furthermore, he integrated the theory of money with the theory of the process of income change. If the interpretation presented in this paper is correct the *Treatise* must be regarded as a paradigm in so far as its relation with previous works is concerned. In the next chapter the post-*Treatise* developments shall be considered. Study of these developments will strengthen our conviction that the *Treatise* should be regarded as a paradigm.

## CONCLUSIONS

This chapter has shown the need for a revision of our views about the *Treatise*. The evidence given in this chapter proves that the proponents of the standard interpretation have distorted the facts because they would not fit a theory which was accepted on a priori grounds. The *General Theory* has been accorded the honour of being the book that revolutionised economic theorizing. The *Treatise* has always been considered as a "transitional" work that contained some brilliant ideas. As Schumpeter said "everybody" saw its points.

Whenever it is discovered that the *Treatise* contains something (the bearishness theory, for example) that it "should not contain" it is said that Keynes' thinking was very confused at the time. If other economists maintained that they were spelling out some of the implications of the *Treatise* which it "should not contain" it is said that they were "really" writing parts of the *General Theory*. In 1931 Keynes made a radio address in which he urged the people to spend more and to reduce their saving. According to Klein this policy prescription was made "not because of but in spite of" the theoretical model embodied in the *Treatise*. The evidence given in this paper should dispel any residue of doubt that may remain in the reader's mind that Klein's view is utterly mistaken.

Kuhn's theory tells us that "facts" alone can never refute a paradigm. In spite of the incontrovertible evidence given, many readers who have not made the *Gestalt switch* will still be unconvinced. They will remain unconvinced because they will continue to read the *Treatise* with their minds shackled and limited by the standard interpretation. Of course, the proponents of the standard interpretation have "evidence" to support the Gestalt with which they approach the book. They will quote the lines from the Preface of the *General Theory* in which Keynes said that he "failed to deal thoroughly with *changes* in the level of output". They will point out that Keynes used the market rate–natural rate terminology of the Wicksellians. They will assert that it was Kuhn who first developed the theory of the multiplier, the idea, that is to say, that investment and consumption can expand *together*.

Using these "facts" the proponents of the standard interpretation have created an interpretative paradigm which they use when they read the book. All the facts then fall into their place and a consistent picture emerges as is attested by Klein's book. Of course, puzzles arise within the paradigm. How is the bearishness theory to be explained. The paradigm, however, has built-in mechanisms to alleviate dissonance. The bearishness theory can be explained by attributing it to the "confused state" of Keynes' thinking at the time. Other puzzles can be taken care of in a similar fashion.

But is this a sufficient explanation of the fact that the majority of economists believe in the standard interpretation?[72] Accor-

---

[72]The notable exceptions are Burstein and Hicks. In his book *Money* (p. 685) Burstein again says Klein's assertion that the" *Treatise* does not contain a theory of effective demand". In his book *Critical Essays in*

ding to Harrod, one explanation for this state of affairs is that the appearance of the *General Theory* greatly militated against the reading of the *Treatise*. Few people have the time and energy to peruse two ponderous books written on recondite subjects by the same author.[73] And this becomes especially credible when we consider the views of some ardent Keynesians that the *General Theory* made a clean break with the past.

On the basis of Kuhn's theory the prediction can be made that the adduction of "pieces" of evidence inconsistent with the standard interpretation will not be sufficient to undermine belief in its validity. The standard interpretation will be seen to be false only when the new interpretation advanced in this paper is accepted.

*Monetary Theory* Hicks presents an interpretation that is similar to the one advanced here. But his claim that the *Treatise* contains a "profit multiplier" (p. 197) is mistaken. According to Hicks' argument the amount of profits will not be independent of consumption out of profits. But Keynes' famous widow's cruse is designed to show that the amount of profits is independent of consumption out of profits. (See *Treatise*, p. 139.)

[73]Harrod (34, p. 404).

## Appendix 1

After the *Treatise* was published in 1930 Hayek accused Keynes of giving confused definitions of concepts like investment and consumption.[74] The following note is intended to clear up some of the difficulties and ambiguities.

The stock of real goods, or material wealth, of a community consists of fixed capital, working capital, and liquid capital. Capital is said to be fixed when it yields its services or real income over a period of time. The working capital consists of all the goods that are "in process", that is to say, it consists of those goods that have to undergo some further economic transformation before they are in a form or state in which they can be consumed. Liquid capital consists of all those goods that are not actually in use but which are capable of being used at any time.

Fixed capital exists because some goods take time to be fully used up. Working capital exists because some goods take time to produce. Liquid capital exists because some goods are not perishable.

The income yielded by the capital is made up of the *available* income or output and the *non-available* output. The available output consists of the flow of liquid goods and services that are in a form available to be consumed. Current consumption is related to the available output during a period of time, but is not identical with it. The former exceeds the latter when stocks of liquid consumption-goods are drawn upon. Such stocks are referred to as "hoards". Current consumption plus the increment in hoards (or minus the decrement) is equal to *the output of consumption goods*.

*The production of consumption goods* is equal to the available output plus the increment of working capital that will become *available* in the future. This means that part of the production of consumption goods increases the non-available output in the current period.

*The production of capital goods* during any period is equal to the net increment, after allowing for wastage, of fixed capital plus the increment of working capital that will emerge from the economic process as fixed capital. It follows that this concept is narrower than that of the non-available output, because the latter includes, in addition, the increment of working capital that will emerge from the economic process as available output.

*The production of investment goods* is equal to the non-available output plus any additions to hoards or *minus* any subtractions therefrom. Note first that the concept of the production of investment goods is the most comprehensive of all since it includes the non-available output (and this includes the production of capital goods) plus the increments in hoards. Note also that when the available output exceeds current consumption the non-available output is less than the output of investment goods.

[74]F. Hayek (37).

### Appendix 2

## The so-called fundamental error in the first fundamental equation

In order to derive the first fundamental equation Keynes assumed that $I'$ $=E.C/O$. After the *Treatise* was published it was pointed out by Hansen[75] that the fundamental equation is invalid when technical progress is occurring. In order to elucidate this whole question consider the following example. Suppose it takes 100 dollars to produce one unit of investment or consumption goods (this is Keynes' cost definition of output). If 5 units of each kind of good are produced $ER=500\$=I'$. Income $E=1000\$$. Furthermore $I'=E.C/O=1000/2=500\$$.

It might happen, for example, that one physical unit of $C$ can be produced at half the cost as compared with the base year. In that case $C/O$ may increase without any change in $I'$ or $E$. But then $I'$ will not be equal to $E.C/O$. This is what Hansen's criticism amounts to. When there is *differential* technical progress the fundamental equation is only approximately valid. If technical progress occurs uniformly in both sectors the equation is valid.

In his reply to Hansen, Keynes admitted that Hansen had "found him out in a slip" and said that the small error could be easily corrected by adopting a slightly different definition of units which it is not necessary to reproduce here. Professor Adarker(2) contended that Hansen's criticism does not amount to very much because Keynes' theory deals primarily with the short run and in the short run the cost of production of the two kinds of goods does not change much. It seems to us that this controversy over the error in the fundamental equation is much ado about nothing. While Hansen's criticism is formally correct, it seems to us, that the fundamental theoretical apparatus of the *Treatise* is not affected by it.

---

[75] A. Hansen (29).

# Chapter VI

# Keynes' "Treatise" and the Ferment in Monetary Theory (1930–1933)

According to Kuhn when the members of a scientific community acquire a new paradigm there are inter-paradigm debates between those members of the profession who have transferred their allegiance to the new paradigm and those who continue to believe in the old paradigm. In these inter-paradigm debates scientists have a tendency to "talk through each other", that is to say, they use the conceptual and theoretical framework supplied by their own paradigm to view the empirical world. Thus when a scientist declares that a particular theory is incorrect, what he means is that in terms of *his own* theoretical framework the other theory is deficient. But as the proponent of the other theory also thinks in the same way inter-paradigm debates are characterized by *partial communication* among its participants.

It is this aspect of Kuhn's theory that will be tested in the following pages. It was argued in the preceding chapter that the standard interpretation of the *Treatise* is untenable, and that a new interpretation is called for. It is interesting to study the post-*Treatise* debates in terms of this novel interpretation. It shall be shown in the succeeding pages that the proponents of the standard interpretation have misrepresented the nature of the response to Keynes' book.

Our first task is to ascertain the general impressions of the various economists who wrote about the *Treatise* during that time. Disregarding for the nonce what the economists felt about the various particular propositions in the book let us try to see what they felt about the book as a whole. Even here we find that the proponents of the standard interpretation have misrepresented the nature of the response to Keynes' book. If the *Treatise* is a "transitional" work with a very loosely knit theoretical structure, as Klein affirms, is it not natural to expect that economists in the thirties while recognizing that the book has merits, that on various particular problems (such as index numbers or the term structure of interest rates) it considerably extends our knowledge, could not regard it as a *paradigm* for future research. Their attitude to the basic theoretical structure of the book could not be favourable. The *Treatise* could not draw scientists away from competing modes of scientific activity. The proponents of the standard interpretation feel that the *Treatise* could not act as a paradigm. But whether or not it could act as a paradigm it is asserted that it *did not in fact* operate in that way.

This contention of the proponents of the standard interpretation is not acceptable. It is not acceptable for the simple reason that it does not accord with the facts. The contention has been made plausible by a misrepresentation of the evidence and by ignoring facts that do not fit or accord with the standard interpretation. Thus Schumpeter[1] says that "the *Treatise* was not a failure in any ordinary sense of the word. Everybody saw its points, and, with whatever qualifications paid respect to Keynes' great efforts". This description of the response to Keynes' book is false. Furthermore, as will be proved in this paper, it is simply not true that "everybody" saw its "points".

Our contention is that the *Treatise* did have the characteristics of a paradigm when it appeared in the thirties. It split the profession into two parts: the part that believed that the fundamental theoretical structure of the *Treatise* was erroneous and the other part which responded to the book with elation, with the feeling that here is a work that opens up new horizons or dimensions for economic theory. Consider what Sir Josiah Stamp said:

> The academic world is not without its camps and jealousies, and its reluctancies to make admissions of a large and generous order. Nevertheless, private recognitions are rapidly accruing, and no work of this remarkable force can, in an environment of reasonably disinterested intellectuality, and love of truth, fail to strike its mark fairly soon. Indeed the more brilliant of the undergraduate world are, I find, quicker to realize potentialities than the cautious and conservative professors. . . . In many respects I regard Mr. Keynes' work as

[1]Harris (32, p. 89).

the most penetrating and epoch-making since Ricardo.[2]

Sir Stamp, with characteristic English brevity and force, has given us an excellent description of the state of the academic world at that time. It is a description which would apply in toto to the response that was given to the *General Theory.* Sir Stamp is, of course, mistaken in his optimistic belief of the effect of an environment of "reasonably disinterested intellectuality and love of truth", a view which, however plausible it may seem, does not accord with the facts. In fact, one of the most remarkable things about the Keynesian Revolution is the almost miniscule role played by the putative disinterested intellectuality of the scientists. It is our firm conviction that it is precisely at this point that Kuhn's theory enables us to explain a fact that is completely anomalous and unmanageable within the existing historiographical framework. It is only when we re-read Kuhn's book in the light of the Keynesian revolution that we can appreciate the depth of Kuhn's assertion that the concept of "truth" is not useful for historiographical purposes.

Here is what Jack Stafford, a frequent contributor to the journal literature in the thirties, said:

It is, however, Keynes' central thesis around which this book is written, and this, in the author's hand is a most powerful instrument in increasing our knowledge of money....The "Treatise" will be enjoyed by those who like difficult going, and will be the starting point for further studies in money for a long time to come.[3]

This is what Joan Robinson said in her famous article:

The plain man has always found the Theory of Money a bewildering subject, but at the present time many academic economists are as much bewildered by it as the plain man. The reason for this state of affairs is that the Theory of Money has recently undergone a violent revolution....Now that Mr. Keynes has shown us how to crack the egg...why should

[2]Stamp (89, p. 242).
[3]Stafford (88, pp. 31–35).

we not try what progress can be made by thinking in terms of the demand for output as a whole, and its cost of production.[4]

It is Klein's (50, p. 39) view that Joan Robinson was being "overgenerous to the master" and that she was, in fact, writing the essential parts of the *General Theory*. We prefer to believe that Joan Robinson knew what she was talking about. She states explicitly that the *Treatise* model made the crucial break with the old monetary analysis. Klein of course proceeds on the dogmatic assumption that the *Treatise* does not contain a theory of effective demand. If the *Treatise* does not contain such a theory, it is obvious that Robinson could not have been referring to that book. But she does refer to the book, which compels Klein to conclude that she *anticipated* Keynes. But Klein is forced to give this highly implausible explanation only because he proceeds on the false assumption that the *Treatise* did not even *appear*, to some economists at any rate, as a paradigm for monetary analysis. Therefore, when he finds that economists did, in fact, regard the *Treatise* in that light, he is compelled to say that they were anticipating a book which was going to be written three or four years later. As early as 1931 Sir Stamp[5] had said that "we must all feel that recent events have completely bankrupted the old monetary analysis both as a means of explanation and as a practical guide".

This is a very important point. The proponents of the standard interpretation have assumed, without warrant, that the *Treatise* did not even appear as a paradigm to some economists. It is for this reason that nowhere in the works of Klein, Shackle, Schumpeter and others, do we find even a mention of the fact that the book, and the *general approach* that it embodied, elicited a very favourable response. They cannot admit this fact consistently with their principles. They are, therefore, led to contend that the *Treatise* received "rough treatment" from its critics. The allusion here, of course, is to the work of Hayek who believed that the fundamental structure of the *Treatise* is erroneous. Hayek's views will be examined in detail later on in

[4]Robinson (75, pp. 22–24).
[5]Stamp (89, p. 242).

this chapter. But this exclusive concentration on the criticism of Hayek and other members of the non-monetary overinvestment school misrepresents the nature of the response to Keynes' book, as the quotations that we have given above, amply prove. Furthermore, the argument that Joan Robinson did not derive her inspiration from the *Treatise*, that Klein urges upon us, and that, in fact, she was writing the *General Theory*, or certain crucial passage thereof, is not only flatly contradictory to what the authoress herself emphatically asserts, but appears plausible to Klein only because he has dogmatically assumed that the *Treatise* does not have a theory of effective demand and the multiplier, an assumption or conclusion that we stoutly deny.

We are not, of course, claiming that all the reviews of the *Treatise* were favourable. In fact, by the very nature of the paradigm it must be the case that the members of the profession are divided into those who continue to adhere to the old ways of thought and those who declare their allegiance to the paradigm in the belief that the new approach is significantly better than the old. It is instructive, therefore, to learn what Hansen and Tout had to say about the *Treatise* in their annual review of business cycle theory:

> Without making any absolute comparisons we may liken it in some ways to "Das Kapital" of Marx. Here is a work which ploughed deeply into ground lightly dug before, which did so inadequately by developing a fundamentally incorrect theoretical structure, and yet withal a work which contained a multitude of correct ideas. . . . It is impossible not to believe that his critics are essentially right and that the very core of his analysis is fallacious.[6]

Later on, Hansen became an ardent Keynesian and the economist who propagated the Keynesian massage in America as Abba Lerner and Joan Robinson did in England. But in the early nineteen thirties Hansen was a Hayekian whose work was given a favourable review in the article. To be a Hayckian meant a firm belief in the proposition that the real cause of depressions was

[6]Hansen and Tout (30, p. 129).

to be sought in the analysis of the fundamental nature of capitalistic production.

Hayek was one of the leading monetary economists in the early thirties. Claiming intellectual descent from Bohm-Bawerk and Wicksell he expounded his rather abstruse theories in two books: *Prices and Production* and *Monetary Theory and the Trade Cycle*. The essence of Hayek's position is as follows: In the domain of static equilibrium theory, we have, what Hayek calls, a certain "closedness of the equilibrium price and quantity relationships". By the closedness of these systems Hayek means that when supply and demand have determined equilibrium price and quantity, any divergence from the equilibrium due to an outside disturbance is regarded as calling forth forces that restore the equilibrium. Equilibrium theory, therefore, cannot describe the forces that tend to make a system diverge more and more from the equilibrium position. Cyclical phenomena display just this set of characteristics. Consequently a theory of closed systems is inapplicable to these phenomena. A general theory of non-closed systems is needed. The problem, therefore, is to find a force or set of forces that is capable of breaking the closedness that is characteristic of equilibrium price and quantity relationships. According to Hayek it is the interest rate that is capable of producing such an effect. But does'nt the interest rate equate the demand and supply of capital on the capital market?, and if it acts in this way how can the closedness of equilibrium price and quantity relationships be broken? Hayek's answer is that it is indeed true that the interest rate acts in this way. But the banking system has control of the money supply. According to Hayek, the banking system exhibits an inherent elasticity or volatility. This imminent elasticity of the banking system makes it possible for the banks to add to the supply of capital that originates from the voluntary saving of the people. In this way the banking system can control the interest rate.

According to Hayek, any theory of non-closed systems must include the elasticity of the banking system as an essential component. But such a purely monetary theory of the cycle can never explain the facts. A fundamental proposition of the Austrian theory of capital is that a fall in the interest rate lengthens the structure of production, i.e. lengthens the average time that elapses between the employment of the uninvested services of land and labour and the time when these intermediate products start "maturing out" into a flow of consumable goods and services and that a rise in the interest rate has the opposite effect. This means that any general theory of non-closed systems has to be based on an analysis of the structure of production.

When the banking system increases the money supply and augments the total of savings flowing into the capital market, the first effect is a fall in the market rate of interest. As it will become profitable to lengthen the structure of production entrepreneurs will use the new money to entice some of the *non-specific* factors of production such as labour from the lower stages of production to the higher stages of production. The effect of this will be that relatively to a given volume of goods more money will be circulating in the higher than in the lower stages of production. As there is full employment prices will rise in the higher and fall in the lower stages of production. This narrowing of the price margins, or a fall in the rate of interest, will induce entrepreneurs to increase their production of goods needed to complete the longer structure of production. For example, more plants for making machines to make other machines will be laid down.

Meanwhile the rise in prices and the transference of the non-specific factors to the higher stages will have imposed forced saving on the people. But the people will not acquiesce in or consent to this reduction in their consumption. In the "next round", therefore, consumers will increase the amount of money spent for buying consumer goods. But this means that insufficient money will be circulating in the higher stages of production where, let us say, more plants for making machines for making other machines are being laid down.

If only the lengthened structure of production could be completed the increased demand in the higher stages could be accommodated without an excessive transference of the non-specific factors of production, because when these plants that we have been talking about start producing machines entrepreneurs in the lower stages will be able to use a more capitalized technique to produce consumer goods. But the essence of Hayek's thesis is that the demand for consumer goods will increase *before* the lengthened structure of production has been completed, assuming of course that the initial expansion was started by an inflationary injection of more money by the banks. In this case, therefore, entrepreneurs in the higher stages will have to abandon their projects and lay off workers.

Workers will be laid off in the higher stages of production. But, although demand has increased in the lower stages it will not be possible for the entrepreneurs in the lower stages to absorb these men. They will not be absorbed because of a shortage of intermediate products in the lower stages which has been occasioned by the attempts of the entrepreneurs in the higher stages to instal a lengthened structure of production. If more workers have been used during the upturn of the cycle to make plants to make machines then after the crisis has occurred there will be fewer intermediate products (raw material) at the lower stages of production which the labourers who now have been laid off in the higher stages of production have to use in the lower stages of production to meet the increased demand for consumer goods. Hence there will be unemployment. This, according to Hayek is the only adequate explanation of unemployment.

According to Hayek it is essential to distinguish between the effects on the structure of production of an increase in the money supply and the effects of a voluntary increase in the savings of the community. An increase in voluntary savings has none of the undesirable effects that we have detailed above because the people are prepared to make the sacrifice of refraining from the consumption of goods until the new longer structure of production has been completed. But if there has been no such increase the increased demand for consumption will necessarily bring about a crisis to be followed by a period of unemployment.

Of course, the banking system has to take the necessary steps to counteract any changes in either the velocity of circulation or the coefficient of monetary transactions. And other departures from a policy of neutral money is bound to be disastrous. Conversely if banks can only be persuaded to follow a neutral money policy the economy will take care of itself and there will be no crises, depressions and unemployment.

It is essential for our purposes to note that Hayek had a *demand-shift* theory of unemployment. Unemployment is fundamentally due to the fact that when entrepreneurs in the higher stages of production lay off workers the entrepreneurs in the lower stages are not able immediately to absorb these men.

Now Keynes could not accept such a theory of unemployment and effective demand and in the *Treatise* Keynes presented an essentially different theory though he continued to use the terminology employed by the neo-Wicksellians. Hayek regarded this neo-Wicksellians theory as being irrefragably correct. Consequently he could not conceive that Keynes was presenting an alternative explanation. Consider, therefore, what Hayek had to say about the book as a whole:

> Indeed, so strongly does it bear the marks of the effect of the recent discovery of certain lines of thought hitherto unfamiliar to the school to which Mr. Keynes belongs, that it would be decidedly unfair to regard it as anything else but experimental . . . . And even if to a Continental economist this way of approach does not seem so novel as it does to the author, it must be admitted that he has made a more ambitious attempt to carry the analysis into the details and complications of the problem than any that has been attempted hitherto.[7]

It is clear from this passage that Hayek regards Keynes' work as being in the Wicksellian tradition. This being the case it is only natural that he should say that he does not regard the approach as novel as it appears to Keynes. But what, according to Hayek, is the approach of the *Treatise* that he does not consider as being completely new? The answer to this question will be given in a few pages. But before we do that it is advisable to consider Keynes' views about the way in which his critics had interpreted his work. This will enable us to get a better understanding of the state of monetary theory at the time.

> As he frankly says, he has found his difference with me difficult to explain. He is sure that my conclusions are wrong (though he does not clearly state which conclusions) but he finds it "extremely difficult to demonstrate the exact point of disagreement and to state his objections". . . . I think I can show that most of my alleged terminological inconsistencies are either non-existent or irrelevant to my central theme.

[7]Hayek (37, p. 270).

But when I have done this I feel sure that I shall have made little progress towards convincing Dr. Hayek. For it is not really my use of language or the fact that my treatment falls far short of a complete analysis (as it certainly does) which is troubling him. It is something much more fundamental.[8]

During the four or five years following the publication of the *Treatise* Keynes found himself in the position of the Indian philosopher who felt that God could only be defined in a negative way. Whenever one of his pupils suggested a particular definition of God, he replied that that is not the correct definition. Whenever any of his critics stated that this is the basic thesis of the *Treatise* and then argued that this thesis is either not original or that it is erroneous, Keynes said that those who were wedded to the classical ways of thought could never accept the fact that he was asking them "to don a new pair of trousers".

Before we go on to examine and discuss those propositions in the *Treatise* that gave so much trouble and caused so much confusion, let us recapitulate. Our basic contention is that the evidence shows that the *Treatise* is a paradigm in Kuhn's sense of the word. It presented to the economics profession a method of approach to macroeconomic phenomena that some enthusiastically accepted and others repudiated. The creator of the paradigm was himself not very clear about the nature of the revolution he was carrying through. At the same time there is no doubt at all that he felt that he had made an important discovery. Furthermore, Keynes felt that those who were wedded to the old ways of thought, including himself, found it extremely hard "to don this new pair of trousers". That the *Treatise* was open-ended cannot be disputed. Even the implications of its central message were not clear to Keynes and had to be spelled out by those economists who accepted these ideas. The proponents of the standard interpretation argue that the *General Theory* made the definite break with the past. The evidence indicates that the *Treatise* should have that honour. The *General Theory* merely spelled out the inchoate vision of the earlier book. This is a controversial proposition and one that is very hard to accept. But the facts compel us to accept it.

[8]*Economica*, Nov., 1931, p. 387.

## THE ROLE OF CAPITAL THEORY IN MONETARY ANALYSIS

In our statement of Hayek's theory we saw that Hayek insisted on the fact that any general theory of non-closed systems must be based on an integration of capital theory and monetary analysis in the way that we have described above. Both Keynes and Hayek repudiated Mill's famous assertion that "there is nothing so intrinsically insignificant in the economy of society as money". Both of them agreed that money is "important". But they disagreed on the role that capital theory should have in a description of "non-closed" processes. Consider what Hayek said:

> Mr. Keynes seems never to have been concerned to study the fundamental non-monetary problems of capitalistic production. . .even if we have no quite satisfactory theory we do at least possess a far better one than that on which he is content to rely, namely that of Bohm-Bawerk and Wicksell. That he neglects this theory, not because he thinks it is wrong, but simply because he has never bothered to make himself acquainted with it, is amply proved by the fact that he finds unintelligible my attempt to develop certain corollaries of this theory.[9]

This criticism was in response to Keynes' description of Hayek's book *Prices and Production* as "one of the most frightful muddles that exists with scarcely a sound proposition after page 45". Naturally, Hayek did not take kindly to this criticism and accused Keynes of being ignorant of capital theory. It is interesting to note that Keynes substantially conceded Hayek's point. He felt, however, that for much that he had to say he did not find it necessary to work on capital-theoretic lines. He felt that phenomena such as unemployment and movements of income could be explained on the basis of a model that used only some elementary principles of capital theory. Hayek fundamentally differed from Keynes on this point and practically all his criticisms of the *Treatise* model stem from this fact.

[9]Hayek (37, pp. 401–402).

Let us consider some examples. According to Keynes, whenever savings exceed investment there will be profits in the consumer industries and these profits will induce entrepreneurs in these industries to expand their output and hence income of the community will rise until equilibrium is restored. Hayek's objection to Keynes' theory of profits is that profit is not a purely monetary phenomenon. It is partly a real phenomenon. Profits can also arise when changes occur in the relative supply of goods in the higher or lower stages of production and when these supplies of goods are met by different money streams in the different stages of production. It may be the case, Hayek argues, that the effects that Keynes attributed to the emergence of profits may arise even when total profits are zero. Suppose that when the banks increase the money supply the market rate is lowered below the natural rate. Entrepreneurs will commence the lengthening of the structure of production. But consumption demand will increase sooner or later. When it increases, less money will now flow in the higher stages of production and more in the lower stages. Losses will be made in the higher stages and workers will be laid off. Profits will increase in the lower stages and, therefore, total profits will be the same. But there will be unemployment as the workers laid off in the higher stages cannot be absorbed in the lower stages due to a shortage of intermediate products. Hayek contends that it is this "real" maladjustment in the structure of production that causes unemployment and not merely the excess of saving over investment as in the Keynesian theory.

Keynes maintained that he had a different theory. Hence only confusion can result if his theory is translated into Hayekian ways of thinking, and it is asserted that Keynes does not draw conclusions that he should draw. But why assume that the Keynesian theory is Wicksellian? What evidence does Hayek give to substantiate his assertion?

## SAVING-INVESTMENT AND THE PROBLEM OF HOARDING

Hayek said that the approach of the *Treatise* is not so novel as it appears to the author. But what is this approach?

The fact that more (or less) money is being invested than is being saved is equivalent to so much money being added to (or withdrawn from) industrial circulation, so that the total of profits, or the difference between the expenditure and receipts of the entrepreneurs, which is the essential element in the second term of the fundamental equations, will be equal to the net addition to (or subtraction from) the effective circulation. It is here, according to Mr. Keynes, that we find the monetary causes working for a change in the price-level, and he considers it the main advantage of his fundamental equations that they isolate this factor.[10]

We can now understand why Hayek thinks that the approach of the *Treatise* is not so novel as it appears to Keynes. In the Hayekian system, saving and investment can never get out of line because savings are always invested. If savings always get invested it follows that only if the banks do not deviate from a policy of neutral money, the economy will never experience depressions and unemployment. On the other hand, if the banking system departs from this policy we will necessarily have all the effects we described earlier. Because of his own beliefs Hayek concluded that in the *Treatise* model the differences between saving and investment is necessarily constituted by changes in the effective circulation of money. If we assume that the quantity of money is held constant, any excess of saving over investment necessarily means that there is an increase in the amount of inactive deposits or an increase in the amount hoarded, and an excess of investment over saving necessarily means a decrease in the amount that is hoarded. This implies that the excess of saving over investment is necessarily related to the quantum of idle funds.

But the theory contained in the *Treatise* is very different from this. Keynes denied that the relation between saving and investment is in any way connected with the actions of the banks. In other words, Keynes denied that the departure of the banks from a policy of neutral money is both a necessary and sufficient condition for saving to get out of line with investment. In the Keynesian system savings *may* not get invested. Consequently,

[10]Hayek (37, p. 291).

saving could exceed investment even without any action on the part of the banks. In the Wicksell-Hayek system this could not happen because savings necessarily get invested. If money is not spent in one way it is spent in another. But it was essential for the purposes of Keynes to deny this sophisticated version of Say's Law. Keynes says:

> *My* analysis is quite different from this; as it necessarily must be, since in my view, saving and investment (as I define them) can get out of gear without any change on the part of the banking system from "neutrality"... there being no automatic mechanism in the economic system (as Dr. Hayek's view would imply that there must be) to keep the two rates equal, provided the effective quantity of money is unchanged.[11]

The automatic mechanism that Keynes refers to is, of course, the interest rate mechanism. In view of this passage it is indeed very startling to find that Klein thinks that the *Treatise* contains a saving investment theory of interest. The fact is that it is Keynes' repudiation of this theory that caused so much bewilderment and confusion, and made it hard to see what he was really driving at.

Both Hansen and Shackle, after comparing two approaches of Hayek and Keynes, concluded that Keynes' arguments were erroneous, that is to say they agreed with Hayek's assertion that the banks are responsible for any discrepancy between saving and investment. Shackle, for example, said:

> It has been shown that except under conditions of panic where the rate of interest ceases to operate in the manner contemplated by equilibrium theory, conditions which are the result rather than the cause of disturbance the volume (of money) cannot be changed without affecting investment.[12]

It has been seen above that Keynes disagreed with the Haye-kians of the role of the banks in generating and discrepancy between saving and investment. He also disagreed with them on

---

[11]*Economica*, Feb. 1931, p. 393.
[12]*Review of Economic Studies*, 1933, p. 33.

the nature of the effects produced on the economy by an excess of saving over investment. According to the Wicksell-Hayek theory an increase of saving will lower the rate of interest and make it more profitable for entrepreneurs to lengthen the structure of production. Because consumption demand has been reduced less money will flow in the lower stages of production and more will flow in the higher stages (including the ones that have just been added due to the fall in the rate of interest). The losses in the lower stages will be counterbalanced by profits in the higher stages. Keynes denied that saving *in itself* will have these effects.

The first effect of the increase of saving will be that the second term of the first fundamental equation will become negative, i.e. saving will exceed the cost of investment. The entrepreneurs in these industries will make losses and the savers will find themselves with an increment of wealth. But this increased saving will not necessarily give rise to new investment. *An increase in the amount of money hoarded is not necessary to explain this fact.* Even if there is no increase in the amount of money hoarded the increased saving may not give rise to new investment. The reason is that the entrepreneurs who have made losses will seek to recoup their losses by selling non-liquid assets on the market and the savers who wish to embark their wealth in securities will purchase them from the entrepreneurs. An excess supply of money will be met by an excess supply of securities. The savers are willing to hold securities at the existing price of securities and the entrepreneurs desire to sell their securities. Hence the price of securities will not change as it has equilibrated the desire to hold cash with the available quantum of cash. Hence there will be no incentive for entrepreneurs to increase their output of investment goods. The result will be a fall in the income of the community.

But it is precisely this sort of analysis that gave rise to all sorts of problems. Let us consider what Robertson had to say about this. Robertson felt that it is precisely this part of the *Treatise* that is fundamentally defective. It is defective because it is not based on the "Fisherine bedrock of a flow of money meeting a flow of goods". Keynes did not write an equation for the determination of the price level of investment goods. Instead he said that the price of these goods is determined by the banking system and the sentiments of the public. The prices of securities (or new investment goods since they are subject to the same influences) will be at that level which equates the desire to hold inactive cash with the available quantity of "inactive" cash.

For it is on page 145 that the conclusion is reached that, if *P* declines owing to an excess of saving over investment, then, *even though there is no increase in the disposition of hoard money unspent*, there need be no counterbalancing rise in the price of investment goods....But the fact which this argument suppresses is such a state of affairs cannot come about except as a result of an act of "hoarding"... on the part of someone.[13]

Hayek, Robertson, Shackle, Hansen and others found great difficulty in understanding and accepting this argument of Keynes. All of them reverted to the classical idea that if less money is spent on consumption goods more money will be spent on investment goods, assuming of course that there is no increase in the amount of money hoarded. Keynes had this to say to all his critics:

I have found that some readers of my book have supposed that an excess of saving over investment is necessarily accompanied by an equal increase of inactive deposits, so that— presumably—an excess of saving would be impossible if the banking system were to behave in such a way as to keep the excess of the total deposits over the active deposits at a constant figure . . . . Their interpretation seems to be that an excess of saving is only another way of talking about an increase in inactive deposits; an increase of inactive deposits means a decrease in the velocity of circulation; thus when I say that an excess of saving leads to a fall in the price of consumption goods, I am only repeating in a very complicated way the old story that a fall in the velocity of circulation must bring prices down, other things being equal. *But, truly, this is not what I am saying.* The volume of inactive deposits has in my view no

[13]*Economic Journal,* 1931, pp. 399–400.

particular relation to an excess of saving.[14]

Here again we find that the Keynesian argument was misinterpreted by his critics, and that Keynes had to resort to his favourite reply "but, truly, this is not what I am saying". Keynes was given credit for the way in which he had analysed the role of "hoarding" in the business cycle. It was granted by his critics that this problem had not been sufficiently analysed before and that such "hitching up of money streams" is more important than the classical economists realized. Keynes felt that this sort of hitching up of money streams, though important, was not what he was trying to describe. The important point that the *Treatise* was trying to make is that the amount of "hoarding" is determined by the banking system. The sentiment of the public determines the price of non-liquid assets or "securities" at which the aggregate desire to hoard is equal to the available quantity of hoards. An excess of saving in the Wicksell-Hayek system would lower the rate of interest and make investment more profitable. This automatic mechanism ensured that saving would be equal to investment. Keynes denied that there is any such automatic mechanism. When there is an excess of saving, entrepreneurs in the consumer industries make losses, and will reduce their output. But there is no reason why investment should increase because there is no reason why the rate of interest should fall. The excess of saving, therefore, does not reduce interest rates, it reduces the income of the community. If at this lower income saving still exceeds the cost of investment, income must fall again as necessarily follows from the theory of profits. Even at this stage there is no reason for the price of investment goods or the interest rate to change because the excess demand for securities on the part of the savers is met by an excess demand for money on the part of the losing entrepreneurs. The natural rate is defined by Keynes as that rate of interest at which saving is equal to investment. During the process of income deflation that we have been describing, saving exceeds investment, or, in other words, the natural rate is below the market rate. Equilibrium will be restored when income has fallen to such an extent that the amount of saving out of that

[14]*Economic Journal,* 1931, p. 416, (emphasis added).

income is equal to the cost of investment. The amount of saving at low incomes is small and this will tend to raise the natural rate. On the other hand the income deflation will reduce the requirements of the Industrial Circulation and this will tend to lower the market rate unless compensatory action is taken by the banks. This is the theory that Keynes put forward in the *Treatise*. Consider what Hayek said:

The most curious fact is that from the outset, all of Mr. Keynes' reasoning aims at proving that an increase in saving will not lead to an increase of non-available output and wants to *prove* that saving will not lead to the necessary shift.[15]

But it is not true that Keynes set out to study the shifts between available and non-available output. This problem is important only in the Wicksell-Hayek system. Hayek is right when he says that Keynes wants to prove that saving does not lead to investment. The inconsistency only arises when one insists that "to a Continental writer, this approach is not as novel as it appears to the author". The plain fact is that Hayek did not understand it because he could not conceive that an excess of saving leads, not to a shift between available and non-available output, but to a decline in income. Income changes to bring saving into equality with investment.

But how can we explain the fact that Hayek thought that Keynes had set out to explain the shifts between available and non-available output, when Hayek himself states explicitly that Keynes' most important conclusion is that savings do not get invested and that there is automatic mechanism to equate the two at a *given level of income*? Enough evidence has been given in this paper to show that economists in the "classical" tradition experienced great difficulty in understanding the central message of the *Treatise*. Their belief in certain "classical" propositions was so strong that they could not accept the fact that Keynes was saying something both valid and original. Hayek started out by assuming that the approach of the *Treatise* is not so novel as it appears to the author. Having imputed what he regarded as irrefragably correct views to Keynes he is startled to find that

---

[15]*Economica*, Feb. 1932, pp. 31-32.

Keynes' most important conclusions are inconsistent with those views. Robertson who insisted on the soundness of proceeding on the "Fisherine bedrock" could not accept Keynes' denial of the proposition that what is not spent in one way is necessarily spent in another. He commended Keynes for demonstrating that an increase in the amount of money hoarded is an important factor in depression. Keynes thought that Robertson had missed his central point that excess savings have nothing to do with the amount of inactive deposits and that it is essential to distinguish between the propensity to hoard, the actual amount of hoards and changes in the propensity to hoard.

The fact that some of his central contentions were misunderstood by his critics must have bothered Keynes and in his reply to Hayek he offers an explanation:

Since Dr. Hayek has not been alone amongst competent critics of my "Treatise" in falling into this misapprehension ....It must be my own fault, at least in part. I suspect that it may be partly due to the fact that when I first began to work on Book 111 of my *Treatise* I believed something resembling this myself. *My ceasing to believe it was the critical point in my own development and was the germ from which much of my eventual theory was worked out. It is extra that I should not have made this clear, because I was acutely conscious of the difference of general outlook which the change of view involved* .... Yet I doubt if it is all my fault. For anyone brought up in the old Quantity-of-Money, Velocity of Circulation schools of thought... this seems to be, for some obscure reason, a difficult transition to make. Indeed I found it so myself. If the true theory were what Dr. Hayek believes it to be, the transition would be easy. If, on the other hand, my theory is right, not only is the angle of approach different, but it is difficult to see just what the relationship is between the new view and the old. Thus those who are sufficiently steeped in the old point of view simply cannot bring themselves to believe that I am asking them to step into a new pair of trousers, and will insist on regarding it as nothing but an embroidered version of the old pair which they have been wearing for years.[16]

[16]*Economica*, 1931, pp. 389–390.

CONCLUSIONS

The central point that this paper has made is that the *Treatise on Money* was a paradigm in a very real sense. It caused much confusion and bewilderment in the profession. Even its critics were not sure if they had understood that "extraordinarily difficult book". In fact, throughout his paper Hayek reminds the reader that his criticisms are really questions put to the author asking for clarification. After all the evidence that has been given in this paper few will dispute the suggestions that the *Treatise* was an open-ended book. It certainly did not definitively solve all the problems. In fact, much work had to be done by economists, including Keynes, to clarify the meaning of its central contentions.

It is very hard to accept the suggestion that the *General Theory* merely spelled out in an explicit form the inchoate vision of the *Treatise*. It is hard to believe that Keynes departed from tradition in the earlier book. The proponents of the standard interpretation have created the impression that the *General Theory* represented a clean break with the past and that Keynes repudiated the theoretical apparatus developed in the earlier book. The image of the *Treatise* that we gather from their writings is that it was a "transitional" work that got a rough reception from its critics. This chapter has presented evidence to loosen the hold of this belief on our minds.

# Chapter VII

# Conclusions

The subject of Keynesian economics is so vast that a study of this sort can scarcely be expected to cover all of it. No claim of exhaustiveness is made for the investigation just undertaken. But it is to be hoped that enough evidence has been adduced to prove that the Keynesian Revolution was a revolution in the sense of Kuhn.

All that remains to be done in this concluding chapter is to briefly consider the questions that will necessarily arise if the main theses of this study prove to be correct, and to pose problems for further research.

First, there is the question of the *Treatise*. On the basis of the evidence given in the last two chapters it is surely reasonable to conclude that the *Treatise* appeared to economists of the thirties as a new paradigm. It embodied an approach to macro-economic phenomena that was significantly different from the old approach. It was accepted enthusiastically by some members of the profession even though they did not fully understand the central theory contained in that "extraordinarily difficult book". The clamorous critics of the book carped and cavilled at venial faults of exposition and inaccuracies of expression. But they missed what was fundamental.

If the interpretation presented in this study is correct we must conclude that the *General Theory* merely actualized the promise contained in the earlier book.

This conclusion is certainly hard to accept. We have all been brought up on the view that Keynes "saw the light" only in the *General Theory*. The *Treatise* has always been regarded as a "transitional" work. How is this "let's-forget-the-*Treatise*" view to be explained? This question is even more intriguing when it is realized that Keynes himself played an important part in popularizing this view.

While no definite answer is possible, the following explanations are not altogether implausible. First, Keynes seems to have had an emotional preference for the *General Theory*. It was

his favourite brain-child. Second, it should be noted that
although Keynes was partly responsible for the view that the
*Treatise* is not an "important" book Klein's interpretation has
had a much greater influence. Klein's book on the Keynesian
Revolution has long been regarded as the authoritative treatment
of the subject. Klein's book has solidified the image of the
*Treatise* as a "transitional" work with a few brilliant ideas.
Subsequently this image has been widely accepted. As it is, as
Harrod has pointed out, few people have the time and energy to
read two ponderous works written on such rarefied subjects. It
must have been easy to solace one's scholarly conscience for not
reading the *Treatise* by the reflection that Klein had shown that
it was not really an "important" book. Furthermore, even those
assiduous scholars who read the book did so on the basis of the
"interpretive paradigm" that Klein had done much to develop.
As people read the *Treatise* with very strong expectations of what
it should contain it became really difficult to see the true nature
of the *Treatise* arguments.

But why were Klein's views accepted so readily? The answer is
that the *General Theory* generated a very intense emotional climate
among economists. Ardent supporters of the Keynesian theory
felt that that book made a clean break with the past. Explicit
revolutionary claims had been made by Keynes in the opening
pages of the book. Practising economists must have derived all
their inspiration for actual research from the *General Theory*.
There was no need to be concerned with the erroneous doctrines
of an older science once Keynes had shown them how to crack
the egg. Consequently, most practising economists ignored the
*Treatise*. Klein's view took root in a very fertile ground.

For these and for other reasons, the *Treatise* has not been
given the attention and importance it deserves. The responsibility for this state of affairs rests primarily on the post-*General
Theory*. Keynesian economists who, in their ardour for the new
economics, were most struck by the explicit revolutionary
claims made by Keynes in the *General Theory*. Although the
*Treatise* theory contains the same insight into the working of
macroeconomic processes (assuming, of course, that the new interpretation presented in this dissertation is correct), Keynes did
not fully realize the implications of its central message. The
finished character of the *General Theory* greatly impressed

Keynesian individualistic historians of economic thought. Strongly believing that revolutions in science occur at particular points of time it was only natural for these historians to accord to the *General Theory* the honour of revolutionizing economic theory, and to downgrade other works appearing in the immediately preceding period as merely adumbrative of the ideas expressed for the "first" time in the *General Theory*.

Once the "individualistic" approach is abandoned the problem of determining the exact date on which a revolution occurs simply disappears.

It was contended in the previous chapters that the *Treatise* should be regarded as the paradigm for Keynesian normal science. This does not mean that Keynes made a clear break with the past in the *Treatise*. On the contrary, the primary purpose of chapters 3 and 4 was to show that Keynes' response of the crisis problem took place in an environment of nascent perceptual styles in the formation of which men like Hobson and Foster and Catchings played an important part. The objective of those chapters was to demonstrate Kuhn's thesis that knowledge grows by a *social process*. Within such a framework the question of anticipators and so forth is really unimportant. New paradigms necessarily result from the interaction of members of the scientific community that has been affected by the crisis. Keynes' *Treatise* necessarily incorporated the ideas that were being put forward at the time; what differentiated it from other works of the time is not that it completely departed from tradition, but its analytical comprehensiveness and incisiveness and its ability to convince sufficiently many members of the profession of its fecundity for producing puzzles and its success in solving the crisis problem.

But still the fact remains that the *Treatise* did not convince many eminent economists who were converted to the new approach after the *General Theory* was published.

The reason for this is not that the *General Theory* made a "clean break with the past". The *Treatise* contained essentially the same insights. But the hold of the classical paradigm was so strong that the *Treatise* could not effect a mass conversion. A more persuasive work with a more revolutionary flavour was needed. A work was needed, that would concentrate all its forces on themes that were so indifferently and discursively treated in the *Treatise*. This is precisely what the *General Theory* did.

According to Leijonhufvud it is the "income-expenditure "interpretation of the *General Theory* that has created the illusion that the models of the two books are entirely different. Leijonhufvud's work brings us to the second problem-area that has not been touched upon in this study, namely Keynesian normal science. A Kuhnian investigation of the development of economic theory from the *Treatise* to modern times is a very important desideratum. Such an investigation would have to deal with the following sorts of problems. It would have to explain how the paradigm-shift affected the community structure of economics. Why did Fisher become so disenchanted with the new orientation in economics that he was unable to do Keynesian normal science? Why did Hayek, whose technical virtuosity was unquestioned, cease to be an economist a few years after the *General Theory* was published? Did these economists reject Keynesianism for political reasons? Is the history of economic thought an epiphenomenon of ideological change? How is it that economists such as Hanson and Shackle were not persuaded by the *Treatise*? While Joan Robinson and Hicks were articulating the theory contained in the *Treatise* (i.e. doing normal science) Hansen and Shackle felt that its fundamental theoretical structure was erroneous. They became normal scientists much later. Why?

These are the sorts of questions that will have to be dealt with. In the past ten or fifteen years there has been much talk of a "neo-classical resurgence". The old quantity theory of money has been resuscitated, so at least the Chicago school maintains. Neo-Fisherine approaches to money have been developed. Do these developments disconfirm Kuhn's theory? Is post-Keynesian economic theory based on one paradigm or two? Is economics a "dual-paradigm" science? These are difficult questions which cannot be answered simply by examining the "facts". Historians need a theory before they can tackle such questions. Kuhn's theory is the most useful for this purpose.

If this study has successfully applied the ideas of Kuhn to the Keynesian Revolution historians of economic thought may be encouraged to apply this theory to other episodes. The mercantilist paradigm, the Jevonian revolution and the "mathematical revolution" are obvious candidates for Kuhnian research. It is hoped that this study has whetted historians' appetite for such research.

# Postscript

In the few years since this work was completed there have been important developments in the subject-matter it treats. The objective of this postscript is to indicate the main lines along which my own thought has been evolving and to assess the implications of these recent developments for the methods and conclusions of the book. In its essentials, my viewpoint is very nearly unchanged. I am strongly of the opinion that Kuhn's historiographical framework is better than its rivals for explaining the nature of the transformation that took place in macroeconomic theory in the twenties and thirties and the subsequent development of macroeconomics. But I am more conscious than before of the difficulties that may arise in the application of Kuhn's ideas to economics.

With regard to the *Treatise*, my views have naturally undergone some modification after the publication of the *Collected Writings* of Keynes by the Royal Economic Society. These volumes contain a large amount of information about the evolution of Keynes' thought and some of this information has been obtained from people who were very closely associated with Keynes at the time. I would still maintain that the *Treatise* is an important book whose role in the Keynesian Revolution has largely been ignored by economists. I still think that the antecedents of the multiplier theory are to be found in the *Treatise*. After the large amount of evidence given in our book there is scarcely any doubt that Keynes did discuss *variations of output* in the *Treatise*. The inclusion of the quantity-adjustment mechanism in the basic theoretical model of the *Treatise* differentiates it sharply from the other models that were put forward at the time. Furthermore, the theory of the variation of output in the *Treatise* is closely integrated with the theory of money in the form of the bearishness theory of the price of securities. Consequently, in consonance with the main argument of chapter five, I still firmly support the view that the *Treatise* contains, in some form, "a monetary theory of production".

But my views *have changed* with respect to the relationship between the *Treatise* and the *General Theory*. The impression that may be created on reading the book is that the *General Theory* had nothing to do with the Keynesian Revolution. Even at the time I wrote I certainly did not support such an extreme position. But there are passages in the book which may suggest that I do (or did at that time). I think it is true that the relationship between the *Treatise* and the *General Theory* was described in oversimplified terms. I am now aware that the problem is much more complex than I had hitherto thought. I do not think that an acceptable account of the relationship between the two books and the evolution of Keynes' thought from one to the other, is to be found in the literature.[1] In fact, I am currently working on this problem and hope to report on the results of this research within a short period of time.

## DEVELOPMENTS IN KUHN'S THEORY OF SCIENCE

It is not an exaggeration to say that there has been an explosion of interest in Kuhnian thought among social scientists in the past five or six years. In fact, Kuhn's historiographical framework has itself functioned as a paradigm for philosophers of science and social scientists. Some political scientists have talked about a "massive conversion experience" to Kuhnian thought and a historian has stated that "all of us have gone berserk over Kuhn".[2]

In spite of the tremendous interest in Kuhnian thought among social scientists, only economics, the most developed and exact of the social sciences, can pass Kuhn's criteria for normal science. Kuhn himself grants a special place to economics among social sciences. "It may be significant," he writes, "that economists argue less about whether their field is a science than do practitioners of some other fields." This permits detailed and recondite research because agreement on the nature of economics has been obtained.[3]

---

[1]For a modern account see Patinkin, "J. M. Keynes: From the Tract to the General Theory", *Economic Journal*, June, 1975.

[2]For an account of the enthusiastic reception of Kuhnian ideas in the social sciences see John Heyl, "Paradigms in Social Science", *Society*, July/August 1975.

[3]Kuhn, *The Structure of Scientific Revolutions* (p. 161).

Among economists there has been considerable interest in Kuhn's ideas. The views of economists with respect to the relevance of Kuhn's ideas for economics can be divided into four groups. In the first group there is Gordon.[4] According to Gordon, who was the first economist to introduce Kuhn's ideas to economics, the maximization principle or rationality postulate is the basic paradigm for economics. This paradigm is to be found in the works of Adam Smith. Much of economic theory, argues Gordon, from Smith to modern times has been concerned with the derivation of the implications of this paradigm in the theory of production, consumption, and so on. Gordon thinks that there have been no real revolutions in economics as the maximization principle has not been supplanted.

In the second group are economists who have more or less directly transplanted the Kuhnian framework and ideas to economics.[5] These economists feel that there have been revolutions in economics and that the Keynesian Revolution has been a revolution in the sense of Kuhn so that it can be adequately explained on the basis of the Kuhnian categories. To this group belong Benjamin Ward, Coats, and the present author.

In the third group there are economists such as Bronfenbrenner and Kunin and Weaver.[6] These economists are not critics of Kuhn. But they feel that a direct transplantation of Kuhn's ideas to economics is not very useful. They feel that the history of economic thought presents some special features which distinguish it from other disciplines and which necessitate modifications in Kuhn's ideas.

Bronfenbrenner first considers the uniformitarian and catastrophic approaches to the growth of science. He rejects the uniformitarian or incrementalist approach because that approach cannot explain the dramatic transformation associated with

[4]D. Gordon, "The Role of the History of Economic Thought in the Understanding of Modern Economic Theory", *American Economic Review*, May 1965.

[5]See B. Ward, *What's Wrong With Economics*, Macmillan, 1972; and A. Coats, "Is There a 'Structure of Scientific Revolutions' in Economics", *Kyklos*, 1969.

[6]M. Bronfenbrenner, "The 'Structure of Revolutions' in Economic Thought", *History of Political Economy*, Spring 1971; and L. L. Kunin and S. Weaver, "On the Structure of Scientific Revolutions in Economics", *History of Political Economy*, Fall 1971. Also see S. Karsten, "Dialectics and the Evolution of Economic Thought", *History of Political Economy*, 1973.

the theories of Keynes (Keynesian revolution) and Milton Friedman (Chicago counter-revolution), to mention only a few of the upheavals that have convulsed economics. Unlike Gordon, Bronfenbrenner does not deny that the Keynesian Revolution was a revolution in the sense of Kuhn. But he thinks that the catastrophic theory of Kuhn does not explain the facts as well as a Hegelian dialectic approach of thesis–antithesis–synthesis. There are two reasons for this. First, the catastrophic theory maintains that paradigms, once displaced, are displaced definitively. But in economics, Bronfenbrenner argues, outmoded ideas are never definitively displaced. Second, advances in economics tend to be major accretions without a rejection of existing paradigms. But, according to Bronfenbrenner, this is inconsistent with Kuhn's catastrophic theory. The Hegelian dialectic approach is able to take care of these special features of economics and, therefore, provides a better explanation of the principal facts than Kuhn's theory which is a special case of Bronfenbrenner's dialectical theory; Kuhn's theory being applicable only in the special case in which the old outmoded ideas have been definitively and completely displaced.

In commenting upon these views, note first that Bronfenbrenner is not a critic of Kuhn's methods and ideas. All he wants to do is to modify Kuhn's framework to make it more relevant to economics. Is he successful? I do not think so. Bronfenbrenner's interpretation of the catastrophic position is of questionable validity. If catastrophes occur only when "outmoded" ideas are completely displaced, then may we not conclude that the concept is vacuous. Perhaps there have been no catastrophies in this sense of the term. But let us accept Bronfenbrenner's interpretation of the catastrophic position. Does it follow that Kuhn is a catastrophist in this sense? I do not think so. Kuhn has often been misrepresented as maintaining that revolutions are complete and unaccountable breaks with the past.[7] As this view is quite common it is worthwhile to give evidence from Kuhn's own writing to determine his exact position.

First, the new candidate must seem to resolve some outstand-

[7]This accounts for the reluctance of economists to apply his ideas to the marginal revolution. See Mehta, "The Marginal Revolution in Economics", *Philosophy of Social Science*, 1974.

ing and generally recognized problem that can be met in no other way. Second, the new paradigm must *promise to preserve a relatively large part of the concrete problem-solving ability that has accrued to science* through its predecessors. *Novelty for its own sake is not a desideratum in the sciences* as it is in so many other creative fields. As a result, though new paradigms seldom or never possess all the capabilities of their predecessors, *they usually preserve a great deal of the most concrete parts of past achievement.*[8]

An important argument of Kuhn's book is that science, as a whole, does not produce progressively more "truthful" statements about reality. But this means that functional progression in science (improvements in puzzle-solving ability of paradigms) may be accompanied by ontological regression.

I do not doubt, for example, that Newton's mechanics improves on Aristotle's and that Einstein's improves on Newton's as instruments for puzzle-solving. But I can see in their succession no coherent direction of ontological development. On the contrary, in some important respects, though by no means all, *Einstein's general relativity theory is closer to Aristotle's than either of them is to Newton's.*[9]

An example of ontological regression has already been given in our book. It was argued that the Keynesian theory is ontologically closer to the mercantilist position (in its emphasis on the importance of money) than the classical theory. But no one has denied that the classical thory is *analytically* superior to the mercantilist theory.

It is now clear that Bronfenbrenner's identification of Kuhn's theory with the so-called catastrophic position is incorrect. Even in physics and astronomy, the most developed of all the sciences, "outmoded" ideas continue to exist. Furthermore, even in the natural sciences the new paradigm does not definitively and completely displace the old paradigm. Often large parts of the past achievements of scientists are preserved in the new paradigm.

---

[8]Kuhn, *op. cit.*, p. 169, emphasis added.
[9]Kuhn, *op. cit.*, pp. 206–207, emphasis added.

Often a new paradigm merely consists in looking at the same things in a different way. For example, Herschel's discovery of the planet Uranus constituted a minor paradigmatic change. In this case, the Gestalt switch consisted in seeing as a planet what for a hundred years before 1781 was seen either as a star or a comet. In this revolution, all the elements of the old paradigm were maintained intact. The revolution consisted in arranging them in a different way.[10]

Enough has been said to cast grave doubt on Bronfenbrenner's identification of Kuhn's theory with the so-called catastrophic position. It may be true that "outmoded" and displaced ideas continue to exist in economics. Bronfenbrenner gives two examples of this: modern income policy proposals are based on elements of the medieval notion of just price, and mercantilist notions continue to exist in spite of their displacement by classical economists. But these "facts" can easily be accommodated within the Kuhnian framework. In fact, the *novelty* of his approach consists in the demonstration that there are no such things as "*outmoded ideas*" per se. Ideas can only be "outmoded" *relative to a given paradigm*. It appears, therefore, that Bronfenbrenner's concept of "outmoded ideas" is itself "outmoded".

"Outmoded ideas" may also appear to exist because the community of economists is not sufficiently differentiated from the amorphous group of "practical economists". The development of a science can be measured by the esoteric nature of its research. In the early stages of a science its research is easily accessible to the lay community at large. As it develops its research becomes more esoteric and inaccessible to the layman. Economics is rapidly changing in this respect. The first stage of its separation from the informed lay community took place with the professionalization of economics and the concomitant acceptance of marginalist ideas in the two or three decades after 1870. In recent years the "mathematical revolution" has almost completed this process of separation. Nevertheless, for economics as a whole, this process of separation is not nearly as complete as that in the natural sciences. This may account for the continued existence of "outmoded" ideas since the views of real economists can easily

---

[10]Kuhn, *op. cit.*, pp. 115–116. Also see Kuhn's neglected work, *The Copernican Revolution*, Cambridge, Massachussets, 1957.

be confused with the pseudo views of "practical economists" in government or industry and even with the garbled notions of the man-in-the-street.

Our conclusion is that Bronfenbrenner's attempted "generalization" of Kuhn's framework has not been successful. If Kuhn's theory can itself explain the continued existence of "outmoded" ideas in economics and the fact that advances often tend to be accretions, there is no need for a "generalization" or "reconstruction" of his ideas. It may appear that, in this case, the two approaches are equivalent. But they are not. In fact, Kuhn's theory tells us that a key concept of the Bronfenbrenner approach, namely, the concept of "outmoded" ideas as such, is of dubious validity. "Outmodedness" can be defined only relative to a given paradigm.

The upshot is that Bronfenbrenner's views about the nature of revolutions in economics may be correct. It may be the case that ideas are not definitively displaced in economics because of the difficulty of obtaining clear-cut evidence. This is much more so in economics than in a hard science such as physics. But the difference is only one of degree. What has been challenged here is Bronfenbrenner's interpretation of Kuhn's theory and his claim that the dialectical approach is superior to the Kuhnian approach.

The views of Kunin and Weaver are similar. They agree with Bronfenbrenner that the dialectical approach is superior to the paradigm approach as far as economics is concerned. They are also critical of any direct transplantation of Kuhn's ideas to economics. Their main contribution is to show that economists study a nonconstant historically conditioned universe. This differentiates economics from many of the natural sciences. It also means that the nature of paradigm change in economics has certain special characteristics. It means, in particular, that anomalies in economics do not necessarily have their origin in normal science. They may emerge from *outside* the normal scientific tradition. Again a careful reading of Kuhn's book indicates that he is aware of such a phenomenon in the natural sciences.

In addition, I would now point out what the absence of an adequate discussion of community structure has obscured above: crises need not be generated by the work of the community that experiences them and that sometimes undergoes revolution as a result.[11]

This fact has been discussed at length in our book. In our discussion of the crisis in macroeconomic theory in the twenties, it was pointed out that one of the most important features of this crisis was that it has its origin *outside* the normal research tradition. It was argued there that the crisis was caused by the existence of unemployment in Britain in the nineteen-twenties and the attacks made upon the classical paradigm by the "underworld" economists. A similar argument is given by Ward.

Economics is influenced by more than its puzzles, however, and the Keynesian Revolution clearly exemplifies the role that current issues can play in such a science. For the great factual anomaly of the period was the persistence of massive unemployment.[12]

We agree with Kunin and Weaver that there are both endogenous and exogenous factors influencing the development of economics. Some of the puzzles of normal science may fail to come out right due to changes that take place *outside* normal science, as the Keynesian Revolution exemplifies. This may be, in part, a consequence of the insufficient differentiation of the community of real economists from the amorphous group of "practical economists". This partial overlap of the two groups not only permits the "outmoded" ideas a continued existence. It also makes possible the consideration of deviant and unconventional views that are rigidly proscribed by normal science. Changes taking place in the institutional structure of society may first be sensed by these deviant groups. This awareness may be absent initially among the real professional economists whose expectations are based on the paradigm orientations that have been internalized during the training and socialization process and later confirmed by paradigm-based practice. The sense of anomaly may be communicated to the professional economists by the "underworld" economists. The interaction of these two

[11]Kuhn, *op. cit.*, p. 181.
[12]Ward, *op. cit.*, p. 36.

groups is a complex social process whose description cannot be attempted here. But note that the reception accorded to these unconventional ideas is unlikely to be uniform over the whole group of real professional economists. The deviant views supported by a minority group are likely to have the greatest impact on the professional economists whose thoughts have already been tending in that direction. The younger generation of scientists are also likely to be more receptive to new ideas and alternative ways of viewing the economic system.

Kunin and Weaver are right in directing the attention of economists to this mode of paradigm change in economics. But they are mistaken in thinking that the force of Kuhn's thesis is greatly attenuated by this phenomenon. In the first place, Kuhn himself is aware that the stimulus for paradigm-change may originate from outside the normal scientific tradition. Kunin and Weaver maintain that this stimulus is not only outside the normal scientific tradition. It is external to science because it arises from changes taking place in the economic universe being studied.[13] But there is a epistemological problem here that is similar to the one we encountered in discussing Bronfenbrenner's concept of "outmoded" ideas. Ideas can be "outmoded" only relative to a given paradigm. Similarly, there is no paradigm-independent way of determining the real nature of the economic universe. Consequently, there is no paradigm-independent way of determining *changes* in the economic universe. But this means that changes in the economic universe can only be known to exist if the puzzles of normal science do not come out right. Normal scientists may not be aware of any anomaly, as in the case of the General Glut controversy in the 1820's. The awareness of dissonance or anomaly may, in the initial stages, be limited to minority groups. If the normal scientists are able to extend the paradigm and to make the puzzles come out right, we must conclude that, in essential respects, the economic universe has not changed. If, on the other hand, normal scientists are unable to make the puzzles come out right and the anomalies become accentuated, as in the case of the Keynesian Revolution, and a new paradigm eventually emerges, then we must conclude that in essential respects the economic universe has changed.

[13]Kunin and Weaver, *op. cit.*, p. 395.

We conclude then that both endogenous and exogenous sources of paradigm-change manifest themselves in essentially the same way. The effect of both of them is to create more puzzles for normal science or to complicate the existing puzzles. The effect of the discovery of new elements in a "constant universe" (for example, the discovery of new planets and the puzzles they created for Ptolemaic astronomers) is similar to the effect produced on a paradigm by a change in a "historically conditioned universe" (for example, the essential identity of the saving and investment functions in the economic system of the early nineteenth century, and the puzzles created for normal economists, such as Pigou, by a change in the economic system which made these functions essentially different).

Kunin and Weaver concede that natural scientists do not have a direct access to an independently existing material universe. Hence, their perceptions of this universe is conditioned by paradigms. But the same thing is also clearly true of the social scientists who have no direct access to an independently existing economic or social universe, or to changes in that universe. Hence, the fundamental fact is that scientists, in both natural and social sciences, are "imprisoned" within their paradigms. Their construction of the essential properties of the universe which they study is itself based on the ruling paradigm of the time. Their knowledge of the universe or changes in that universe is ineluctably conditioned by paradigms. The fact that changes in the economic universe may necessitate changes in paradigms does not imply (and this is where Kunin and Weaver err) that economists have a paradigm-independent access to these changes of the economic universe. But then the effect of a changing economic universe is the same as that of a discovery of new elements in an unchanging universe.

Let us now proceed to consider the fourth group of views concerning the applicability and relevance of Kuhn's ideas in economics. Economists in this group do not base their views on some fundamental difference between economics and the natural sciences. They are critics of Kuhn in the sense that they reject his methods and conclusions even with respect to the natural sciences. They are incrementalists who repudiate the notion of paradigm-based science and the catastrophic facets of Kuhn's historiographical framework not only in the social sciences such as economics, but also in the natural sciences. The views of the incrementalists must be clearly differentiated from the dialectical approach. The dialecticians do not deny the existence of revolutions in economics. In fact, they explicitly repudiate the incrementalist thesis of continuous change. The incrementalists reject Kuhn's central thesis of revolutionary change. The dialecticians are Kuhnians as far as the natural sciences are concerned. They are "modified Kuhnians" when it comes to economics.

The incrementalist thesis that scientific advance is gradual and continuous has a strong appeal for economists.[14] The incrementalist denies that Keynes effected a revolution in economics. He supports his contention by demonstrating the existence of Keynesian or non-Sayian ideas within the domain of Sayian economics. Similarly, by showing that there were anticipators and adumbrators of the marginalist ideas, the incrementalist concludes that there was no marginal revolution. Our whole book is intended to be a critique of the incrementalist or uniformitarian position and it is hoped that the Kuhnian approach has been demonstrated to be superior to the incrementalist approach. My position on this matter is unchanged. So it is unnecessary to say anything more regarding the incrementalist position.

## THE ROLE OF THE TREATISE IN THE KEYNESIAN REVOLUTION

After the publication of the *Collected Writings of Keynes* by the Royal Economic Society much more information is now available about the evolution of Keynes' thinking from the *Treatise* to the *General Theory*. It is worthwhile now to look again at the question of the role of the *Treatise* in the Keynesian Revolution. The book's discussion of this question can now be seen to be oversimplified. An attempt will be made in this section to use some of this information to give a more accurate account of evolution of Keynes' views from the *Treatise* to the *General Theory*.

[14]See, for example A. Coats, R. Black, C. Goodwin, *eds.*, *The Marginal Revolution in Economics*, Duke University Press, 1973. Most of the contributors to this book are incrementalists. Also see M. Blaug, *The Cambridge Revolution: Success or Failure*, Institute of Economic Affairs, 1974. pp. 79–86, and M. Blaug, "Paradigms versus Research Programmes in the History of Economics", *History of Political Economy*, Winter 1975. See also, T. Sowell, *Say's Law*, Princeton University Press, 1972.

First, there is the question of the criterion of disequilibrium in the *Treatise*. Keynes did not clearly and consistently adhere to a rigidly defined concept of disequilibrium. From the fundamental equations it is clear that disequilibrium manifests itself by a divergence of price from the cost of production. An excess of saving over investment, for example, means that the price of output is less than the cost of production. The question one may ask is why the system responds to a disturbance by a price adjustment. This point was discussed by Keynes in his epistolary exchange with Hawtrey before the publication of the *Treatise*.[15] Hawtrey asked if demand can increase output directly without first raising prices. Hawtrey argued that the cause of disequilibrium is a change in demand which leads to a change in the stocks of goods with the dealers. When stocks change, dealers curtail or increase the orders placed with the manufacturers. Increased demand *first* affects output and *then* price.

In his reply to Hawtrey Keynes said that he did not mean to leave out variations in the stocks of goods in the hands of the dealers. When fixed investment declines relatively to saving, Keynes argued, there may be an increase of liquid investment (stocks of liquid goods) in the hands of the dealers. The increase in liquid investment mitigates the decline in fixed investment, and price does not fall as much as it would have in the absence of changes in liquid investment. In the extreme case, there will be no change in price. Keynes agreed with Hawtrey that in such cases the change in stocks is a symptom of disequilibrium. But this means that the system may respond to the demand disturbance by an output adjustment.[16] This shows, that even in 1930 Keynes could obtain a result by using the *Treatise* apparatus in which the system responds by quantity adjustments.

But the fact that the *Treatise* model enables the system to respond to demand disturbances by quantity adjustments does not mean that the *Treatise* contained a theory of the complete set of forces explaining the exact amount by which output would change following a demand disturbance. This is what Keynes said to Hawtrey:

---

[15]*The Collected Writing of J. M. Keynes*, Royal Economic Society, Macmillan, Volume 13, pp. 139–169.
[16]*The Collected Writings of Keynes*, Vol. 13, p. 142.

I am not dealing with the complete set of causes which determine the volume of output. For this would have led me an
endlessly long journey into the theory of short-period supply
and a long way from monetary theory; though I agree that
it will probably be difficult in the future to prevent monetary theory and the theory of short-period supply from
running together. . . . I have left on one side the question
*how much* output is affected.[17]

This was in a letter to Hawtrey at the time of the publication
of the *Treatise*. The letter shows that as early as 1930 Keynes
was aware of the need for a "monetary theory of production".
In the *Treatise* he made a start on this intricate task by showing
that the system responds to disturbances by quantity adjustments
either directly, as in the case considered above, or indirectly
via a change in price. But the *Treatise* model did not contain a
description of the complete set of causes determining the level
of output.

It has been said that while a discrepancy between saving and
investment in the *Treatise* provokes a change in output, there is
nothing to show what effect the change of output will have on
the discrepancy.[18] But it is not true that there is *nothing* to show
what reaction the change of income will have on the discrepancy
between saving and investment. We have already given ample
evidence in the book to show that when income changes, two
equilibrating mechanisms are brought into operation: the "saving
effect" and the "Keynes effect" of the change in the requirements
of the Industrial Circulation on the Financial Circulation. The
"saving effect" reduces the quantum of saving and the "Keynes
effect" transfers resources from the Industrial Circulation
(where they are not needed due to the income deflation in the
commodity market) to the Financial Circulation. If the financial
market is not a bear market with a consensus of opinion, investment may be stimulated due to a fall in the price of securities.
If the financial market is a bear market only a severe income
deflation will eliminate the discrepancy.

But to say that the changes of output and income in the

[17]*The Collected Writings of Keynes*, Vol. 13. pp. 145–146.
[18]R. Harrod, *The Life of Keynes*, pp. 433–434. Also see Patinkin, *op. cit.,*
256.

*Treatise* operate upon the discrepancy between saving and investment via the "saving effect" and the "Keynes effect" is not to say that Keynes had more than an inchoate theory of the consequences of the change of output. An early version of Kahn's famous paper on the multiplier was known to Keynes before the publication of the *Treatise*. In the final version, which was more elaborately worked out, Kahn showed precisely how investment "finances" itself by raising income to just that extent that is necessary for the "alleviations" or "culs-de-sac" to be equal to investment.[19] It is certainly true that Kahn's analysis filled an important lacuna in the *Treatise* model. It was a lacuna, however, that Keynes was fully aware of.

> The question *how much* reduction of output is caused, whether by a realized fall of prices or an anticipated fall of price, is important, but not strictly a monetary problem. I have not attempted to deal with it in my book, though I have done a good deal of work at it.[20]

The question how much output changes when there is a demand disturbance clearly depends upon the reaction a change in output has upon the discrepancy between saving and investment. It also depends upon the supply curve of output, a fact which Kahn emphasized in developing the multiplier theory. In the *Treatise* the first term of the fundamental equations measured the response of prices to changes in demand conditions. Much evidence has been given in the book to show that Keynes was aware that income deflation (a rise in $E/O$) is more likely to take place at higher levels of employment due to the stiffening of the attitude of the factors of production. It was left to Kahn to develop from these ideas of the *Treatise* the concept of the supply curve of output as a whole. The supply curve of output will determine the extent to which demand disturbances get dissipated in price changes, and the amount by which output will respond.

Even as early as 1930 Keynes knew that a "monetary theory of production" would have to consider the following four questions. (1) What is the supply curve of output as a whole? (2) Are

---

[19]R. Kahn, "The Relation of Home Investment to Unemployment", *Economic Journal*, June 1931.

[20]*The Collected Writings of Keynes*, Vol. 13, p. 145.

changes in stocks a symptom of disequilibrium and will the system respond to demand disturbances by quantity adjustments? (3) How much does output change when a demand disturbance impinges on the system? (4) How does a change in output react upon the relationship between saving and investment? The *Treatise* itself contained the answer to some of these questions. Question three was not answered in the *Treatise* although it indicated the lines on which the answer may be found. The other three questions were, at least partly, answered in the *Treatise*. But there is no doubt that even as early as 1930 Keynes was already at work on these questions.

As the *Treatise* did not completely answer these questions (and others like them) it is an exaggeration to say that the *Treatise* was a paradigm for Keynesian normal science. The *Treatise* was not completely successful in constructing a "monetary theory of production". It only made a beginning in this direction.

# Bibliography

1. ABBATI A. H., *The Final Buyer*, London, P. S. King and Son Ltd., 1928.
2. ADARKAR B., "Mr. Keynes' Treatise on Money", *American Economic Review*, May 1932.
3. AGASSI J., *Towards a New Historiography of Science*, Gravenhage, Mouton, 1963.
4. BECKER C. and BAUMOL W., "Classical Monetary Theory", *Quarterly Journal of Economics*, November 1952.
5. CLOWER R., ed. *Monetary Theory*, Penguin, 1970.
6. COATS A., "Is There a Structure of Scientific Revolution in Economics?", *Kyklos*, 1969, pp. 289-294.
7. COLE G. D. H., ed. *What Everybody Wants to Know About Money: A Planned Outline of Monetary Problems by Nine Economists from Oxford*, New York, A. A. Knopf, 1933.
8. DEAN E., *The Controversy Over the Quantity Theory of Money*, Boston, E.C. Heath and Co., 1965.
9. DOUGLAS C. H., *The Control and Distribution of Production*, London, Cecil Palmer, 1922.
10. DOUGLAS C. H., *Social Credit*, London, Cecil Palmer, 1924.
11. DOUGLAS C. H., *Monopoly of Credit*, London, Chapman and Hall Ltd., 1931.
12. DOUGLAS C. H., *The Douglas Theory: A Reply to Mr. J. A. Hobson*, London, Cecil Palmer, 1922.
13. ELLIS H., *German Monetary Theory: 1905-1933*, Cambridge, Massachusetts, Harvard University Press, 1937.
14. ESHAG E., *From Marshall to Keynes: An Essay on the Monetary Theory of the Cambridge School*, Oxford, Blackwell, 1963.
15. ESTEY J., *Business Cycles*, New York, Prentice-Hall, 1950, 2nd edition.
16. FESTINGER L., *A Theory of Cognitive Dissonance*, Stanford, California, Stanford University Press, 1957.
17. FISHER I., *The Purchasing Power of Money*, New York, Macmillan Company, 1911.
18. FISHER I., *Booms and Depressions*, New York, Adelphi Company, 1932.
19. FOSTER W. and CATCHINGS W., *Business Without a Buyer*, New York Houghton Mifflin, 1928, 2nd edition.
20. FOSTER W. and CATCHINGS W., *Profits*, New York, Houghton Mifflin Company, 1925.
21. FOSTER W. and CATCHINGS W., *Money*, New York, Houghton Mifflin 1930, 3rd edition.
22. FOSTER W. and CATCHINGS W., *The Road to Plenty*, New York, Houghton Mifflin Company, 1928.

23. GALBRAITH J., "Came the Revolution", *New York Times Book Review*, May 1965.

24. GLEASON A., "Foster and Catchings: A Reappraisal", *Journal of Political Economy*, 1959.

25. GORDON D., "The Role of the History of Economic Thought in the Understanding of Modern Economic Theory", *American Economic Review*, May 1965.

26. HABERLER G., *Prosperity and Depression*, Atheneaum, 1963.

27. HANSEN A., *A Guide to Keynes*, New York, McGraw-Hills, 1953.

28. HANSEN A., *Business-Cycle Theory: Its Development and Present Status*, Boston, New York, Ginn and Company, 1927.

29. HANSEN A , "A Fundamental Error in Mr. Keynes' Treatise on Money", *American Economic Review*.

30. HANSEN A. and TOUT H., "Annual Review of Business-Cycle Theory", *Econometrica*, June 1932.

31. HANSON N.R., *Patterns of Discovery: An Enquiry into the Conceptual Foundations of Science*, Cambridge, England, Cambridge University Press, 1958.

32. HARRIS S., ed., *The New Economics: Keynes' Influence on Theory and Policy*, New York, A Knopf, 1947.

33. HARROD R., *Money*, London, Macmillan, 1969.

34. HARROD R., *The Life of J. M. Keynes*, New York, Harcourt Brace, 1951.

35. HAYEK F., *Monetary Theory and the Trade Cycle*, Translated from the German by N. Kaldor and H. Croome, New York, Augustus Kelley, 1966.

36. HAYEK F., *Prices and Production*, New York, Macmillan, 1932.

37. HAYEK F., "The Pure Theory of Money of Mr. Keynes", *Economica*, 1931.

38. HAZLITT M., ed. *The Critics of Keynesian Economics*, Princeton, New Jersey, Van Nostrand, 1960.

39. HEGELAND M., *The Quantity Theory of Money: A Critical Study of Its Historical Development and Interpretation and a Restatement*, Goteborg, Elanders, 1951.

40. HEGELAND M., *The Multiplier Theory*, New York, Augustus Kelley, 1966.

41. HENDERSON H., *Supply and Demand*, Chicago, University of Chicago Press, 1958.

42. HICKS J. R., *Critical Essays in Monetary Theory*, Oxford, Clarendon Press, 1967.

43. HICKS J. R., "Suggestions for Simplifying the Theory of Money", in *Reachings in Monetary Theory*, London, George, Allen and Unwin, 1949.

44. HOBSON J. A., *Economics of Unemployment*, London, George, Allen and Unwin, 1922.

45. HOBSON J. A., and MUMMERY A. F., *The Physiology of Industry: An Exposure of Certain Fallacies in Existing Theories of Economics*, London. J. Murray, 1889.

46. HUTCHISON T.W., *The Significance and Basic Postulates of Economic*

*Theory*, London, Macmillan, 1938.

47. KEYNES J. M., *The General Theory of Employment, Interest and Money*, London, Harcourt Brace, 1935.
48. KEYNES J. M., *A Treatise on Money*, 2 Volumes, New York, Harcourt Brace and Company, 1930.
49. KEYNES J. M., *Monetary Reform*, New York, Harcourt Brace, 1924.
50. KLEIN L., *The Keynesian Revolution*, New York, Macmillian, 1947, 2nd edition.
51. KNAPP G. F., *The State Theory of Money*, Abridged edition, translated by H. Lucas and J. Bonar, London, Macmillan, 1924.
52. KUHN T., *The Structure of Scientific Revolutions*, Chicago, University of Chicago Press, 1970, 2nd edition.
53. LAKATOS I. and A. MUSGRAVE, eds., *Criticism and the Growth of Knowledge*, Cambridge, 1970.
54. LEIJONHUFVUD A., *Keynesian Economics and the Economics of Keynes*, New York, Oxford University Press, 1968.
55. LEKACHMAN R., ed. *Keynes' General Theory: Reports of 3 Decades*, New York, St. Martin's Press, 1964.
56. LEKACHMAN R., *The Age of Keynes*, New York, Random House, 1966.
57. LINDGREN H., *Introduction to Social Psychology*, New York, Wiley, 1969.
58. MARGET A., *The Theory of Prices: A Re-examination of the Central Problems of Monetary Theory*, 2 Volumes, New York, Prentice-Hall, 1938-42.
59. MARSHALL A., *Money, Credit and Commerce*, New York, Augustus Kelley, 1960.
60. MILL J. S., *Principles of Political Economy: With Some of Their Applications to Social Philosophy*, ed. with an Introduction by W. J. Ashley, London, Longmans Green, 1920.
61. MILL J. S., *Essays on Some Unsettled Questions of Political Economy*, New York, Augustus Kelley, 1960.
62. MINTS L., *A History of Banking Theory in Great Britain and the U.ᶜ.*, Chicago, University of Chicago Press, 1956.
63. MISES L., *The Theory of Money and Credit*, translated from the German by H. E. Batson, New Haven, Yale University Press, 1953.
64. MYRAL G., *Monetary Equilibrium*, London, W. Hodge and Company Ltd., 1939.
65. NEMMERS E., *Hobson and Underconsumption*, Amsterdam, North Holland Publishing Company, 1956.
66. PATINKIN D., *Money, Interest and Prices*, Evanston Illinois, Harper and Row, 1965, 2nd edition.
67. PIGON A., *The Theory of Unemployment*, London, F. Cass, 1968, Reprint of 1933 edition.
68. POLANYI M., *The Tacit Dimension*, London, Routledge and Kegan Paul, 1966.
69. POLANYI M., *Personal Knowledge: Towards a Post-Critical Philosophy*, University of Chicago Press, 1958.

70. ROBERTSON D., *Banking Policy and the Price Level: An essay in the theory of the trade cycle*, New York, Augustus Kelley, 1949.

71. ROBERTSON D., *Money*, Chicago University Press, 1959.

72. ROBERTSON D., *A Study of Industrial Fluctuations*, London, London School of Economics and Political Sciences, 1948.

73. RICARDO D., *The Works and Correspondence of David Ricardo, Volume I, on the Principles of Political Economy and Taxation*, ed. P. Sraffa and M. Dobb, Cambridge, 1951.

74. ROBINSON E. A. G., "J. M. Keynes: An Obituary", *Economical Journal*, 1946.

75. ROBINSON J., "The Theory of Money and the Analysis of Output", *Review of Economic Studies*, October 1933.

76. SAULNIER R., *Contemporary Monetary Theory*, New York, Columbia University Press, 1938.

77. SAY J. B., *A Treatise on Political Economy*, New York, Augustus Kelley, 1964.

78. SAY J. B., *Letters to Mr. Malthus on Several Subjects of Political Economy and on the Cause of the General Stagnation of Commerce*, translated from the French by Richter, London, George Harding's Bookshops, 1936.

79. SCHAAF W., *Mathematics: Our Great Heritage; Essays on the Nature and Cultural Significance of Mathematics*, New York, Harper, 1948.

80. SCHUMPETER J., *History of Economic Analysis*, Edited from manuscript by E. Boody Schumpeter, New York, Oxford University Press, 1954.

81. SCHUMPETER J., *Ten Great Economists from Marx to Keynes*, New York, Oxford University Press, 1951.

82. SHACKLE G., *The Years of High Theory: Invention and Tradition in Economic Thought 1926-1939*, Cambridge, Cambridge University Press, 1967.

83. SMITH A., *An Enquiry into the Nature and Causes of the Wealth of Nations*, ed. with an introduction, notes, marginal summary and an enlarged index by E. Cannan, New York, Modern Library, 1937.

84. SODDY F., *Money versus Man: A Statement of the World Problems from the Standpoint of The New Economics*, New York, E.P. Dutton and Company Inc., 1933.

85. SODDY F., *Wealth, Virtual Wealth and Debt: The Solution of the Economic Paradox*, London, George, Allen & Unwin, 1933.

86. SODDY F., *The Role of Money: What it Should be Contrasted With What it Has Become*, London, George Routledge and Sons, 1934.

87. SODDY F., *The Arch-enemy of Economic Freedom: What Banking Is*, Knapp, Enstone, Oxon, The author, 1943.

88. STAFFORD J., "Mr. Keynes' Treatise on Money", *Manchester School*, Volume 2, No. 1, 1931.

89. STAMP J., "Mr. Keynes' Treatise on Money", *Economic Journal*, 1931.

90. STEWART M., *Keynes and After*, Harmondsworth, Penguin, 1967.

91. STORER N., *The Social Systems of Science*, New York, Holt, Rinehart and Winston, 1966.

92. WICKSELL K., *Interest and Prices*, Translated from the German by R. Kahn, London, Macmillan, 1936.
93. WINCH D., ed. *James Mill: Selected Economic Writings*, Chicago, University of Chicago Press, 1966.
94. WRIGHT L., "The Genesis of the Multiplier Theory", *Oxford Economic Papers*, 1956.
95. YNTEMA, "Say's Law: A Restatement and Criticism", *Studies in Mathematical Economics* and *Econometrics* ed. by Lange, McIntyre and Yntema, Chicago, University of Chicago Press, 1942

# Index